POWER AND PURPOSE
AFTER THE COLD WAR

Le Temps Mondial/World Time Series

Edited by Zaki Laïdi, *Centre National de la Recherche Scientifique (Centre d'Etudes et de Recherches Internationales), Paris*

Previously published title in the Series:

Power and Purpose after the Cold War
Edited by Zaki Laïdi

Le Temps Mondial / World Time Series

POWER AND PURPOSE AFTER THE COLD WAR

Edited by

Zaki Laïdi

Forward by

William Zartman

BERG

Oxford/Providence

English edition
first published in 1994 by

Berg Publishers Ltd

Editorial offices:
221 Waterman Street, Providence, RI 02906, USA
150 Cowley Road, Oxford, OX4 1JJ, UK

English edition © Berg Publishers 1994
Originally published as *L'ordre mondial relâché*
Translated from the French by permission of the publishers
© Presses de la Fondation nationale des sciences politiques
Translated by Helen McPhail

Library of Congress Cataloguing-in-Publication Data
A CIP catalogue record for this book is available from the Library of Congress.

British Library Cataloguing in Publication Data
A CIP catalogue record for this book is available from the British Library.

ISBN 0 85496 807 5 (cloth)
     1 85973 077 9 (paper)

Printed in the United Kingdom by WBC Book Manufacturers, Bridgend,
Mid Glamorgan

CONTENTS

Acknowledgements   vii

Notes On Contributors   ix

Foreword
    William Zartman   xi

Introduction: Imagining the Post-Cold War Era
    Zaki Laïdi   1
    Post-Cold War: Not One but Several   3

1   Power and Purpose in the International System
    Zaki Laïdi   7
    The Decoupling of Power and Purpose   11
    Polarity: Neither Single nor Multiple   19
    The Ambivalence of World Time   27

2   The Purpose of German Power
    Anne-Marie Le Gloannec   35
    Paradoxes of the Economic Model: Admired but not easily
    Transposable   37
    How can Germany Create Purpose?   41
    How is Germany Maximising her Power?   45
    A New German Universality?   49

3   Japan and the Quest for Legitimacy
    Jean-Marie Bouissou   55
    Japan within the Cold War: A Potentially Variable Alignment   57
    Collective Attitudes as a Factor Inhibiting the
    Promotion of a Worldwide Purpose for Japanese Power   62
    Internal Constraints on the External Game: The Process of
    Decision-Making and Public Opinion   68
    Hypotheses for Japan in the Loosened World Order 73

4   The Middle East after Cold War and Gulf War
    Elizabeth Picard   83
    The 'Useful Zone' and its Margins   84
    A New Strategic Deal   90
    World Time and Regional Mishaps   98

5 The Evolution of the International Trade Régime:
A Three-Bloc Trading System?
Helen Milner — 107
Economic Data on Trade Flows, 1958–89 — 109
Politics and Trade Patterns — 114
Conclusions — 123

6 The Loosening of China
Jean-Luc Domenach — 125
The Chinese 'Advance' — 127
The Great Loosening — 128
The End of the 'Strategic Triangle' — 130
Internal Loosening — 133
Spaces and Flux — 138

7 The Far East: The Meaning of Prosperity
Jean-Louis Margolin — 141
The Age of Bipolarity — 143
The Birth of Complexity — 145
Loosening and Reorganisation — 150
In Time to the World Rhythm? — 156
Japan: Relative Power, Limited Purpose — 159
The Far East: A Model of Original Development? — 164

8 The Inter-American System after the Cold War
Georges Couffignal — 167
Traditionally Unequivocal and Asymmetric Relationships — 169
The Emergence of Ethics and Rights — 171
The Birth of a Self-governing Latin American Diplomacy — 176
Towards a New Inter-American Order — 180
Ideological Void and Ambivalent Relationships — 184

9 Africa: Adjustment and Conditionality
François Constantin — 189
The Faded Flowers of Bipolarity — 192
Ambivalence in the World Time — 197
Unimaginable Marginalisation — 204

ACKNOWLEDGEMENTS

This book expresses the ideas developed through collaboration within a research group over more than twelve months. Such team work would have been impossible without the great cooperation of the participants who were occupied on other matters and without the exceptional working conditions offered by the Centre d'études et de recherches internationales de la Fondation nationale des sciences politiques. I would like to thank the authors of this book as well as Rachel Bouyssou, who contributed greatly to its speedy production.

Zaki Laïdi

NOTES ON CONTRIBUTORS

William Zartman is Jacob Blaustein Professor of International Organization and Conflict Resolution and Director of the International Relations Program at the Nitze School of Advanced International Studies at the Johns Hopkins University.

Zaki Laïdi is a Senior Research Fellow at the Centre National de la Recherche Scientifique (Centre d'Études et de Recherches Internationales), Paris

Anne-Marie Le Gloannec is a Senior Research Fellow at the Centre d'Études et de Recherches Internationales (Fondation Nationale des Sciences Politiques), Paris

Jean-Marie Bouissou is a Senior Research Fellow at the Centre d'Études et de Recherches Internationales (Fondation Nationale des Sciences Politiques), Paris

Elizabeth Picard is a Senior Research Fellow at the Centre d'Études et de Recherches Internationales (Fondation Nationale des Sciences Politiques), Paris

Helen Milner is a Professor at Columbia University, New York

Jean-Luc Domenach is Director of the Centre d'Études et de Recherches Internationales (Fondation Nationale des Sciences Politiques), Paris

Jean-Louis Margolin is a Lecturer at the University of Provence and Associate Fellow at the Centre d'Études et de Recherches Internationales, Paris

Georges Couffignal is a Professor at the University of Paris-III (Institut des Hautes Études d'Amérique latine)

François Constantin is a Professor at the University of Pau et des Pays de l'Adour, Pau

FOREWORD

WILLIAM ZARTMAN

It is enough to read the newspapers these days to realize that the earth is without form and void, and darkness is upon the face of the deep. The informal bipolar order has collapsed and the formal replacement order based on the equality of states is not even a myth. The bipolar order had its myths and meaning, imparted to it by the reality of power, both within the blocs and between them. The collapse of these blocs, of the system of world order which they constructed and even of the possibility of existence outside of them sweeps away with it all the previous myths and norms of international relations. Regionalism has triumphed over globalism, but without bringing with it any order or meaning of its own.

The collapse of the bipolar system of world order is well known, but its consequences for power and meaning are less well studied. During the Cold War, the superpowers kept in form by training against each other, conducting isotonic exercises. But once the opposition has been vanquished, the current power has weakened, showing itself to be of a form inappropriate for its new tasks. The powerful West, winner in the long Cold War against communism and in the short hot war against Saddam Hussein, is incapable of consummating either victory. The great powers of Europe are powerless to handle the rebellions on their own continent or to achieve their self-declared goal of unity among themselves. The countries of Africa, hoping to find their strength in unity, face instead their inability to assure their own existences. There were greater capabilities in all these directions during the Cold War, which was criticised for blocking the same goals, than there are today. Currently, power is found only in resistance and rebellion, not in accomplishment and control.

Similarly, but even less studied, the collapse of world order has also brought about the evaporation of mythologies and meanings. Not only are ideologies worn out and bereft of their miraculous powers, but even the images which give context and connotation to events have lost their ability to organise. Where before Cold War, or for the Third World conspiracy theories, clearly told people who their friends and enemies were, they have now lost not only that assurance but also the certainty that there are reliable friends and constant enemies at all. Long accustomed to interpreting world events as a function of the forces that threaten them – communism, capitalism or both – people no longer have a standard for judging the world around them. Any expectation of a new world order to replace the old is premature. When a structure falls down, it takes a while for the dust to settle, the rubble to be cleared and preparations to be made to erect a replacement. Yet contenders for the succession tend to appear immediately and inchoately, at the same time as the reality of current power shapes the dust, the rubble and the preparations. The following chapters of this book lay out the main themes of the collapse in world order on the dual levels of power and meaning, and then analyse the world's regions as they try to come to terms with that collapse. But before developing the notion of collapse and analyzing its effects on the regions, it is worth searching in the debris for indicators of contending structures that reflect current power and impart meaning to world events.

There are at least seven potential world orders vying for recognition as the world heads into the mid-1990s. Each has some significant features; none is salient enough to provide the dominant structure that the Cold War (or before it, the colonial system) was able to impose.[1] The first model is unipolar, the result of the collapse of one side of the former bipolar world. Victor in the struggle, the United States is still the largest national economy and the foremost nuclear military power, the leading initiator and the ultimate enforcer ('the world's policeman') in international affairs.[2] But it is only *primus inter pares* and a contested *primus* at that, challenged by other economic, nuclear or diplomatic powers independently pursuing their own goals, and it no longer has the heart and mind to exercise hegemonic power as it did during the last collapse in world order systems after World War II.

The second contender, therefore, is a multipolar system, regulated by the centuries-old mechanism of the balance of power, a pattern of action whereby the rise of a potential hegemon triggers other states into an alliance to balance it until the hegemonic threat wanes.[3] The world of the 1990s is indeed characterized by a number of great powers or power centres whose dominance is even institutionalised in the annual G-7 meetings and (with a different but overlapping membership) in the UN Security

1. On these two regimes, see Donald Puchala and Raymond Hopkins, 'International regimes' in Stephen Krasner (ed.), *International Regimes*, Ithaca Cornell University Press, 1993.

2. Robert Gilpin, *War and Change in World Politic*, 1981; Robert Koehane, *After Hegemony*, 1984; Zaki Laïdi, 'De l'hégémonie à la "prédations"?' Paris Les Calviers du CERI no. 1, 1991.

3. Kenneth Waltz, *Man, The State and War,* Columbia University Press, 1954, ch. VII; Kenneth Waltz, *Theory of International Politics*, Random House, 1979, esp. ch. 6.

Council. Balance-of-power theory would predict that the US position as the apparent hegemon after the collapse of the Soviet Union would lead other powers, notably European states and Japan, to seek greater autonomy of action and to combine their efforts (particularly among European states) to limit American initiatives, as is now happening. Yet balancing power is not a dominant characteristic of the world today, current international interaction is a far cry from security alliances, and the very weakness of model I (unipolar hegemony) makes model II (multipolar balance) equally weak as the key to systemic dynamics.

The third contender is the world institution designed to overcome the ill effects of the first two classic systems, the United Nations.[4] Freed of its Cold War paralysis, the UN is often seen as the potential new world government, prepared to handle security problems around the globe as the real 'world's policeman'. Its day has come. But the brief post-Cold War experience of the UN in trying to fill this role has brought out an old and a new lesson, neither yet fully learned. On the one hand, the UN is still a place, not a thing. It has little capability and leeway as a corporate actor and is above all a collection of states who decide and enable according to their individual interests, not according to a sense of collective order and responsibility. Nor is the UN a source of meaning and identity for the world's population, any more than it is an independent source of power. On the other hand, even when authorised, UN operations cost money and, whatever elements of decision and initiative the UN may have, it has no independent source of financing. UN operations in the 1990s have quickly run up against the limitations of members' contributions.

So a fourth model of world order presents itself as a more accurate reflection of reality, a world legislative forum of sovereign states.[5] Whether operating in the UN or in the increasingly broad and intrusive global conferences, such as UNCLOS (the third UN Conference on the Law of the Sea between 1973 and 1982),[6] or GATT (General Agreement on Tariffs and Trade, meeting since 1986 in its Uruguay Round),[7] or the UNCED system

4. Perhaps the clearest statement is the 1992 Agenda for Peace of the UN Secretary General Boutros Boutros Ghali.

5. Approximations of his model are found in Alice Rivlin, David Jones and Edward Meyer, *Beyond Alliances*, Brookings, 1990; I. William Zartman (ed.), *Cooperative Security: Reducing Third World Wars*, Syracuse University Press, 1994; Gunnar Sjosted, Bertram Spector and I. William Zartman (eds), *Negotiating International Regimes*, Graham & Trotman, 1994; I. William Zartman (ed.), *Many Are Called but Few Choose: International Multilateral Negotiations*, Jossey-Bass, 1994.

6. James Sebenius, *Negotiating the Law of the Sea*, Harvard University Press, 1984; Robert Friedheim, *Negotiating the New Ocean Regime*, University of South Carolina Press, 1992.

7. Gunner Sjostedt, 'The Uruguay Round' in I. William Zartman (ed.), *Many are Called but Few Choose: International Multilateral Negotiations*, Jossey-Bass, 1994.

(focussing on the 1992 UN Conference on Environment and Development),[8] states large and small are in almost continuous overlapping sessions. But this system has no structure, no dominant power configuration, no identity or belief system. It is a form of activity, not yet a system of world order.

Quite the opposite is a fifth contending model, the divided North–South (or West–East) world.[9] This is a perceived world order, a structure of identity and beliefs rather than of power, although some believers would argue that it reflects power too. With the Second (communist) World gone, the First (developed West) and Third (underdeveloped South) Worlds are left alone to face each other. To some interpreters, this model also has a structure, primarily economic, topped by the leading countries of the world capitalist system operating through the international financial institutions (World Bank and Monetary Fund) and exploiting the underdeveloped Third World base.[10] Some Western and Southern representatives even agree in going so far as to see the North–South (or more specifically West–East) conflict as World War IV after the end of World (Cold) War III; this is particularly true when the East is identified with political Islam, giving it a perceived ideological coherence. Most observers would agree, however, that either the economic or the ideological version is a caricature of reality (as all ideologies are), containing some characteristics of current international relations like the other contenders but highly exaggerated in its internal coherence or its Manichaean polarity.

A looser alternative, model VI, continues to structure the world on the values of the Cold War – democracy, human rights, market economy – without attributing ideological coherence to the 'other' side.[11] Converting societal values into foreign-policy goals, it moves on to structure the world into 'dos' and 'do nots', recreating a loose bipolarity and launching a gentle crusade. It seeks to turn a world now finally safe for democracy, human rights and free enterprise into a world *of* those values. This is the ultimate world order of organising beliefs, with no specifically related power structures other than those of the states qualified by these values (or their opposite). As such, it is a cognitive and purposive device, but not yet a world order system.

The last contender, then, is a system of no global structure at all but a

8. Gunnar Sjostedt (ed.), *International Environment Negotiations*, Sage, 1993.

9. Richard Feinberg and Delia Boylan, *Modular Multilateralism*, Washington, Overseas Development Council, 1991.

10. Immanuel Wallerstein, *Capitalist World Economy*, Cambridge, 1979; Zaki Laïdi, *Enquête sur la Banque Mondiale*, Fayard, 1989.

11. Max Singer and Aaron Wildavsky, *The Real World Order*, Chatman House Publishers, 1993.

world of regions, where order in terms of power and identity is found only in the sub-global level, and each of the major world islands and peninsulas retreats within its own protectionism, its own security system, its own identity and its own kind.[12] Europe becomes its own Community, concerned with its own security and identity, depending for 60 per cent on its own internal market. North America becomes its own free-trade area; Africa, the Arab world and Latin America turn to themselves first for the solutions to their problems. But the model has already as many holes as realities: the rest of the world is hard to regionalise, the Arab League does not cover its region and the Organization of American States covers more than the Latin region, African and Arab states trade little with each other, and so on. A world order based on regions presently structured is little order at all, even if the regions as conceptual baskets can be the useful frameworks for analysis as the following chapters show.

All of these characterise the world today; none of them dominates it. There is, of course, no reason – other than for academics with curious minds and others with orderly minds – why there has to be a sharp, clear and compelling system of world order. All transitions are somewhat disorderly, and history has sometimes seen periods of weak or confused world order patterns. But two characteristics make for the disquieting insecurity of the current period. One is the combination of vacuum in power and beliefs, criss-crossed with the contenders for order in both structure and meaning. The result is uncertainty and confusion, an inability to know the players in the new situations and to devise policies to deal with them.

The other is the sharpness of the previous order which has just disappeared. As we emerge from the Cold War spaceship, where everything had its place and life was ordered and without surprises, and set foot upon the face of the moon, there are suddenly no rules, no orders, only surprises, and the contrast makes the new situation all the more unsettling. Unsettling, uncertain and confused is the shape of the world this book elucidates.

12. W. Howard Wriggins (ed.), *Dynamics of Regional Politics*, Columbia University Press, 1992; Patrick Cronin (ed), *From Globalism to Regionalism*, National Defense University Press, 1993.

INTRODUCTION: IMAGINING THE POST-COLD WAR ERA

ZAKI LAÏDI

The euphoria that followed the Fall of the Berlin Wall gave rise to the hope that the international system was at last ripe for a complete overhaul: the time had come to change its organisational principles and ground rules. The assumption was that everything could be explained in terms of the Cold War; it stood to reason then that once it came to an end everything would get resolved automically. As soon as 'market democracy' was established as the undisputed norm, the hurdles associated with economic interdependence, cultural interpenetration, the globalization of trade and environmental hazards would vanish of their own accord. Ideological quarrels hindered international cooperation, so it was felt that when these came to an end, it would receive a natural boost. This then was how the post-Cold War brave new world was conceived; the removal of ideology and globalisation would mutually reinforce each other, heralding in a world government which, through the United Nations, would manage the common fund of mankind.

Unfortunately this Kantian vision, liberally sprinkled with references to the Enlightenment, has had to contend with international realities that stubbornly refuse to fit into any teleological scheme. For want of a new international order, what we have today is a loose international system whose distinctive feature is not 'disorder', a necessarily relative and mainly descriptive term, but the growing tension between the dynamics of power which under economic pressure are pushing towards globalisation and integration and the problematic of meaning which, ever since it lost its teleological base, appears to be progressively divisible, flaky and transient. The divergence between meaning and power finds its strongest and most visible expression in the contrast between the rapid globalisation of markets and the rise of an ethnic, cultural or regional sense of identity. The *end of geography* coincides with the revitalisation of micro-histories. However, interpreting this divergence is not as easy as at it appears at first sight. Indeed, while the phenomenon of withdrawing into one's identity (infinitely small) may be seen as a reaction to globalisation (infinitely big), it becomes clear that in practice this apparent symmetry leads us nowhere. Certainly, obvious that the 'end of History' versus the 'return of History' debate is a non-issue as both these processes are complementary. We can however well and truly speak of the end of History, not in the sense of the culmination of a process of transformation in the evolution of human societies, but in the sense of a finalised and teleological promise (Hegel's *Endzweck*) held out by one or several States – a journey with a starting point and an end point, a trajectory between what Kosselek called the field of experience and the horizon of expectations. Today, any conceptualisation of the post-Cold War means dwelling on the implications of the 'end of a historical cycle that began with the French Revolution', as Fran_ois Furet has so rightly emphasised. Symmetrically, we may speak of a 'return to History', that is to say return to the theme of roots. But appart from the fact, as we have seen, that it is extremely difficult to go back in time and link this return to the most elementary constraints of the present, there is the fundamental question of how this return is to be dated: a return to History, but to which history? To begin with, the spontaneous tendency is to situate it in the period preceding the advent of communism. Now, in Russia, in the Balkans and in China too, 'freezing the image' at the pre-Cold War period is somewhat arbitrary. In the case of the Balkans, one would have to go back to at least the Treaty of Versailles; in the Russian case still further back to the fifteenth century at the time when Russia – then the grand duchy of Muscovy – was without an Empire. All this amply proves that the 'reconstruction of meaning' and its linking up with the exercise of power cannot be settled through any ideological or teleological deintoxication which the proponents of Popper's 'open society' seem to be advocating at times.

For all that, the divergence between meaning and power cannot be reduced to the tension between the integrating logic of the economy and the disintegrating dynamic of identity. It triggers off a 'chain' reaction affecting all the factors related to the exercise of political sovereignty of nations, the most important of which being the military instrument. For the entire period of the Cold War, the connection between *military power* and *military policy* (meaning) did not pose any major problem. In the Western camp, absolute priority was given to *containment* of Soviet forces particularly through nuclear deterrence, even if the doctrines regarding the use of nuclear arms varied from one player to another (United States, France) or displayed significant shifts (the complete and exclusive sanctification of French territory was in practice given up even before the end of the Cold War).

In the Soviet camp, the Warsaw Pact mechanism was on the other hand resolutely offensive. Today, the perception of a radical change in the balance of power in Europe has less to do with strictly military considerations

(Russia remains by far the leading military power of Europe) as with the way we perceive danger. In other words, the way we view the collapse of Russian power is governed less by its inherent weaknesses than by the fact that today there is no underlying plan to this power. Which leads us to the commonplace but nonetheless essential observation: a military power, no matter how large, suffers a considerable loss of meaning the moment it is unable to connect power with a military police. The divergence between military power and military policy affects not just Russia but, symmetrically, all its former Western adversaries.

The military power-policy connection raises two sets of problems for all the inheritors of the Cold War. The first is related to the relationship between defence and security. During the Cold War, the two terms corresponded almost naturally. With the end of the Cold War, the dissociation of the two terms became more apparent. This is because on the one hand security is being perceived in increasingly general terms and includes within it's ambit technologies and information. On the other, and more importantly, security problems are no longer systematically linked and identified with any politico-military player. Today, there is probably a greater feeling of *insecurity* in Europe than during the Cold War despite the fact that the military threat has never been weaker. In other words, the military responses (defence policy) to insecurity appears to be both inadequate and tentative. Defence policies are no longer adequate when it comes to formulating security policies. The second set of problems relates to the dissociation between defence and nation. During the Cold War, defence was exclusively national. The rationale of alliances made no difference to this overriding reality. Today, one may well ask whether this equivalence has not been called into question. The widening of perspective in the European case is the result of at least three factors: the absolute necessity to share the cost of military research programmes; the quest for collective supranational identities – weakened by the absence of a collective military instrument; and the fact that national solutions are unrealistic in a context where threats arise more from political contagion (the political disintegration of the East is spilling across the West) than from a clash of state wills. It is this last change which is the most difficult to conceptualise and organise.

Post-Cold War : Not One but Several

While the divergence between meaning and power appears to be durable, it is still not possible, on the basis of this conceptual hypothesis, to construct a stable architecture of the international system. On the contrary, the latter lends itself to increasingly fluid and elusive interpretations; to pretend otherwise would be futile. Still, the speed at which our post-Cold War representations change and sink into confusion leaves one perplexed. That is why we would do well henceforth to speak not just of a post-Cold War but of *several*. The recourse to chronology, though necessarily arbitrary, proves to be very instructive here.

The first post-Cold War began with the fall of the Berlin Wall and ended with the beginning of the Gulf crisis. This was a euphoric period when Kantian and Hegelian propositions of lasting peace and the triumph of reason were sprouted out liberally. In retrospect, we may smile at such an evaluation. But it would be wrong to reduce it to a simple expression of naivety. The end of the Cold War was indeed an exceptional moment. It was for the first time, in the history of the modern international system, that one began talking of a new international order, of a new global deal, without the preceding one (the Cold War) having resulted in a military clash between the dominant powers of the international system. It was, above all, the time when one thought that the liquidation of the Cold War would represent *a moment manageable in time and space*. The Cold War was viewed as a bad memory that had to be forgotten and the process of its mental evacuation was facilitated by the widespread failure of communism. The West like the elite in the East tended to interpret the end of the Cold War as a 'purge', a kind of *reverse normalisation*.

The fact that the civil societies of the East showed themselves to be utterly incapable of advancing any new ideas on the organisation of the post-Cold War, that the dissidence in the East had been more social (Poland) and more moral (Czechoslovakia) than political. The fact that the transition to the market had never been envisaged by the East European or Soviet dissidence was interpreted to a greater or lesser degree not as a structural handicap but rather as short-circuit towards 'market democracy'. Even if all this did not provided a theoretical framework, the guiding spirit of the first post-Cold War was a great liberal voluntarism, based on the idea that the rejection of communism and the political vacuity in the East – reflected by an infantile idealisation of the West – were the best assets of 'market democracy'. Manageable in time, the post-Cold War appeared just as manageable in space. One was lulled to believe and hope that there existed an *optimum level of political disintegration* in the East: this was not likely to damage the territorial structure of the Cold War (excluding East Germany and the Baltic countries), and, better still, would remain confined to East Europe. During and after the Cold War, the United States never wished the political and territorial destruction of the USSR. *Dismantling the Cold War, nothing but the Cold War*, this was to have been the reasonable agenda of the new world order.

With the beginning of the Gulf crisis in August 1990, the international system entered the second post-Cold War. The effect of this crisis was to amplify and extend to the South the vision of a major and rapid restructuring of the world on new principles. Western euphoria was heightened, as this crisis prefigured the political disappearance of the USSR. There was neither any ideological alternative left – something one knew since the fall of the Berlin Wall – nor any strategic alternative, a fact that the southern countries – or nearly all of them – discovered to their great dismay. This period was to see the idea of a 'new world order', based on the triumph of international law and reason, flourish. In truth, it was less a question of building a 'new world order' than framing the rules of a *new public order* founded on a new and optimal connection between principles and means in the East as in the South.

As far as means are concerned, the Gulf war saw the principle of coalition take root, combining the advantages of political consensus and leadership exercised by a dominant player.

At the level of principles the war, through resolution 688, consecrated the principle of interference even if in practice the 'founding text of interference' contained any number of ambiguities. This second 'moment' consecrated superficially at the international level – and not just in the East – the idea of a manageable, decipherable and qualitatively superior post-Cold War.

The Moscow putsch, followed by the collapse of the USSR in December 1991, a year after the start of the Gulf crisis, was to put paid to this post-Cold War representation. In this phase, two new realities emerged which erased completely the previous euphoric perceptions.

The first consequence of the splintering of the USSR was to demonstrate that the principle of *reverse normalisation* was no longer acceptable. Decomposition was not going to stop at the doors of the Cold War but was going to bring down the entire pre-Cold War edifice. Indeed, decommunisation has lead not only to the disappearance of the GDR and the Soviet Union but has also caused the breaking up of the Czechoslovak federation, the disintegration of Yugoslavia, the extension of ethnic cleansing to all the East European or former Soviet states which had in their midst non-national minorities, and the exacerbation of the question of identity within the Federation of Russia itself. In other words, not only did the disintegration rationale not stop where one hoped or expected it would, but there seems to be no way to stem the tide.

The second consequence, even more worrying than the first, was the realisation that political disintegration was not going to remain restricted to the former socialist countries but was bound to spread to the West where regional movements with separatist overtones are gaining ground in Belgium, Italy and Canada.

Indeed, the end of the Cold War was largely responsible for the breaking up of Belgium because of the interplay of two factors : the abolution of the draft which limits 'interethnic' mixing between the Flemish and the Walloons and the demonstration effect that the amicable split of Czechoslovakia had on this country. To this one may add a third factor which flows to a large extent from the devalorisation of the socialist idea, that is to say the legitimacy of a redistribution of wealth between regions of very different levels of growth (Wallonia/Flemish Country). The imperative, within the same nation, of 'paying for the others' just because 'the others' do not speak the same language or share the same history does not hold any more. The 'politically thinkable' post-Cold War field is trying to shake itself free from territorial (national) and social (sharing) constraints, and this goes far beyond the Belgian case. The measure of this problem is of fundamental importance for the post-Cold War and post-Maastricht Europe. Indeed, one of the aims of the European Union Treaty is to respond to the dual challenge of the territoriality crisis and redistribution out of a kind suprastate voluntarism. At the economic and monetary level, national space has been done away with to some extent (single market, Central European Bank) or deemed to be of little relevance. At the social level, the Europe of Maastricht proposes to reinforce the redistribution of wealth from the rich countries to the poor countries. Now, it is this two-pronged attack that is causing problems, for it has to contend with the residual sovereignty of States as well as increasing public intolerance of redistributive and *a fortiori* supranational policies. The few cases discussed above show that we have yet to gauge the full impact of the collapse of communism. Conceptualizing the post-Cold War is by no means an easy task.

1

POWER AND PURPOSE IN THE INTERNATIONAL SYSTEM

ZAKI LAÏDI

The international order that was born in the ashes of Hiroshima and buried in the ruins of the Berlin Wall can be read, retrospectively and approximately, as a vertical and bipolar system regulated by three main principles. Nuclear deterrence was the ultimate instrument of control between East and West, politico-strategic factors predominated over economic constraints, and peripheral conflicts were subordinated to those at the centre. Nuclear force *protected* the international system against the excesses of conventional warfare, political solidarity *contained* economic disputes, the central theatre *dominated* peripheral conflicts. These three points require clarification.

Nuclear deterrence rapidly became identified with the East-West conflict, not only because the two superpowers gradually acquired the notorious power of Mutual Assured Destruction, but also because nuclear weapons provided an umbrella of deterrence protecting the main allies of each side. Occasionally the guarantee even extended to the periphery, as when the Americans had recourse to a nuclear alert against China and Korea in the 1950s. Over the years, however, the increasing stability of deterrence made explicit nuclear threats obsolescent, as if the deterrence culture had finally been internalised by the two blocs.[1] This concept of the *common culture of deterrence* can be seen as fundamental for, as we shall see, its extension to the South raises some delicate questions.

The pre-eminence of the politico-military factor in the management of international relations is related to a multiplicity of facts. The first of these is that the military hierarchy of nations, itself strongly influenced by the possession of nuclear weapons, was long identified with the hierarchy of world power (the five permanent members of the Security Council are nuclear powers). In 1971 the normalisation of Sino-American relations

1. Ernst-Otto Czempiel, James N. Rosenau (eds), *Global Changes and Theoretical Challenges. Approaches to World Politics for the 1990s*, Lexington, Lexington Books, 1989, p. 178.

symbolically confirmed the triumph of this image: the concept of a strategic tripolarity (Washington, Moscow, Beijing) appeared considerably more significant at that time than an economic tripolarity which included Japan.

The second truth is that, in most cases, the dominant powers in each bloc have shown their whole-hearted willingness to accept certain economic sacrifices in the name of what they see as overriding political imperatives. For example, the United States not only funded Japan's security but urged Europe to open its markets to Japanese products, while attempting at the same time to play down the political content of their commercial differences with Tokyo, despite the arsenal of justifiable economic criticisms directed at Japan from the 1950s onwards.[2]

Correspondingly, the prevailing political logic of security – as opposed to market freedom – meant that an alliance's political basis could not be permanently undermined by any substantial internal economic dispute.[3] Even after 1966 and ceaseless denunciation of the over-privileged dollar, Gaullist France had no intention of questioning the basis of her political alliance with Washington. Bonn's spectacular refusal to subsidise the financial laxity of the United States in the late 1970s did not affect German-American relations during the Euromissile crisis a few years later. This management of priorities was glaringly obvious in the Eastern bloc, where Moscow's allies had virtually no room for manoeuvre, and where economic constraints were consistently sacrificed on the altar of political ideology.

Finally, the primacy of political considerations did not escape the definition of North-South relations. The economic aid poured out by the central nations to those on the periphery followed a diplomatic-strategic reasoning which left the socio-economic modalities of its use to the beneficiaries' discretion. Within the Western camp the discipline of the UN vote took precedence over respect for market signals.

At the same time this bipolar logic rested on the almost total lack of any link between the central front, considered to be frozen, and a peripheral zone seen as less stable and more disputed. Hence a profusion of regional conflicts which were costly in human terms, and very often dependent on the symbolic and material resources of the East-West matrix, but which were remarkably contained by it.[4]

2. Cf. Warren Hunsberger, *Japan and the US in World Trade*, New York, Harper and Row, 1964.

3. Robert J. Art, 'A Defensible Defense. America's Grand Strategy After the Cold War', International Security, 15 (4), Spring 1991, p. 33.

4. The regional conflicts during the Cold War probably created nearly 40 million victims. Perception of bipolar stability is therefore very relative. Cf. Robert S. MacNamara, *The Post-Cold War World and its Implications for Military Expenditures in the Developing Countries*, Washington, World Bank, 1991, p. 27.

These hierarchical principles were underpinned by a relative cohesion between ideology, economy and policy. In effect, and starting with the Cold War, the Soviet Union and the United States presented themselves explicitly as *generators of purpose* well beyond their frontiers. They asserted their capacity to provide a global and coherent response to 'the world enigma' and to deploy the symbolic and material resources essential for its resolution.

The bipolar structure thus rested on a relative cohesion between the capacity to *define purpose* (to deliver a universalist message) and the capacity to *generate power* (economic and military). Depending on the circumstances, Islamic or Third World attempts to escape from this corset by operating together with autonomous signals and resources were nullified, restrained or broken.

The specific reason for recapitulating these elements of the Cold War tableau is that today they are seriously undermined by two complementary but separate developments: the end of the ideological East-West conflict, and the inescapable transformation of the rules of the international game. It is important to understand that the complexities of decoding international reality are the result not only of the implosion of communism but also of the coincidence between this fundamental event and the accelerated transformation of the rules of the pre-1989 international game. It is therefore useful to consider the cumulative nature of these two developments. Equally, starting from the concept of a decoupling of purpose from power, it seems appropriate to reflect on what we call the *loosening of the world order*.

Three approaches illuminate the hypothesis of a relaxation in the international order. The first leads to debate on the validity and viability of an international system based on the potential disconnection between power and purpose; the second encourages self-questioning concerning the best way to study a complex, ambivalent and volatile international system with its continually conflicting patterns of unification and fragmentation, on the assumption that the multipolar approach as a substitute for bipolarity is, in our view, empirically and conceptually too narrow to provide a comprehensive solution; and the third leads to an examination of the fundamental ambivalence in the loosening of the international system – attempting, for example, to show how the unification of the world ideological market through market democracy does not necessarily lead to the uniform or irreversible globalisation of the democratic rules of the game and of the market.

Next, this chapter – like the subsequent contributions – will consider the central question of contemporary international relations: the relationship between hierarchy and values, between purpose and power.

Definitions

For relatively simple reasons, the analysis of international relations is more naturally inclined to deal with the logic of power than that of purpose. As the offspring of history and of law, it instinctively expects to quantify material forces (weapons arsenals, GNP) in an institutionalised framework (the nation-state). Yet even in this respect there must apparently be change. Much of the debate on American decline is fuelled by the fact that the calculation of power becomes increasingly more delicate in a world of currents without fixed physical or national roots. The main difficulty in comprehending the American-Japanese conflict lies less in the interpretation of the actors' game than in the nature of the stakes. At a time when the 'added value' of certain Japanese cars made in the United States is more American than that of American cars made from parts imported from Japan, are the concepts of sovereignty or commercial deficit still relevant? The range of arguments extends in both directions.

Be that as it may, the question of purpose traditionally tackled by anthropology raises problems of methodology even more formidable than the assessment of power. Three provisional and unequal expressions of the concept of purpose exist in the international system; the order in which they are shown here does not imply any ranking of their importance.

The first is an overall representation of the world resting either on an identification of one's own values with universal values and thus seeking 'self-aggrandisement' (Tucker), or on a 'right to manage the world', to quote Thomas Mann's famous expression.[5] The two may come together naturally in a single actor within the international system; but the first tends to rest on hegemony (domination legitimised by means other than coercion) while the second seeks primarily to impose itself.

The second is an ambition to disseminate values which one sees as universal even if they are limited to a particular domain. Such values, which generate purpose, may be the natural counterpart of a material power, but may equally be largely independent of it. As Fernand Braudel stressed, the musical primacy of Germany and Italy was historically evident at times when their economic dominance in Europe was less than secure.[6] France's cultural influence – a useful field for generating purpose – has far outstripped her material power. If we are to believe Marc Fumaroli, French cultural expansion since Malraux has been planned and considered as an

---

5. Louis Dumont, *L'idéologie allemande, France-Allemagne et retour*, Paris, Gallimard, 1991, p. 83.

6. Fernand Braudel, 'Civilisation matérielle, économie et capitalisme XV–XVIIIe siècle', in *Le Temps du monde*, Paris, Armand Colin, vol.3, 1979, p. 54.

instrument of international politics designed to compensate for the loss of empire.[7] Similarly, British *savoir-faire* today in terms of financial development is incomparably superior to British material power.

The final expression of purpose is an ability to resolve problems of political, economic or social organisation without any real intention of extending their 'benefits' to the rest of the world, but with a domestic success-rate that encourages external operators to follow suit.

These necessarily broad meanings raise at least one essential question touching on the traditional stumbling-block of international analysis: that of the relationship between state and non-state actors.

For one simple reason this should not be seen as a fundamental difference: in the modern international system, values projected externally by significant non-state actors are virtually never in radical opposition to the values of the state. The supremely important promotion of market values beyond the American frontiers has barely been affected by the clash of American multinational firms with the American state in certain specific situations. The fact that the French intelligentsia of the Left exercised a quasi-monopoly in the export of French cultural values between 1945 and 1981 has in no way harmed the diffusion of a message perceived in other nations as that of 'France'.

The Decoupling of Power and Purpose

Although the Gulf War contradicted analyses of the obsolescence of war in international relations, it undoubtedly increased the tension between economics and politics, the two bulwarks of power. Moreover the proposition or imposition of a new hierarchy of power, based on a new combination of strategic diplomacy and economics, is a fundamental characteristic of the new world order. It occurred as soon as the two earlier controlling politico-military systems (first the 1939–45 victors, then the Cold War protagonists) proved incapable of dealing with the many limitations of the international system.

In straightforward terms, the end of the Cold War has removed the *ultima ratio* for crude distinctions between friends and enemies, between primary and secondary conflicts. The result has been a structural modification of the international stakes, from a *vertical* pattern (conflicts are not all of equal importance) to a more *horizontal* logic (conflicts are too complex and too specific for their settlement to be fungible). Politico-military primacy diminished with the fading of the nuclear threat; world economic

7. Marc Fumaroli, *L'Etat culturel. Essai sur une religion moderne*, Paris, Bernard de Fallois, 1991, p.188.

competition sharpened correspondingly. Yet here too the end of the Cold War cannot be held wholly responsible for the change; in reality it is only hastening the fundamental *non-fungibility* of vectors of power. In other words, the gains accumulated by an actor in a particular field (diplomatic strategy, for example) become less and less transferable to another field (economic or commercial).[8] Economic power and political power would thus tend to develop along increasingly divergent lines. This non-fungible characteristic of power is reinforced by the international system's increasingly volatile nature, now permanently open to renegotiation. Any rules that may be established are quickly seen as obsolete. Stable 'international régimes', dominated by one actor or another for long periods, have virtually ceased to exist, to be replaced by provisional and partial arrangements renegotiated at regular intervals.

Even if it reaches a positive conclusion the Uruguay Round cannot be seen as an exclusively United States product, nor can it have a life-expectancy comparable to the former post-1945 financial or trade régimes. It will never be possible to talk of the Uruguay Round system as one used to speak of the Bretton Woods system.[9]

Can we, however, envisage the lasting emergence of an international system split between politico-military powers and economic powers, between creators of purpose and generators of power? The response must involve a consideration of the interplay between the will of the actors, the constraining weight of world competition and the influence, sometimes decisive, of circumstances.

Firstly, it is reasonable to doubt whether a power such as the United States will resist the temptation to strengthen its comparative natural advantage (politico-military protection) in an attempt to sustain the fungible nature of power. Taken to extremes, this logic would lead the United States to make full use of its political trump cards in an exceptional context (the collapse of the Soviet Union) in order to preserve its own standing. The exploitation of this 'niche' would slow down the economic adjustments still affecting the United States. The striking contrast between the United States' international *savoir-faire* on the diplomatic-strategic level, reinforced by the Soviet collapse, and the growing erosion of the sources of its internal economic prosperity (over-consumption, disinvestment, the absence of any industrial policy other than military and space research, and the exhaustion of the Ford-inspired model of mass production) supports the hypothesis of a disconnection between purpose (ordering the

8. Joseph S. Nye Jr, *Bound to Lead. The Changing Nature of American Power*, New York, Basic Books, 1990, p. 182.

9. Susan Strange, 'States, Firms and Diplomacy', *International Affairs*, 68 (1), 1992, p. 14.

world around legitimate dominant values with universalist appeal) and material power. The consequence would appear to be an extended redefinition of the concept of 'burden-sharing', forcing the 'dependent powers' not only to assume the cost of their own protection, whether direct (Europe) or extended (the Gulf), as so often stated, but also to renounce certain economic and financial choices. This would enable American society to prolong its life of structural imbalances, without adjustment. The cost of the protection would thus be singularly high, because it would affect the growing *structural power* (in Susan Strange's meaning) of the 'dependent nations' in the world economy. Germany's reluctance to modify its monetary policy, despite the exhortations of the United States to do so in the name of a 'solidarity cemented' by the Gulf crisis, is an indicator of this slide.[10] The Gulf War does not, in any case, appear to have disproved the principle of the non-fungibility of elements of world power. Apart from the politico-military field of the Atlantic alliance – where their advance was foreseeable – the United States have not so far managed to affect the direction of German or Japanese financial policy, or impose new or excessive commercial concessions on Europe and Japan.

Secondly, this division might derive increased significance from its origins, extending beyond a pure exercise of will. Present-day international economic competition tends towards a complete separation of military and economic research networks, distinguishing clearly between economic and military powers. The trend towards a diminishing spin-off from military research to civil research undermines one of the most functional mechanisms of American power.[11] The excessive militarisation of US research is becoming a source of rigidity, even of decline, whereas only twenty years ago it was a symbol of its vitality.[12] Some writers take this reasoning further and perceive a negative correlation between levels of military research and international manufacturing competitiveness.[13] Even so, when civil and military research converge on common uses, the purpose of their relationship will tend to change. Civil innovation will lead to military innovation, but no longer the other way round.[14] The nature of the Soviet Union's collapse tends to sharpen international perception of this shift. This being so, the United States' ability to extend its comparative

10. *Financial Times*, 2 May 1991.

11. John Zysman, 'US Power, Trade and Technology', *International Affairs*, 67 (1), January 1991, p. 100.

12. Philippe Delmas, *Le maître des horloges. Modernité de l'action politique*, Paris, Odile Jacob, 1991, p. 304.

13. Mary Kaldor, *Problems of Adjustment to Lower Levels of Military Spending in Developed and Developing Countries*, Washington, World Bank, 1991, p. 5.

14. Zysman, 'US Power', p. 99.

advantage in the politico-military domain, to appear to be the only state capable of giving purpose to some event of international significance (the Gulf, the Balkans) cannot conceal the central fact that, like the majority of the great Western societies, American society is confronted with *three simultaneous and complementary losses of purpose:* (1) the 'loss of an adversary', forcing the United States to relinquish the 'friend/enemy' Manicheism which formed the basis of its foreign policy as well as part of its internal cohesion; (2) the public power's struggle to see itself and to operate in a context which de-legitimises it in two ways: through the ending of the Cold War (and thus of the great investment programmes combining public powers and the private sector) and the globalisation which undermines the implementation of purely national strategies; (3) the breaking of the balance between the US politico-military external focus and the growth of American material wealth. Most observers seem to agree that America must choose between external and internal demands, and also that most of the United States' problems are strictly self-induced.[15]

Developing powers will therefore see the possession of a military tool of prime size as an obstacle to a better standard of living, reinforcing their traditional political inhibitions. In the specific cases of Japan and Germany such inhibitions would reflect not only simple historical and moral guilt but the persistent difficulty of creating hegemony, in other words domination without coercion.[16] Purely economic considerations would be added to cultural or historical concepts to sustain – at least provisionally – ambitions opposed to political Messianism. The fashion for 'the Swiss model' in Germany is an example.[17]

As soon as the exploitation of principal strengths appears unrealistic or uneconomic for powers in the ascendant, the very meaning of world competition will be modified. Rather than the exercise of a global function of control it will concern patterns of organisation, sharing and balance between security and prosperity. As power becomes less fungible, the hierarchy of nations will double or, at the very least, become more complex. The end of the classic mechanism of *global relay* between ascending and descending powers, which Edward Carr has shown so well with reference to the United States and Great Britain, will undoubtedly be the essential trademark of the late twentieth-century international system.

<hr>

15. Cf. *Building Competitive America. First Annual Report to the President and Congress,* Competitiveness Policy Council, March 1992.

16. Edward H. Carr, *The Twenty Years' Crisis, 1919–1939,* London, Macmillan Papermac, 1991, p. 236. Ian Buruma, 'The Pax Axis', *New York Review of Books,* 25 April 1991; Peter Schneider, *L'Allemagne dans tous ses états,* Paris, Grasset, 1991, pp. 220ff.

17. *Financial Times,* 4 January 1991

Thirdly, serious analysis of the transformed international system requires full recognition of the changed rhythms of its various altered parameters. Patterns of erosion develop more slowly in the politico-military field than in the increasingly rapid cycles of economic innovation because politico-diplomatic dynamism is not rooted in material accumulation alone. The pressures of history, the vitality of a diplomatic apparatus or the capacity to exploit political opportunities introduce significant power differentials. In this connection the evident promptness and success of the United States' decision to 'deal with' the Mexican problem by integrating their southern neighbour into their own economic system are revealing; particularly when, like Paul Kennedy, one can see the decision creating an almost inexhaustible series of problems for the United States.[18] The capacity of actors to elicit, even permanently, a 'political added value' from the management of world affairs should therefore not be seen only in terms of its economic significance. The level of American political influence on Israel, for example, is wholly unaffected by variations in American power. There will always be a political temporality independent of economics which some nations will manage to operate more effectively than others. This is the case in France, whose capacity to *create purpose* (*politique de grandeur*) has traditionally exceeded its material capacity (humanitarian diplomacy). Today, with the ending of the Cold War, France is attempting to turn this 'humanitarian diplomacy' into an essential instrument of her diplomatic redeployment and the maintenance of her individuality in the world. This move has the advantage of creating purpose at a relatively low cost – in other words a strong symbolic presence can be sustained for a minimal economic price. President Mitterrand's spectacular visit to Sarajevo, for example, helped to disguise France's very modest contribution to the reception of Bosnian refugees. Perhaps humanitarian diplomacy conceals an inability to act politically. Within this hypothesis it would be premature, or perhaps inaccurate, to see 'humanitarian diplomacy' as a fundamental trait of the world politics of the twenty-first century, or a significant means of creating purpose on the international scale. It is equally possible that the Russia of the late twentieth century will eventually come to resemble nineteenth-century Russia and recover political influence matching its geography, history, military power and impressive capacity for harm.

Fourthly, three major significant developments in the international system have apparently increased this gap between patterns of material production and the production of purpose: the Soviet Union's political

18. Paul Kennedy, *The Rise and Fall of the Great Powers*, New York, Random House, 1987, p. 517.

collapse, the emergence of the European Community and the growth of Japan, which since 1985 has both caught up with the United States and subsidised its hegemony.[19] Even though they appear radically different in cultural and historical terms, these three 'moments' illustrate and reinforce the current tendency within the international system towards more rapid organisation economically than in terms of political image. Europe is having difficulty both in synchronising its economic and political development and in creating common values, a universalist model greater than the simple aggregation of national good intentions.[20] Europe will not convince the world of its ability to create purpose until it invents a new combination of collective security, national sovereignty and economic integration. Links between national and supranational elements must be considered, as well as between economic and political factors.

The current danger of disunity between military security and economic integration offers two further disadvantages: of increasing Europe's political insecurity and reducing the continent to a simple free-exchange zone. Even in the latter case, however, the relationship between power and purpose would have to be faced one day. Should we consider Europe only with a regard to its becoming more competitive on a world scale, or should we be concerned with the sanctity of the marriage between economic and social factors – the basis, after all, of its specific character? While these two major questions remain at least partially unresolved, it is possible to speak of a disconnection between purpose and power in Europe.

At first sight the Maastricht Treaty appears politically capable of bridging this gap between purpose and power, provided it undertakes to raise Europe from the level of a trading group to a global political project. In the event the Maastricht debate seems – at least temporarily – to have shown up this gap rather than reduced it. The Maastricht Treaty concentrates very much more on how to construct Europe than on the purpose of this construction. Europe's political, cultural and philosophical aims are very largely ignored and the geographical limits of the Community are equally disregarded. The European Union project has thus been defined more by what it is than by what it aspires to. This difficulty in expressing power and purpose is largely the result of the extreme difficulty experienced by the drafters of the Treaty in finding a universally acceptable compromise. Discussion of the 'European model' – as distinct from the American or Japanese models – is therefore likely to reveal temporary splits at the heart of Europe. This bare explanation is, however, inadequate. The construc-

19. Robert Gilpin, *The Political Economy of International Relations*, Princeton, Princeton University Press, 1987, p. 328.
20. Jean-Marie Domenach, *Europe: le défi culturel*, Paris, La Découverte, 1990, p. 145.

tion of Europe is foundering on a major contradiction of our times. In order to carry weight, public opinion needs a strong theme, requiring a certain amount of simplification, issues seen to be at stake, and a debate. Yet public opinion is equally cautious about generalised discourse with no definite objective. The consequence, both for the actors directly involved and for the ordinary citizen, is the great difficulty of finding a satisfactory half-way point between the debate's technicality (an antidote to romanticism but a potential obstacle to mobilisation) and teleological initiatives (a source of strong feelings but equally possibly of scepticism). The debate on monetary union does little to avoid this contradiction, for although its extreme technicality removes it from any teleological drift, it nevertheless has difficulty in appearing as a real question requiring a solution. Here, too, the technical debate on the best way to maximise European power fails to give this power any strong purpose.[21]

This gap penalises Europe in diplomatic-strategic terms as well as in its economic relations with the rest of the world. The roots of Europe's weakness in commercial negotiations with the United States, for example, do not lie in any economic imbalance (the two blocs are similar in size) or in the 'magical effects' of American leadership following the Gulf War, but in Europe's political atrophy. The representatives of the American state – who have a wide range of prerogatives and are therefore capable of enlarging the scope of their discussions with Europe at will – confront a European Commission whose mandate is strictly limited to the consideration of commercial questions. Problems therefore arise less from the absence of cohesion between Europeans than from their (temporary?) difficulty in thinking of themselves in political terms, even in the field of international economic relations. As Anne-Marie Le Gloannec emphasises in this book, however, we should recognise that Europeans within the Community hold a perception of their own collective identity which differs – perhaps fundamentally – from the Eastern European concept of Europe. Seen from Prague or Budapest, the Europe of the Community constitutes an essential pole of democratic reference. For this reason it seems difficult to agree with Cornelius Castoriadis that Western societies offer the rest of the world a 'counter image' dominated by a 'void totally without meaning'.[22]

This *lack of purpose* appears even more flagrant in the case of Japan, with its explicit imbalance between the national cultural model and its globalisation. Japan appears incapable of visualising the world (which

21. Cf. Laurent Cohen-Tanugi, *L'Europe en danger*, Paris, Fayard, 1992.
22. Cornelius Castoriadis, 'Le délabrement de l'Occident', *Esprit*, December 1991, p. 39.

would make it an *importer of purpose*), and, in addition, she rejects the possibility of such visualisation, in order to preserve her 'otherness'. Japan appears to lack those *substantive beliefs* which, combined with material inducements, enable a dominant power to develop the means for global socialisation.[23] This would indeed be a true expression of power without a message, the ultimate illustration of the disconnection in the international system between power and purpose, since the expression of its action on the international level would be economic rather than diplomatic-strategic or cultural.

The central question is whether, through its material power, Japan will lead the world towards a *devaluation of purpose* (seen as an obstacle to material prosperity), or whether its *domination without purpose* will make that domination even less tolerable to the rest of the world.

Between these two extremes several intermediate possibilities can of course be envisaged, which would reduce the gap between purpose and power, and also abrogate Japan's uniqueness.

The allocation of purpose between its creators and its seekers has, in fact, never been absolute or static. Eighteenth-century Amsterdam did not present itself to the world as a model capable of reproduction. Its initial fame was based on naval and commercial achievements, with the concept of 'trust' emerging gradually from the developing confidence between merchants (basis of the mechanism of the letter of exchange) that material interest guaranteed human security more effectively than weapons. Europe learned gradually from Amsterdam that the sword no longer ruled the world and that weapons were not the answer to every problem.[24] This example alone shows clearly that a pre-stated claim to universality is not essential for ensuring the successful diffusion of one's message. A multitude of Japanese micro-strategies, of procedures and of initiatives, can therefore be imagined, spreading ever further through the world and gradually creating purpose in the eyes of their potential users. A deliberate intention to create purpose for others is thus not necessary as a precondition for such creation. The fact that the Japanese social model may be neither 'attractive' nor exportable does not prevent Japan from offering the model in terms of 'human development' (education, health).[25] The fashion for the Japanese model of *just in time* compared to the old American mass-

---

23. G. John Ikenberry and Charles A. Kupchan, 'Socialization and Hegemonic Power', *International Organization*, 44 (3), Summer 1990, p. 285; Masaru Tamamoto, 'Japan's Search for a World Role', *World Policy Journal*, 7 (3), Summer 1990, p. 502.

24. Henry Méchoulan, *Amsterdam au temps de Spinoza. Argent et liberté*, Paris, Presses Universitaires de France, 1990, p. 75.

25. The latest report of the UNDP on human development places Japan first in the world, *The Economist*, 25 May 1991.

production model reveals how far others may be constrained to follow an alignment by the 'simple fact' of its having become the most successful, as is shown by Jean-Marie Bouissou in his contribution to this book.

Elsewhere, it now seems to be accepted that the era of pre-assembled models, exported 'ready to drive away', has passed. True, there are still universal points of reference which are currently enjoying an accelerated globalisation (democracy, market, human rights): but the particularism of national or infranational situations has never been so great. The weight of history, of tradition, or of the accidental, has never fully explained the success or failure of a project or an experience. The debate about France's introduction of the German pattern of apprenticeship ended abruptly when it was realised that German success in this domain was the result less of a 'benevolent strategy' requiring only thought, than of a group of interconnected choices rooted in the German enterprise culture. Ralf Dahrendorf has stressed, moreover, that the German social market economy – a tempting new model in some eyes – is not a pre-existing intellectual construction, but 'a hybrid of ideas and personalities'.[26] In fact we are entering a world where external borrowings are increasing but where ready-made models are rejected even when they lay claim to a certain balance between the economic and the social, as is seen in the setback suffered by 'third ways' and the exhaustion of the Swedish model. In other words, perhaps the point at issue no longer lies between passive acceptance and positive rejection of a particular model but in the optimum combination of the universal and the particular.

In other words again, the export of one's own values today depends less on asserting their specificity abroad, planting the flag or selling one's label by encouraging the receiver to adopt the sender's principles, than on demonstrating a willing and ready response to specific demanding expectations.

Polarity: Neither Single nor Multiple

The end of the bipolar system has almost inevitably revived the taste for multipolarity, a theme which very many writers took for granted in the 1970s in the threefold context of Soviet-American détente, Sino-American rapprochement and the emerging oil powers of the OPEC nations. In this respect we must now guard against what Hirschmann calls the 'danger of hindsight', i.e. over-emphasis of the bipolar era's cohesive stability in order to show up more clearly today's 'instability' or 'lack of coherence'. Is this thinking constructive in the post-Cold War context?

26. Ralf Dahrendorf, *Reflections on the Revolution in Europe*, (`Counterblasts' series), London, Chatto and Windus, 1990.

If by multipolarity we understand a greater distribution of the means of power in the world, the concept appears pertinent but in no way new: its merit may be limited to its descriptive value. Beyond that its application appears more complex in terms of both method and analysis.

Firstly, by adopting the hypothesis of an international system in *transition*, we must in effect follow Gilpin in conceding that the appropriate level of analysis lies less with the static distribution of world power than with the interaction between the actors. In other words, an interest in syntheses, processes and tendencies should replace the scrupulous inventory of arsenals and the everlasting debates about *equality of purchasing powers* versus the rate of exchange as the best way to evaluate GNPs. Because international relations obey a logic of demand more than of supply, statistical and accounting battles over calculations of power or decline are of only relative interest.[27] From this point of view, the 'polarity' approach tends to treat matters as fixed when they are in full evolutionary spate and to crystallise forms which are fluid and manifold.

Secondly, the concept of multipolarity arises from the classic view of an international system which can be reduced to single nation-states of equal strength within it, pursuing the same goals and springing promptly into a mechanistic game of alliances at the first sign of individual ambition.[28]

The current international situation challenges the validity of such an approach. The decoupling of purpose and power described above prevents any possible competition between nations in the form of a struggle between units sharing the same objectives or at least employing the same channels to maximise their positions. Moreover, even before the end of the Cold War this difficulty in comparing different poles restricted regularisation of the concept. Power would lie less in overall domination than in a coordinated selective choice. It would be as significant to *avoid* certain responsibilities as to *acquire* them. A major part of the American criticisms addressed against Japan rests precisely on the latter's refusal to assume certain costs of power.

The use of the concept of multipolarity raises even more fundamental objections. Although the state still remains a powerful actor in the international system, its monopoly of stimulus is much reduced. The need to bal-

27. The financial re-evaluation of American shares abroad which considerably reduces the United States' rank as net debtor, or the taking into account of exports of American branches overseas to the United States – allowing a relativisation of the economic range of the American commercial deficit – have only a negligible influence on the political interpretation of the American decline.

28. Kenneth H. Waltz, *Theory of International Politics*, Reading, Mass., Addison-Wesley Publishing Company, 1979, p. 118.

ance a developing power with an alliance strengthened by traditional powers exists in economic terms but does not necessarily coincide with the frontiers of nation-states. Nor should one consider transferring the problem of the state to commercial management, for here again reality is even more complex. Business management operations resemble those of states only superficially; furthermore – and contrary to certain theories fashionable during the 1970s – they resist any 'move into politics'. It cannot be claimed that the aggravation of commercial tensions between Japan and the United States encouraged the Americans to resolve their differences with Europe in a friendly fashion. The operational application of multipolarity is reduced in many ways: by the inappropriate nature of the *balance of power* concept in the economic field, the fragmented nature of the stakes in international politics, and the imperfect coincidence of economic and political sovereignty – not to mention the political heterogeneity of the poles, for Europe is not politically sovereign in the same way as the United States or Japan. In this book, for example, Helen Milner stresses the improbability of a commercial tripolarity based on three clear-cut blocs. Finally, even if it were accepted that multipolarity represents a functional specialisation between economic and military poles rather than a static distribution between comparable powers, its operation would stumble over fresh difficulties.

The consideration of Japan as the world's leading financial power should not obscure the fact that it lacks two essential attributes of financial supremacy: that of lender of last resort and that of nation of international currency reserve.[29] This 'functional semi-paralysis' may reasonably be seen as temporary; but Japan may nonetheless continue to resist the assumption of such responsibilities. This single example shows clearly the uncertainties of classification defining the differences between economic or financial strength and political strength. In virtually all areas of strength, the dominant state and non-state actors hold ever-wider responsibilities (globalisation), but these are also increasingly shared responsibilities. No single actor can now dominate an entire international process, and this includes the United States in the military domain. In short, we would be faced with a multipolarity which is new, incomplete and heterogeneous. New, because it would be based neither on a categoric differentiation of functions nor on an equal division of global power; incomplete, since it would

<hr>

29. R. Taggart Murphy, 'Power without Purpose: The Crisis of Japan's Global Financial Dominance', *Harvard Business Review*, March-April 1989, pp. 75–6; Georges S. Tavlas and Yusuru Ozeki, 'The Japanese Yen as an International Currency', working document of FMI-WP 91, Washington, IMF, 1991; Jean-Marie Bouissou, Guy Faure and Zaki Laïdi, *L'expansion de la puissance japonaise*, Brussels, Complexe, 1992.

not allow any actor to be the absolute master of a process; and heterogeneous through establishing relations between political entities of different natures (the European Community, the United States).

It is, in fact, reasonable to consider whether the sources of power should be sought not in poles, where it may be difficult to define the area of responsibility, but in the *combinations* pre-eminent in certain processes or certain geopolitical areas. This combinatory approach would direct the problematics of polarisation in two ways: firstly, in emphasising that, more than ever before, power is generated by the *interaction of the actors* rather than by the actors individually; secondly, by emphasising that combinations are shaped by the elements or processes under consideration rather than the reverse.

An International Post-Modern System?

We must be clear about this. An essential question – the meaning of the post-Cold War international system – is ignored in refinements of systematisation and classification. On this level, post-modernity may be helpful.

Firstly, it is important to avoid possible misunderstandings: there is no fully accepted definition of post-modernity. Nor, fortunately, is there any global problematisation of the post-modern international system.[30] However, the analyst of international relations can draw freely on certain interpretations of post-modernity. Rather than interpreting the overall international system according to a post-modern model, it is thus a matter of accepting the possibility of analysing certain of its dynamics starting from the post-modern situation. In other words, the recourse to post-modernity responds primarily to a need to understand new empirical situations for which classic readings no longer provide the answer.

Reasoning in post-modern terms means attempting to reflect on everything which now appears, in practical terms, to be characteristic of the disintegrated world order: *the transitory, the unstable, the disconnected, the ambivalent.* It means attempting to understand the unstable and question the unequivocal.[31] The post-Cold War world would appear to be post-modern in its tendency to break with the principal characteristics of modernity: the linear and constructed model-types (the Cold War), based on direct and predictable causality. Three hypotheses sustain this view.

Firstly, the complexity of the world cannot be reduced to a 'new enig-

30. Cf. Pauline Rosenau, 'Once Again into the Fray. International Relations Comforts the Humanities', *Millennium*, 19 (1), Spring 1990.

31. Cf. the very stimulating work of David Harvey, *The Condition of Postmodernity*, Oxford, Basil Blackwell, 1989. Many of the reflections in this book are applicable to the field of international relations.

ma' with a hidden meaning capable of being grasped at the cost of sustained intellectual effort: nothing that we see today – facts without any firm foundation, self-contradictory processes, management plans with blurred and overlapping outlines – indicates a temporary state which will eventually and inevitably be settled, stabilised or clarified. A very lengthy transition may be imagined, with purpose emerging slowly. To quote Steiner, the 'meaning of the world' is neither 'stabilised' nor 'saturated'.[32]

Secondly, the international dynamics seen in juxtaposition – co-existing, interpenetrating and confronting each other – prefigure not a 'remix' of the central ingredients in classic terms, but an era in which we will learn to combine representations or categories hitherto in opposition. Timothy Garton Ash's invented 'portmanteau words', which he used with reference to post-communist Eastern Europe (*'refolutions'*, *'demotatorship'*), illustrate the process clearly. Examples of post-modernity in international relations appear in most of the contributions to this book. Thus, even without using the exact term, Georges Couffignal emphasises that it has now become impossible to define relations between the United States and Latin America in terms of 'autonomy' or 'dependence' because the two dynamics are symmetrically engaged. Certainly in Latin America, as elsewhere, there is nothing new in this ambivalence; but today it presents a new and more closely defined character. The implementation of autonomous strategies stems not from any mechanistic need to offset a sense of economic inferiority but from the impossibility, even for the United States, of taking on the whole of Latin American dynamics. The attempt to create an independent political self-image coincides with the search, by other methods, for integration into the sphere of American wealth.

Finally, the third hypothesis consists in accepting that in general terms explanations are neither firm nor unequivocal.

Specific illustrations are helpful when considering sketchy definitions which may be too abstract.

Let us take first the number of polarities within the international system. We emphasised above that it was pointless to imagine that, with some genuine effort, one would eventually establish a precise figure. It is therefore more productive to see the international reality as simultaneously unipolar, multipolar and, in many cases, 'a-polar', leaving only reflection on the intersection and interaction of these polarities. The current map of Europe illustrates this situation. Rather than debating whether Community logic will overcome Atlantic or federal logics we would do better to consider how they might co-exist without an inescapable 'clarification' immediately intervening. In the study of international relations it will be less a

32. George Steiner, *Real Presences*, Chicago, University of Chicago Press, 1989.

matter of classifying and simplifying than of interpreting what is mobile and contradictory. This extreme complexity, together with many other factors, leads, at the very least, to reservations and scepticism about the emergence of any UN-style legitimacy capable of employing principles recognised by all its actors to create a new and definitive purpose out of the international system. In the new world order, as in the old, it will be the most powerful participants who continue to supply elements of purpose.

Consideration of the Japanese problem also corresponds reasonably well to this post-modern step, for it forces us to think of concepts or categories, which we have customarily considered as opposites, in association with each other. It can be said simultaneously of the Japanese economy that it is both powerfully regulated and alarmingly competitive within its own frontiers; that the state is heavily represented within it, yet that Japan is a society without a state, that political pluralism exists but that the logic of the single party is strong, that the originality of the Japanese production system is to invert the order of factors between producers and consumers to the advantage of the latter but – also simultaneously – that the Japanese consumer is very often the victim of producer cartels, etc.

Reflection on hegemony, and particularly on regional hegemony, also lends itself to post-modern problematics. Classically, the hegemonic aspirations of an actor were measured by his capacity to control a national space, to identify resources (whether material or symbolic) essential to the exercise of a durable strategy of influence, and to design a political plan for 'mobilising support'. This problematisation of power is still relevant in many cases. For example, the Turkish regional game could be interpreted as the expression of a 'traditional' regional plan. This would see Turkey as seeking to construct a sphere of influence among Turkish-speaking peoples on the basis of a genuine economic prosperity, with its 'model of modernity' (Picard) based on material prosperity, its special capacity for intercession with the West, and its model of the democratic integration of Moslems into economic and political activity. The Soviet Azeris' (temporary) political preference for Ankara rather than Teheran would reinforce this view.[33] This could be seen as an existing model of a rise to power in which economic success and bipolar disintegration operate cumulatively to reduce political inhibitions among newly emancipated actors. On the best hypothesis, Ankara would employ its stabilising role of tutor to the Turkish-speaking world to advance its political position *vis-à-vis* the West. In this case, we should not minimise the risk that the West might concede the leadership of the Turkish-speaking world to Turkey but covertly pre-

33. Olivier Roy, 'Les limites du nouveau jeu iranien', *Le Monde*, 3 May 1991.

vent her full and unrestricted entry into the closed club of the 'Christian West' to which she so desperately aspires.

It has not, however, been established that this clearly marked path of power now constitutes the most current and appropriate mode of regional affirmation. From Nigeria to India, via Brazil, Iran and China, we are witnessing the emergence of a post-modern structuring of hegemony, founded on disconnections rather than on coherent processes, finding expression in a potential capacity for harm rather than in redistribution, eased by autonomous infranational social actors rather than by embassies, borne along by partial strategies rather than any global design. All of these contradictory accretions clearly correspond to the post-modern approach. Barely ten years ago, Nigeria's regional influence was measured by the yardstick of the redistributional power of her oil wealth and her politico-military control over her neighbours. Today, this classic 'representation' of regional power seems too reductive for a genuine understanding of Nigerian reality. In Liberia, the point at issue is perhaps less to set up a politically docile government than to preserve intact one of the precious channels for the laundering of drugs (valuable as part of the dollar zone).

In China the proliferation of 'economic regions' on the Pudong model – outside the clumsy authority of centralised bureaucracy but, to powerful effect, part of the world market – cannot be interpreted as either asset or weakness. It expresses both realities simply and simultaneously; for as well as undermining still further the political authority of the octogenarian *nomenklatura* in Beijing, this proliferation offers the Chinese government and its extended clientèles both an effective – and therefore convertible – economic tool and a valuable 'geopolitical hinterland' which inhibits the making of excessively drastic choices between economic openness and political pluralism. China's national regionalisation occupies a central place in her relationships with the West and prevents an over-simplified Western attitude towards Beijing. The effect of Chinese geopolitical atomisation is to force others to atomise their own interests in response.

The existence in Beijing of a powerful, autonomous and effective military-industrial complex sustains a similar interpretation. It confirms the weakening of Chinese political power beyond the ultimate totalitarian circle, but strengthens China's capacity to establish herself at the forefront of competition in arms sales, enabling her to profit from her potential for damage in the export of sensitive technologies. The 'cellularisation of Chinese society', discussed by Jean-Luc Domenach in this book, arises from this same type of ambivalence. It accelerates society's change from the era of 'detotalisation' to that of social entropy; simultaneously it accentuates continental China's synchronisation with the Chinese world overseas. This 'synchronisation' is not in itself *either* harmonising *or* disintegrational, it is simultaneously harmonising *and* disintegrational. Certain aspects are highly integrational in character (drainage of resources through development); others (accentuated phenomena of flight, the abdication of responsibility or the infantile idealisation of the Western world) are extremely destructuralising.

It is a delicate matter to reflect on Chinese world or regional strategy, on the basis of such contradictory facts that have no coherent underlying design, even when, retrospectively, they will acquire a functional character. However, such reflection is probably still worth pursuing. In post-modern terms, China is both much less and much more than a regional power.

She is less than a regional power because the 'Chinese model' appears more repellent than attractive. Chinese society expects infinitely more from the outside world than that world can offer it. Even on a classical political register, such as that of Cambodia, China must share its influence with increasingly demanding partners such as Thailand. Nevertheless, China preserves her regional status by default, as the result of the unprecedented political collapse of her two great rivals, the Soviet Union and Vietnam. The potential risk of a strategic void in Asia, the fragmentation of the Asia-Pacific area, the partial disappearance of the Chinese menace in certain lands such as Indonesia, the extraordinary vitality of anti-Japanese feeling – all these are elements which nourish, there too 'in the void', China's potential influence. Finally, thanks to her diplomatic status (she is a permanent member of the Security Council), her fragmented economy and her military-industrial complex, China is a world power which her peers, and particularly the United States, see as having great 'nuisance value'.

Iran is a different case; yet she too provides a moderately sound illustration of this post-modern problematic, where traditionally disparate or hierarchical elements cling together without any pre-existing rationale. Iran's pretensions to Islamic hegemony, moreover, were shown to be greater than those of the Shah because they bore a religious Messianism which extended beyond the traditional framework of the Gulf region. From Senegal to Pakistan, via Soviet Azerbaijan and Bahrain, Teheran attempted to influence an Islamic zone of Shiite dominance and revolutionary potential. The end of the Gulf War and the crushing of Iraq revived the notion of a more classical Iranian hegemony. Redeployment on these lines would offer Teheran the advantage of combining three registers – ethnicity, religion and non-Arab regional power – while receiving indirect support from the West. Three conduits hitherto judged partially contradictory would come together and thus confirm the flexibility of interplay between hegemonies. Here as elsewhere, however, fragmentation seems likely to win over coherence. In general terms Teheran failed to construct a Shiite geopolitical space. Wherever Shiism manages to attain a significant level of political force, Iran is forced to share her patronage: with Syria in Lebanon and in Iraq, with the Pakistanis in Afghanistan, and with the Turks among the Azeris. In the Sunni subregions, the bounds of its influence remain greater because the external patronage is exclusively Arab.[34]

There will thus be a growing and almost structural flaw in any plan for regional hegemony, to the point moreover where 'the region' as an area and, through it, the concept of 'a regional subsystem', may appear to have lost part of its relevance. This question is not easily answered, for any brief reply would risk being invalidated by multiple counter-examples.

On the other hand, it is easier to state more categorically that 'the region' is no longer automatically an intermediate register between the internal and the worldwide, an essential staging post along the route to a world policy. As we increasingly witness the compression of these different registers in real time, our relationship with traditional geopolitical topography becomes distinctively modified. Certain choices which are recognised as regional are no longer the end result of a laborious balancing of the internal and the worldwide; they constitute rather the regional interpretation of a world strategy elaborated on the national scale. Actors who promote economic activity, such as Japan, Korea or Taiwan, have their own fundamental image of themselves – and on a world scale – which does not stop them using the Asiatic zone temporarily or more permanently as the chosen field for their economic interventions. This perspective may perhaps help us to avoid repeating old debates on the self-centred potentialities of a nation or a region.

The Ambivalence of World Time

To say of today's world order that it has 'loosened' does not imply that it is threatened with complete chaos or the loss of all restraint. In many respects the world order is becoming increasingly standardised and constricting, as is seen in the extreme power of the phenomena of economic and cultural globalisation. This argument can be taken further in considering the unprecedented efforts at collective thought among operators of the modern international system (which extend far beyond the field of international relations), as can be seen in the proliferation of legal norms in the general field of social relations. In economic relations the weight of constraint is still more striking: concepts of autonomy or choice are buried under the burden of interdependence. Business margins for

34. Ibid.

manoeuvre, for example, depend much less on choice than on the speed of reaction to external circumstances. On the North-South axis, constraints operate even more oppressively under the burden of asymmetry: for over a decade now the nations of the North have sought to export their own imbalances to the South, while filtering out with great care any 'retroactive effects' which might affect them. This has been the central point at issue in programmes of structural adjustment established since the early 1980s. Since the liberation of the Eastern nations the logic of conditionality has been extended to the political field: the aim is to link the grant of external economic resources to respect for political pluralism as well as to a programme of economic reforms based on market regulations. In theory this new disposition should be irresistible because, on the world scale, there remains no surviving strategic or economic alternative capable of withstanding it.

However, we must be careful not to let this line of argument lead us into inferring over-simplistic consequences for world organisation. The 'diplomatic-legal' view of the world remains too conventional to be helpful in appreciating the complexity of the international system. Elizabeth Picard's contribution to this book suggests that the regional pattern remains undisturbed by the Gulf War, since the power of domination acquired by the United States in no way implies any capacity for control over this region. The Middle East, she writes, is an area which is dominated but not controlled. In fact, and whatever the multiplicity and intensity of external constraints, the post-Cold War world order presents one major singularity: it no longer rests on an essential principle that is capable of ordering united and simultaneous *hierarchy* and *purpose*, as was partly the case during the Cold War. If the creation of purpose on the world scale remains, despite everything, the business of the dominators, matters of interpretation and application increasingly elude its proponents.[35] The loosening of the international system is an unstable process in which prescribed figures and re-invented ploys confront each other and mingle together. Today the 'exportation of meaning' (to quote Tamar Liebes) is volatile and ambivalent,[36] despite caution over the excesses of a culturalist move which, through insistence on the 'autonomisation of meaning', is falling prey to the opposite problem: the denial of strong relationships on a world scale. Today's 'world time' expresses well this postmodern ambivalence.

35. Bertrand Badie and Guy Hermet, *Politique comparée*, Paris, Presses Universitaires de France, 1990, p. 61.

36. Tamar Liebes and Elihu Katz, *The Export of Meaning. Cross Cultural Readings of Dallas*, Oxford, Oxford University Press, 1990.

The collapse of the Berlin Wall has made us realise a powerful international truth: that of 'world time'. Market democracy henceforward constitutes the world matrix, the legitimate problematic of the international system. We find this change both striking and surprising in the speed of its spread and the extent of its influence. Less than two years after the collapse of the Berlin Wall the claims of 'planned single-party socialism' have become wholly discredited and virtually the exception to the rule.

World time is not only the legitimisation of the market ideology and its political corollary, democracy: it is also the affirmation that they are organically associated, forming a circular relationship between market, development and democracy. This shows an awareness of market signals which will generate development – development which in its turn would be politically 'unthinkable' without scrupulous respect for pluralism. Progress (development), equity (exchange-based market) and liberty (democracy) therefore find themselves locked into a virtuous circle. The starting point of this circle has, however, never been established historically except, *a contrario*, through the conclusive failure of communism. This dominant norm takes over in an exceptional ideological and technological context: the absence of any global alternative to market democracy or any technical obstacles to hinder its world-wide diffusion.

The world time thus finds itself bearing a stabilising universalist message, establishing what Guy Hermet calls 'a world condition recognised as necessary'. Its power lies less in its capacity to convert humanity to the benefits of this new universal and secular belief (the democracy of the market) than in insisting on the need to place oneself, politically speaking, in relation to it. In Latin America, for example, regional specialists are puzzled at the speed with which the 'ideology of the Left' has collapsed within a few years, and the extent to which the economic recovery of Chile and Mexico validates the whole subcontinent's move to the market. This context is probably fragile and volatile; but for certain governments, such as those of Argentina or Venezuela, it constitutes at this juncture a considerable and virtually unexpected political resource which only Brazil appears to utilise poorly or with difficulty. The world time thus reminds mankind of its shared aspirations, even if this entails the illusion that it also shares experience of the same problems and will resolve them in the same way. From this point of view the world time tends to generate a universal culture of instantaneity which legitimises the most unreasonable impatience. No sooner are specific obstacles to market democracy removed than such democracy is demanded *hic et nunc*. The idea of democratic construction, with all its implications of lengthiness, difficulty and danger, becomes unacceptable to those who consume Western television products every day in real time. In this respect, the fashion for the concept of 'civil society' in both the East and the South is evidence of this levelling synchronicity. The whole world refers to it, although there is evidence that it assumes widely differing meanings.[37] In Czechoslovakia, for example, civil society echoes the idea of a second society based on an associative movement; in the Maghreb, on the other hand, it represents social operators, generally from the state apparatus, who are subject to a framework of moral or meritocratic interpretation (probity, independence of thought, technical competence).

In such circumstances, how can one appreciate the residual margins of autonomy of social and governmental operators? How to believe in the loosening of the international system when such a standardising and normed logic crosses so many frontiers?

By enquiring a little more closely, however, it may be seen that the shades of world time are more mixed than they appear, that the 'world enlightenment' is sometimes more apparent than real, more spectacular than effective, and more ambivalent than unequivocal.

The world time does not solve the enigma of the world. There is no resemblance to Hegel's cherished 'splendid dawn of the world', even if it suggests that certain human victories have a character which is both universal and 'cumulative' (Lévi-Strauss). It is therefore much more an approximate and tendential universality than a new Messianism. What this time modifies is therefore less the matrix of world problems than the terms in which it is convenient to reconsider them. At its best the market democracy represents a political ideal, a political system or a 'human construct', but in no circumstances is it a 'ready-made' model.[38] The move to the market in Eastern European countries constitutes a unique historical experience, not to be matched fully or satisfactorily by anything else. The United States' silence on Boris Yeltsin's economic 'shock therapy' is highly revealing of the 'neo-liberal' model's operational limits.

It is therefore helpful to cite certain examples, not so much to provide comparisons between powerful effects of the world climate as to give the latter a more contrastive interpretation.

In effect, at least two implicit but uncertain correlations are apparent behind the concept of market democracy: they concern the relationship between legitimacy and effectiveness, and that between democracy and development.

37. Michel Camau, 'Le Maghreb face aux mutations internationales', contribution to colloquium for translation, establishment of texts and studies, Carthage, Beit El Hikma, May 1990, p. 12.

38. Jean-Luc Domenach, 'Chine: la longue marche vers la démocratie', *Pouvoirs*, 52, 1990, p. 63.

Legitimacy and Effectiveness

Although market democracy is universally dominant, it is far from being universally effective. One must reckon not only with the slowness of the transition process but also with the vitality of forms of resistance which were not automatically eliminated by the ideological collapse of socialism. In Italy or Greece the reluctance of the political class to privatise a powerful and inefficient public sector arises less from an outmoded state-control oriented reflex than from the fear of losing an important source of finance for political parties. It could be said, in fact, that the complex play of acquired interests has no need to structure itself round an ideological principle (socialism) for justification or survival. It can establish or re-establish itself from new factors such as the fear of foreign seizure by means of privatisation. *A contrario*, it would be naive to regard a certain infatuation for privatisation as the mark of a magical conversion to the market. In the Soviet Union, where private property was little known even before the October Revolution, the privatisation of public property appeared potentially like a privileged division of the spoils, sharing out the defunct Soviet system for the benefit of the former *nomenklatura*. Privatisation in such conditions would be no more than a travesty of liberalisation,[39] as is often the case in Africa or the Middle East.

This lack of a correlation between legitimacy and effectiveness appears in another context, that of 'democratic dissymmetry' (Rosanvallon), in other words in the gap between the development of a *political dispute* carried out in the name of democracy and *democratic construction*, that is, the establishment of the institutions and procedures of a constitutional state. And as long as the democratic dispute can be borne along by the world time (the spectacular repercussions of the Ceaucescu effect in Africa, through the media), democratic construction will constitute a deeply endogenous phenomenon even when supported by foreign loans. The world time thus moves from the condition of 'destructive wind' of authoritarianism to that of international 'safety belt' against a possible step backwards. It then becomes less spectacular and more uncertain, for although it disallows certain procedures of authoritarian revenge it can never of itself guarantee democratic advance or market logic. The world time, understood in the sense of a configuration of 'value concepts' of external origin, is more than likely to disintegrate or evaporate if it is not captured and 'encoded' locally. From this point of view it forms part of the problematics of the circulation of ideas in the world as analysed by Louis

39. 'La décolonisation de l'Empire soviétique', interview with Marie Mendras and Olivier Roy, *Esprit*, October 1991, p. 52.

Dumont. The initial impact of an imported novelty is very intense, catching people almost unawares. The generalisation of the process throughout the world then endows it with a power of magnetic attraction which is difficult to control. But very quickly a 'recovery' of 'local time' takes effect which, depending on the country or the cultures, will alter, distort, overtake or contradict the world time.[40]

In Africa, for example, certain writers have ascertained that a genuine intention to introduce political enfranchisement did not exclude a rise in electoral abstention in proportion to the reduced number of candidates, for the local political culture is still impregnated with traditional principles such as 'exclusive leadership' or 'seniority'.[41] This new dynamic is more than purely cultural; it also rests on world geopolitical relationships, which are too often underestimated by culturalist analysis, despite being an integral part of the world time. The problematic of the world time does not therefore eliminate the autonomy of national time, particularly because additional regional or transregional times often lie between these two and have an ambivalent effect on the world time. Today, for example, Islamic time is one of the strongest climatic variables in the Arab-Muslim ensemble. In many ways it appears to compete with the Western time which we call the world time; yet in other respects it complements it. From Algeria to Iran, Muslims have taken political and economic advantage of the state's loss of favour and its excessive control over economic life. Islamic time is one of *laissez-faire*.

Democracy and Development

The connection between legitimacy and effectiveness may not be easily perceived, but the liaison binding democracy and development is even more obscure. Even by reducing the concepts of democracy and development to their simplest readings of pluralism and growth respectively, it is clear that there is no strong empirical correlation between these two parameters. Any link between democracy and development over a long period is the result of repetition and not causality. In Japan economic and technological modernisation very largely preceded political modernisation, which in its turn came before cultural modernisation. The success of the new Asian industrial nations owes much to cohesion and social control, to political voluntarism and, exceptionally, to taking international economic constraints into account – but it owes nothing to the vitality of political pluralism. In this book Jean-Louis Margolin confirms the

40. Dumont, *L'idéologie allemande*, pp. 44–5.

41. Yves-André Fauré, 'l'économie politique d'une démocratisation', *Politique africane*, 43, 1991, p. 44.

ascendancy of market logic over democratic problematics in Asia. The spectacular economic recovery of Mexico owes much to the existence of a 'strong régime' which has taken more care over modernising its authoritarianism than over democratising society. State partisan systems in fact have been powerfully mobilised both to channel the social questions generated by economic reform and to overturn the country's ideological configuration. What is supposed to become irreversible in the eyes of the populace is the 'move to the market' and no longer the 'historic achievement' of the Mexican Revolution. In Mexico the world time plays a fundamental and probably exceptional role in the nation's economic and ideological transformation; but its effects, like its practices, affect democratic construction only slightly. In Africa the fragility of democratic activity is even more apparent. Monopolised by urban groups, this activity excludes the peasants who are the leading element in African life. It may therefore be feared that pluralism is ticking over in neutral and that, apart from the differences experienced in any multiparty modality, urban actors easily come to an agreement to keep the peasants on the fringes of the infant democratic game. On this hypothesis, it would be pointless to see the timid democratisation of public life as the beginnings of a new dynamic of development.

Moreover, in three of the 'great' economic successes of the South in the last ten years (Turkey, Chile, Thailand), it is authoritarianism and not pluralism which has influenced the changes in economic logic – yet there is little reason to accept the contrary hypothesis, of a positive link between authoritarianism and development. In fact, in this matter we are condemned to the most absolute relativism, for there is an infinite number of intermediate examples between the classic models of 'authoritarianism' and 'pluralism'. A significant study, based on the result of the World Bank's policies of economic reform, considers that the distinguishing political variable lies not in the nature of the political régime but in the combination of the appearance of new management teams (democratic or otherwise), the power relationship between socio-economic operators affected by the reforms, and the existence of institutional and administrative structures capable of guiding change and neutralising opposition.[42]

42. Paul Mosley, Jane Harrigan and John Toye, *Aid and Power: The World Bank and Policy-Based Lending*, vol 1, *Analysis and Policy Proposals*, London, Routledge, 1991, pp. 160–1. See also Joan N. Nelson (ed.), *Economic Crisis and Policy Choice. The Politics of Adjustment in the Third World*, Princeton, Princeton University Press, 1990, p. 111.

2   THE PURPOSE OF GERMAN POWER

ANNE-MARIE LE GLOANNEC

The most remarkable consequences of the loosening of the world order and the end of bipolarity can be seen in Europe, and particularly in Germany. Bipolarity was of course at its most rigid in Europe, as the two superpowers faced each other across the line that divided Germany and Europe into two opposing military and ideological systems. As the supreme point of superpower confrontation, Europe was to some degree representative of the international system just as Germany was to some extent a microcosm of Europe. Yet because the dividing line here was unyielding – cemented by the balance of terror – Europe was also an exception, just as from 1945 to 1990 Germany was an exception, perhaps unique – but with its singularity nonetheless set firmly within the European system.

The loosening of the world order, the retreat of the United States and the implosion of the Soviet Union all confirm the ending of this double exception: unity is returning to Europe and Germany, and the nature of German power is changing. Reunited Germany is becoming sovereign and central once more, winning back sovereignty both legally (with the removal of Four-Power rule) and politically (because she is no longer part of that bipolarity which divided the nation, thus forcing the Federal Republic to import security from the United States and to seek compromise with the Soviet Union). While the two German states played a key role – ideologically, politically, economically and militarily (but not geopolitically) – at the heart of each of these systems, reunited Germany is regaining a central place within the continent without losing her status as the keystone of European and Atlantic institutions.

Germany's new strength creates fear among her partners, recalling memories of British and French distrust of reunification. Until the election of March 1990, when the East Germans voted for Chancellor Kohl's party, the French government in particular wanted to restrain or even prevent reunification by setting up counter-alliances. Once reunification was successfully achieved, would not the Federal Republic be tempted to follow a national rather than a European path? At Maastricht on 9–10 December

1991 Chancellor Kohl proved to be the keenest defender of an irreversible monetary and economic union. But could the raising of German interest rates in response to strictly national considerations, together with German recognition of Croatia and Slovenia without any prearranged co-ordination among the Twelve, be the early indications of such a path?

Despite her strength, however, or the disquiet which it arouses, Germany increasingly appears to make sense even to her critics. The German model is popular in France, for example, where Michel Rocard's government wished to reproduce the links between German banks and manufacturing. His successor spoke of imitating German industrial democracy and vocational training: in this respect there is indeed a German design. The post-war years could have led to belief in a blind German economic strength, imposing its constraints on European partners. At the dawn of the third millennium Germany is becoming a model for others: an economic model of moderate liberalism, ensuring both economic competitiveness and social cohesion – as opposed to Reaganism or Thatcherism. For the European Community it also turns out to be a political model, one of subsidiarity and decentralisation as opposed to the Jacobin model.

The purpose of German power should thus be understood as 'a capacity to provide solutions for problems of political, economic or social organisation without any genuine intention to extend its advantages to the rest of the world', according to the third meaning which Zaki Laïdi gives to the word 'purpose'. Yet Germany has been capable of offering meaning in other ways, either through the diffusion of universal values (notably in the nineteenth century) or by proclaiming her right to lead the world, according to Zaki Laïdi's second and first definitions. There is nothing new, therefore, in this question of Germany's purpose, nor in the question of her power, which has been seen by Europe as either too little or too great for over four hundred years.

Even before 1989, the Federal Republic had gained increased power from weakening bipolarity, détente and the second Cold War, together with the assertion of a 'German model' at the heart of a continent of increasing autonomy *vis-à-vis* the superpowers. In the first two parts of this chapter I shall analyse the significance of this model and assess this Federal German policy of expanding autonomy.

After 1989 reunified Germany regained sovereignty, centrality and power: yet the 'post-Yalta' system is neither the 'Yalta' order nor a return to pre-war Europe. The European Community and many more or less integrated or loose groups (NATO, WEU, CSCE) are constructing German power, but this power is civilian rather than military. As the century draws to an end the question remains not whether Germany will or will not expand militarily (through renationalisation of her defence policy, for example) but what the practice and purpose of the new Germany diplomacy will be. I shall consider this question in the second part of this chapter.

Paradoxes of the Economic Model: Admired but not easily Transposable

The idea of a German model appeared during the 1970s, in an attempt to explain the economic miracle of the 1950s and 1960s. The notion of a *miracle* was partly rational, partly emotional, and was disseminated without analysis through Germany and beyond. The notion of a *model* was its counterpart, an intellectual questioning of the miracle's origins and its consequences, in Europe and worldwide; it became established in restricted circles without ever matching the success of the notion of the *German miracle*. Its rationality was blended with occasional elements of fascination or concern.

Above all the German model was to be understood in economic terms: development of the system of production, growth of exports and a growing structural trading surplus. The prosperity of the Federal Republic assured all these factors despite successive revaluations of the Deutschmark (DM), which should have burdened exports, cut down the structural trade surplus and restricted production. At the heart of the German model, which thus defied the laws of classical economics, lay a 'virtuous circle'.[1] German industry specialised in manufacturing durable goods and high-quality chemical products, designed for an inelastic world demand, and these goods found buyers no matter what their price: successive DM revaluations or growing salary costs increased the trade surplus. As was demonstrated by some German and foreign economists, the internationalisation of growth complemented internal stability; the policy of stability exercised internally – wage moderation, the sharing of certain decisions between workers and employers, low growth and controlled monetary inflation – helped exports to grow and, together with monetary revaluation, ensured a growth in purchasing power in real terms and strengthened internal stability.[2]

1. To use Bernard Keizer's expression, cf. 'Le modèle économique allemand. Mythes et réalités', *Notes et études documentaires*, 4549–50, 31 December 1979.

2. Cf. Christian Deubner, Udo Rehfeldt and Frieder Schlupp, 'Deutsch-französische Wirtschaftsbeziehungen im Rahmen der weltwirtschaftlichen Arbeitsteilung; Interdependenz, Divergenz oder strukturelle Dominanz' in Robert Picht (ed.), *Deutschland, Frankreich, Europa. Bilanz einer schwierigen Partnerschaft*, Munich, Piper, 1978, pp. 91–136; Michael Kreile, 'West Germany. The Dynamics of Expansion' in Peter Katzenstein (ed.), *Between Power and Plenty. Foreign Economic Policies of Advanced Industrial States*, Madison, The University of Wisconsin Press, 1978, pp. 192–224; Keizer, 'Le modèle économique allemand.'

The success of the German economic model can therefore be explained by its perfect adaptation of the production apparatus to international constraints, the word 'adaptation' being understood in both its narrow and broad senses. In the post-war era the German economy benefited from favourable conditions such as the under-valuation of the DM in relation to the dollar, the demilitarisation of the Federal Republic until the early 1950s, the Korean War, etc.; yet the Federal Republic's skills enabled it to adapt on a long-term basis to world demand, pursuing Wilhelmine Germany's industrial specialisation. Adaptation to an international environment should also be understood in a broader sense: internal stability and external growth went hand-in-hand and the socio-economic system as a whole responded to international constraints.

Once in the international system, the German model exercised constraints on its environment. As European economies became intertwined at the heart of the European Community and monetary policies were aligned within the 'snake' and then the European Monetary System (EMS), the Federal Republic imposed its stability on its partners despite the inability of their production systems to adapt to world demand. 'The concept of the German model only takes on its full meaning when it is understood as an international norm: West Germany's structural balance of payment surplus enabled her to bring the long-term deficit countries into alignment, in particular France, Italy and Great Britain.'[3]

Thus, from the first the concept of the German model implied constraint, the structural constraint exercised by a dominant economy on its partners.[4] The relationship between the dominant economy and those dominated is reciprocal: 'the permanent improvement in the German Federal Republic entails a corresponding deterioration elsewhere'.[5] Germany's trade surplus is another nation's deficit. Within the European Community this establishes a commercial flux of evolving market shares, trading surpluses and deficits. In these three categories the Federal Republic's absolute and relative gains are expanding steadily. 'On the eve of unification the Federal Republic was the sole and chief beneficiary of community commercial arrangements among the major states of the European Community.'[6]

3. Keizer, 'Le modèle économique allemand', p. 199.

4. Cf. note 2 above.

5. Bernard Keizer, 'La République fédérale d'Allemagne: puissance extérieure' in *Statistiques et études financières. La spécificité du 'modèle' allemand. Trois études sur la RFA*, Paris, Ministry of the Economy, Forecasting Management, 1980, special issue, p. 35.

6. Andrei S. Markovits and Simon Reich, *The New Face of Germany. Gramsci, Neorealism and Hegemony*, Cambridge, Mass., Center for European Studies, Harvard University, Working Paper Series no. 28, p. 26.

From the 1970s to the 1980s this analysis of the German economy as a dominant structure at the heart of the European Community lost none of its validity, and has remained unaffected by German reunification. While the Federal Republic is now embarking on a Keynesian policy of major building projects (investment in East German infrastructure), monetary growth (with the conversion of the East German mark into DM on a one-for-one basis and the financing of public expenditure through borrowing), and a higher rate of inflation, Germany's monetary policy nevertheless continues to affect her partners: the relationship remains asymmetric. Certainly Germany's partners had hoped for domestic and international German expansion and a more flexible policy (in short, that she should act as a locomotive of growth), yet these wishes, disregarded in the 1980s, now appear vain. The chief result of the 1990–91 revival, which was fed by public and private demand in the former German Democratic Republic, has been a rise in interest rates set by the Bundesbank. In short, Germany's partners cannot force her to modify her monetary policy.

The description of this model, which is still applicable to the 1980s, gives a measure of its ambivalence. The concept of a model is concerned on the one hand with broad monetary balance and on the other hand, more broadly speaking, with a social, economic, political and cultural system. The functioning of such a system is based on the division of powers between politics and the economy, with the state, business and banks deciding industrial policy, for example; the *Länder* and businesses concerned with professional training; and unions and employers concerned with wage policy and certain economic aspects, etc.[7]

At a different level of analysis the notion of model is reductive: this model may mean *style*, a specific style of organisation, which is effective in practice and is particularly well-adapted to the international division of labour, whether concerned with economic organisation or, more broadly, with the social, political and cultural system. But the concept of model also refers to the idea of *example*, something to be imitated as the best adaptation to the objective constraints of the international system. The model could then have universal value. In the 1970s, when the term model was used explicitly, its essential aim was to describe the particular in relation to the general or, more precisely, to the group of European nations belonging to the European Community. It therefore relates implicitly to the relationship between the former and the latter and to the constraint which Germany places on its partners. The concept of model understood as

---

7. Cf. Peter Katzenstein's brilliant book, *Policy and Politics in West Germany. The Growth of a Semi-Sovereign State*, Philadelphia, Temple University Press, 1987.

example represents the specific and inimitable; the German model does not, for two reasons. On the one hand, the success of the German economy is the failure of others. 'If the German model were copied successfully by several other nations, one might wonder whether the formula would still be applicable in the Federal Republic. Germany would then be forced to share with other nations the position which she occupies today on the export market and her industrial structures, largely dependent on her exports, would pose problems for her.'[8] Since its success, on the other hand, is explained not only by the adaptation of an industrial apparatus to world demand but also by the whole social, political and cultural system, can the formulae for the German success be applied in other contexts? Can France, for example, adopt the German system of vocational training or German industrial democracy without taking into account the differences between the two nations' political and economic cultures? In fact, the export of the Japanese model comes up against exactly the same types of constraint, as Jean-Marie Bouissou emphasises in this book.

The German model, being specific to one country, therefore appears to suffer from two drawbacks, and criticism of German economic policy extends partly to the broader area of politics and society. One may recall the criticism in the 1970s, when the concept of model was popular, particularly in the intellectual milieux of the Left in Germany and elsewhere. It was concerned at this period with the direction of democracy in the Federal Republic;[9] its sources may have been neo-corporatism (whose functioning lay outside democratic control) or terrorism, which occasionally met with a less than democratic state response: the German model as a negative example. Elsewhere, criticism is aimed more generally at the political plan underlying the Federal Republic's economic policy, notably in its international dimension. The particular, the specific, may in fact be understood as harbouring an ambition which is necessarily expansionist, as it moves from the particular to the general and as it aims at reaching the general through the particular. The German economy's structural constraints upon its partners then become subject to analysis in terms of expansionism. In certain milieux this criticism has been heard ever since the creation of the EMS, and it is increasing with reunification.[10]

8. Gerd Junne and Frieder Schlupp, 'Le modèle allemand et la crise mondiale', Das Parlament, 1 October 1977 (reproduced in *Problèmes économiques*, 1545, 2 November 1977).

9. As an example see Freimut Duve, Heinrich Böll and Klaus Staeck (eds), *Briefe zur Verteidigung der Republik*, Reinbek bei Hamburg. Rowohlt Taschenbuch Verlag, 1977; *Briefe zur Verteidigung der bürgerlichen Freiheit*, Reinbek bei Hamburg, Rowohlt Taschenbuch Verlag, 1978; or again, *A cura dell'istituto Gramsci, Sezione Emiliana: Modello Germania. Struture e Problemi della realta tedesco-occidentale*, Bologno, Zanichelli editore, 1978.

10. The model of this type of criticism is provided by Alain Cotta, *La France en Panne*, Paris, Fayard, 1991.

The notion of the German model, understood as a non-transferable style of economic development, thus reveals its full singularity: the model is economic, even economicist; in fact, it excludes all political vision or, if there is a political plan, it is only 'the pursuit of the economy by other means'. The Federal Republic's history and foundation, the state constitution, its socio-economic structure and its underlying justificatory myths, favoured the economy both in fact and in myth. The Federal Republic was a society before it became a state,[11] in the period when the occupying forces held supreme power; to the outside world they represented Germany, and internally they set it up. The leading actors were the Churches and the unions; the leading powers were the press and economic forces. The state, created in 1949, was conceived as both dependent and as provisional or transitory – dependent on the victorious powers which had not granted it full and complete sovereignty, and provisional or transitory because it would one day dissolve into a reunified Germany and a united Europe. Dependent and transitory, the West German state was, in some ways, absent, a state without a founding ceremony. It was certainly endowed with the symbolic attributes of any state (national anthem and flag, which were nonetheless discreet)[12], as if the West Germans were inclined to be an invisible state because they had once had 'too much state'.

How can Germany Create Purpose?

Among those who set to work to build a new Germany after the war, the 'orthodox-liberal' economists played a significant part. They saw the balanced liberal economy (*Soziale Marktwirtschaft*, social market economy), as the foundation for the future democracy. In this respect the 'economic miracle' preceded the 'political miracle'. In one famous opinion-poll, 33 per cent of Germans questioned in 1959 were proud of their economic system and only 7 per cent of their government and political institutions.[13] Should these figures have been seen as signs of pragmatism, or even of an ultimately apolitical cynicism which was part of German tradition? Was democracy fundamentally nothing more than a guarantee of the fruits of prosperity, simply a factor contributing to sound economic functioning?

The very conditions which prevailed at the establishment of the Federal Republic, and its founding myths, encouraged belief in the 'primacy of the

11. According to the expression of Ernst Nolte, *Deutschland und der Kalte Krieg*, 2nd edn, Stuttgart, Klett-Cotta, 1985, p. 327.

12. Cf. Anne-Marie Le Gloannec, *La nation orpheline*, Paris, Hachette, 1991, ch. 1 ('Pluriel' series).

13. Gabriel Almond and Sydney Verba, *The Civic Culture. Political Attitudes and Democracy in Five Nations*, Princeton, Princeton University Press, 1963.

economy' and therefore concern over the actual substance of German democracy. With the origins of her prosperity rooted in the sharing of growing wealth, perhaps Germany was no more than a fair-weather democracy (*Schönwetterdemokratie*) where economic difficulties could lead to a new Weimar. This was the argument of the British historian Harold James, who identified a continuity between Wilhelmine Germany and the first and second Republics: in Wilhelmine Germany, 'instead of being a cultural community or a political unity rooted in a common culture, the nation became the setting for an economic process which in its turn was the foundation of cultural and political awareness'. Without institutions to create and define German identity, this identity found an anchorage in economic growth and in nationalist wanderings. James foresaw the possibility of a cyclical return of nationalism.[14]

Once the imperatives of reconstruction were settled and the Cold War, which had sustained anti-communism and the American model as founding myths, abated, German society could be described as disorientated. 'The gloss has gone,' said Günter Grass, 'People have suddenly realised that these two [German] States were built on sand, that economic prosperity and social security do not, on their own, provide an adequate foundation, that there is a debt to oneself, to one's neighbour, that one's own vision must be defined in relation to the historical and cultural past. A sort of specification of national identity.'[15] Once again German identity was subjected to questioning from 'below' and from 'above', from society and the élites. On the one hand, Greens, alternative life-stylers, citizens identifying with various 'initiatives', sought to confer on the Republic a purpose which they felt it lacked. On the other hand, political and intellectual élites – essentially conservative groups – sought to 'order' history, both to see order in it and to impose this order on German identity.

Yet political democracy and the economic miracle were indissolubly linked. This was not only (as a number of German or foreign analysts would like to see it) because prosperity made the new political system easier to accept but also because the economic miracle represented the opening-out of society to Western liberal and democratic values and benefited from the modernisation and increased driving force of the resulting social relationships.

With the resurgence of the state, which had been temporarily concealed by Chancellor Adenauer's authoritarianism (paradoxically, he imposed democracy from above), policy did not spring from the restricted domain

14. Harold James, *A German Identity 1770–1990*, London, Routledge, 1989, pp. 3 and 218.

15. Günter Grass, 'Beide deutsche Staaten sind auf Sand gebaut', in Hans Willauer (ed.), *Deutschland – wohin? Gespräche über Deutschland*, Konstanz, Im Verlag des Südkuriers, 1985, pp. 25–6.

of the state, either because it shared the installation, and even the design, of certain policies with economic and social actors, or because it handed them over entirely to these actors. Examples of this are industrial policy and development aid – the first through cooperation between banks and businesses, particularly within administrative councils, and the second through the cooperation between the Ministry for Development, the Churches, foundations close to the political parties, etc. In this respect one may suppose that the diffusion of political power in the Federal Republic leads to the absence of political vision or, on the contrary, to a multiplicity of plans and the transmission of multiple models.

Foundations close to political parties (the Friedrich-Ebert-Stiftung, the Hans-Seidel-Stiftung, the Friedrich-Naumann-Stiftung, the Konrad-Adenauer-Stiftung) have a fourfold mission in the countries where they are established: to gather local information, to establish relations between the German élites and those of their host nations, to mould the host nations to the Federal Republic's political and trade union methods, and to create, sustain and counsel political parties, unions, cooperatives, and so on, in this way diffusing a model, the German model, of democracy. Although the result of this work may be ambiguous it is certainly favourable, particularly for the promotion of Germany's image in the world. If the foundations cannot always claim to have achieved the election of candidates of their favoured political parties, they nonetheless appear to have contributed to the establishment of democracy in Latin America, for example, and to have consolidated German influence there. In this respect the foundations would constitute 'the most powerful diplomatic instrument'.[16]

It is but a small step from this situation to talk of a political model. In the final decade of the twentieth century the Federal Republic is increasingly proving to be a political model for others and therefore for the countries of Central and Eastern Europe which won their freedom from the communist and Soviet yoke in the double revolution of 1989–91. This also applies to the countries of the European Community which, since the Maastricht summit of December 1991 are forming a type of confederation. It is a political model with dual value, by virtue of what it is and/or by virtue of who promotes it.

The nations of Central and Eastern Europe, which were forced to invent their own revolutionary models, are creating their own transformation. But they look both to the West (for example, to the United States) to borrow formulae of economic and political liberalisation, and to the German Federal

16. According to Michael Pinto-Duschinsky, 'International Political Finance. The Konrad Adenauer Foundation and Latin America', paper prepared for the Panel on International Political Finance, Research Committee on Political Finance and Political Corruption, 24 July 1991, Buenos Aires, International Political Science Association.

Republic. Germany, if it is not always the nearest neighbour, is at least the most powerful and sometimes also the most interesting one in its multiplicity of opinions and styles, and is thus finally becoming what it rarely used to be: a *model for political transition to democracy*. Timothy Garton Ash takes up this point in one of his remarkable articles: 'Germany has offered much to East Central Europe over the centuries, but democracy has rarely been among them. Now, however, the German model of democracy is arguably the most relevant of all, because it is a model built on the rubble of a totalitarian dictatorship. It is, one might say, a Western system built on Central European experience.'[17] One could quote certain borrowings (such as the 5 per cent clause, the figure below which no party can enter parliament, or the concept of *constructive no-confidence*, which prevents the dismissal of a chancellor without a replacement being nominated), which were written into the Basic Act of the Federal Republic and which Czechoslovakia and Hungary have adopted,[18] even if in other respects some were attracted by the French presidential pattern. It is interesting to note that this selective rather than universal adoption of a political model operates in the same way in South-East Asia with the Japanese model, as is demonstrated in this book by Jean-Louis Margolin.

Germany may, on the other hand, have value as an example for western European countries (particularly the member states of the European Community) not so much for what she represents as for the way in which the example is disseminated: through the foundations, of course, which, as was said above, constitute a remarkable instrument of German diplomacy; and through the synergy between German banks and industrial sectors, which French banks and industrial sectors are attempting to imitate, following the 'no-no' route: neither privatisation nor nationalisation of the economy.[19] Last but by no means least, with its vertical organisation and subsidiarity as a principle of the devolution of powers between the *Bund* and the *Länder*, does not the Federal Republic as a whole offer a preview of the European Community of today and tomorrow,[20] while a Jacobin

17. Timothy Garton Ash, 'Eastern Europe: après le déluge, Nous', *The New York Review of Books*, 16 August 1990. In fact the foundations have quickly been established in Central Europe, notably in Hungary, the first to welcome them all at the same time.

18. In contrast, the German model adopted by to Yeltsin is strangely reactionary: the Volga Germans had to undertake the economic development of the Kaliningrad belt. In other words they were considered capable of it because they were German, whatever their political or economic culture.

19. In this context the speeches of Edith Cresson are revealing, as is Michel Albert's book, *Capitalisme contre capitalisme*, Paris, Le Seuil, 1991.

20. This provides a further reason for the nations of Central and Eastern Europe to wish to adopt the federalist German model. In France itself a debate is developing between the proponents of the Habsburg empire – the model for European organisation – and the advocates of the Jacobin state.

France would resemble classical France without the Baroque and so remain an isolated European example? Yet it should also be noted that at the very moment of its triumph the German federalist system is in danger from two developments: the addition of new, poor *Länder* to the older richer ones, so that the interests of the two clash rather than support each other; and the construction of Europe, in which the *Länder* feel deprived of their areas of jurisdiction, which the *Bund* has transferred to Brussels.

If, as the century approaches its end, purpose arises not from a *single centre* but from *multiple centres,* is not Germany the winner, by being more skilful at diffusing purpose than at imposing it? If, indeed, one or more German political models should emerge, this would be both a historical novelty and also the triumph of a model granted to defeated Germany in the post-war period. Is the model then German or neutral, universal? Or again, is the model not, at one and the same time, both diffused and also imposed? German domination, as accepted by the Federal Republic's partners via models, would thus finally achieve what it lacked during the 1970s: ideological legitimacy.[21]

How is Germany Maximising her Power?

The Federal Republic's increasing power as the dominant economy and producer of ideological models is present in one or more of the international political systems which successive Bonn governments have wished simultaneously to stabilise and to subvert. In other words Germany – following Japan in this respect – is concerned less with inventing the international system than with maximising her national interests within an international system which she sees as accepted. This may explain why German power appears more visible or more explicit than her purpose, even though the German experience increasingly makes sense to her partners. This double policy of stabilisation and subversion developed from the Federal Republic's extreme dependence on one or more international systems.[22]

In economic terms the Federal Republic has become increasingly dependent with the passage of time. First or second exporting power, depending on the year, she earns more than one-third of her GNP from foreign sales. The economic and political stability of the international system is therefore important to her, as is the liberalisation of trade, which she

21. Cf. Markovits and Reich, *The New Face of Germany.*

22. Understood as functional systems (economic, military, etc), or geographical systems. 'European system' here means the system with its transatlantic dimension, with the United States being a European power.

defended during the 1970s, for example, when the Third World nations were seeking a new international economic order. The Federal Republic was also dependent as the state of a nation divided from 1949 to 1989–90 by the frontier between political, ideological and military systems. The legal limitations on her sovereignty were less constricting than the political ones. Legally, the status of Berlin and the fate of Germany – a hypothetical future at the time – were in the hands of the former victors.[23]

From the 1960s onwards in particular, with the relative decline of the United States (as a result of inefficient public financial management) and the Federal Republic's economic growth, West Germany had to pay for her security. In exchange for security she helped to consolidate the American balance of payments by buying locked-in Roosa bonds (named after their American inventor) and establishing special drawing rights. At the very moment when France was fighting the Bretton Woods system Germany extended it by agreeing not to demand the gold conversion of the dollar.[24] During the Gulf War, in the winter of 1990–91, there was liaison once more between security and financial management: by contributing to American military expenses the Republic gained a measure of security, in the broad meaning of the term, by maintaining her place at the heart of the Atlantic alliance.[25]

During the 1960s and 1970s the link between dependence and security came close to breaking point. On the one hand, the Federal Republic could neither gain independence from her old conqueror (only the end of the bipolar order would make this possible) nor increase her moral respectability. On the other hand, this dependence prevented her from acquiring greater military or political security. When the concept of 'flexible response' was introduced the Federal Republic questioned the reliability of American pledges and with the arrival of détente she questioned whether the United States would wish to take up the cudgels for German unity. In monetary affairs the disappearance of the Bretton Woods system led Germany to seek terms within the European Community, with the establishment of the 'snake' and then the EMS. Politically speaking, Bonn's initiatives at the heart of the European Community, above all where Eastern policy was concerned (*Ostpolitik and Deutschlandpolitik*), extended her scope for manoeuvre.

23. Other limitations included the ban on production of ABC (Atomic, Biological, Chemical) weapons, which is still in effect, and other lesser prohibitions which have been lifted over the years.

24. Cf. Kreile, 'West Germany. The Dynamics of Expansion', p. 196.

25. The Federal Republic also supplied considerable logistical support and deployed troops in Turkey. Nevertheless the exercise was not accompanied by the adoption of clear positions by the government, and it aroused criticism from an active minority in public opinion.

In this respect the EMS, as a zone of stability, was an answer to international challenges: it also helped to correct distortions within the Community. Since trade between the Federal Republic and her partners worked out to the former's advantage, concessions were required: the ability of the weakest elements to pay had to be sustained in order to keep the system stable. Two possible means were available: the Community budget, with the greatest contribution coming from the Federal Republic, and the loans granted by the Federal government during the 1970s, for example to Italy in exchange for Italian entry into the 'snake'.

Successive governments increasingly lost confidence in American power during the 1980s, in particular in her capacity and will to defend German interests: the second Cold War, which was characterised by the Soviet intervention in Afghanistan and the establishment of a military régime in Poland, appeared to prove that the United States were defending their own interests by risking those of Europe. Consequently, Helmut Schmidt's liberal and Social Democrat government and, in a different way, the liberal, Christian Socialist and Christian Democrat coalition headed by Helmut Kohl (from 1982 onwards), continued to buy their security from the United States, but on their own terms. On the one hand, Germany was no longer obliged to import everything that Washington wished to send: Chancellor Kohl obtained from the Bundestag authority to deploy American medium-range missiles in the Federal Republic, despite popular disapproval, but a few years later the Foreign Minister, Hans-Dietrich Genscher, declared his opposition to the modernisation of short-range missiles. On the other hand, Bonn sought an accord with the Soviet Union: rather than a second Cold War, Helmut Schmidt's government and the German Left (and also, to a lesser extent, Helmut Kohl's government) favoured a second European détente.

Ostpolitik and *Deutschlandpolitik,* which had first been conceived by the SPD in Berlin's town hall in the 1960s and then operated by governments from the 1970s to the 1980s, were designed to achieve 'change through rapprochement' (*Wandel durch Annäherung*). The East European régimes had to be consolidated, economically and politically, by financial agreements and negotiations, in order to reassure their leaders and win liberal reforms. Internal openness would be accompanied by a greater openness at frontiers, particularly that between the two Germanies. In fact, this policy of stabilising East European régimes represented a two-pronged approach by Bonn: one advance specifically German and national, the other interstate or international. It was a matter of sustaining family and familiar relationships (and hence the national substance), and also of multiplying circles of dependence to reduce constraints more effectively.

The policy of stabilising East European régimes and systems thus led to the subversion of the European system, a process which benefited the Germans more than the East Europeans and the rulers more than the ruled. More precisely, it extended Bonn's scope for manoeuvre and consolidated East Berlin, helped some East Germans to reach the Federal Republic and concentrated more on inter-German dialogue than on relations with other East European nations; however, it also confirmed Soviet domination in Eastern Europe, by preferring models of evolution from above to revolutions from below. In the end, however, the policy was to overturn Eastern Europe.

To a certain extent, which is not easily determined, the 1989 revolutions were therefore the fruit of an Eastern policy, even though German public opinion and the German political class were not yet ready to face the consequences. Adenauer had calculated on the collapse of the communist system, as had been hoped for by the European Community, and his Social Democratic, liberal or even conservative successors had to a greater or lesser extent wanted to believe in change through rapprochement; but it was the Left rather than the Right, and intellectuals rather than public opinion, which were taken unawares by the revolutions. In fact, the subversion of the European system appeared to mean only the preservation of stability. The 1989 revolutions have undoubtedly upset the European system and transformed the Federal Republic. With the end of bipolarity and with German and European reunification the continent has become sovereign, central, and hence more powerful – even if only relatively, compared with international agreements and, more particularly, with military integration within NATO and politico-economical integration within the European Community. Sovereign, central and powerful, Germany is debating her role: is she to be more European than Atlantic? If more European, will she be tempted by the East or by the West, or by pan-Europeanism? And how is she to redefine her interests?

Since subversion has triumphed, stability now seems to be the prime objective. Despite the collapse of the Soviet system (or because of it), Central and Eastern Europe is a source of economic, social and political instability and therefore a cause for concern in Germany. Not only does the Federal Republic command attention as model for these nations, she is also seen as the nearest, the richest and the most powerful of all the members of the European Community, as an essential supporter and expected supplier of goods and credits, technology and skills, the potential mediator with the Community and even, for the people of these nations, the nearest refuge. Yet Germany cannot fulfil all these expectations: she is suffering from social tensions and disquiet over her immigration policy, she is paying heavily for reconstruction in the former GDR and, finally, memories of the past weigh heavily on relationships, particularly those with Poland, Czechoslovakia and Serbia.

The Federal government apparently expects a dual approach to reduce Germany's expenditure. Firstly, the burden will be spread more widely through enlargement of the European Community to include the EFTA nations and then to former members of COMECON; by combining their resources with those of the Twelve the wealthy non-aligned European states, from Switzerland to Finland, will help to rebuild the new impoverished democracies. Secondly, the deepening of Community integration will bring a sharing of responsibilities. On immigration, for example, the Federal government is seeking a common policy extending beyond inter-governmental cooperation, in order to escape criticism from Germans who call for greater liberality and others outside Germany who would like greater rigour.

A New German Universality?

Broadly speaking, deeper Community integration meets the Federal government's wishes, even though the Maastricht accord of 10–11 December 1991 failed to meet such German proposals as the strengthening of the European Parliament's powers. In effect, not only would the European Community protect Germany from Central and Eastern European institutions, it is already a sort of buffer zone protecting Germany from the uncertainties of the former American superpower. On the economic and monetary level the great European market in 1993 and the creation of a single currency at the end of the century guarantee, and will continue to guarantee, stability in a group of nations which represents the bulk of the Federal Republic's trade.

At the political level, the unification of European defence – even in an embryonic form – should help to make up for American deficiencies. Although NATO remains an essential insurance policy for the Federal government in the face of possibly dangerous convulsions in the former Soviet Union, it is nonetheless seen as too timid in its reforms and also too burdensome, since it exercises a semi-monopoly in Europe. An army, or at the least a European corps, would enable Europe (and therefore, necessarily, Germany) to play a more active role in settling international or European conflicts. Although the Federal Republic does not (for political rather than constitutional reasons) send troops to conflict zones, her membership of a European military grouping would give the government the political means to break this embargo. In short, between American uncertainty and East

European instability the Community would reduce Germany's vulnerable points while maximising her power and independence.

Finally, the Community fulfils a politico-ideological function: that of legitimising German power both to her partners and to the German people. During the post-war years Germany's integration into the Atlantic and European groupings allowed the Federal Republic to regain a certain moral legitimacy at the cost of her sovereignty, and subsequently a certain political legitimacy to match her growing economic power. Following the re-establishment of German unity and sovereignty, the conclusion at Maastricht of agreements on future stages of economic and monetary union and a modest political union offers the Federal Republic gains which are ideological and political rather than economic.

For Germany, in fact, the EMU represents both an opportunity (the single European currency, with the payment facilities that this implies) and a risk (of a currency less stable than the DM). Germans who think in purely economic terms are alarmed by this.[26] On the political level, however, Chancellor Kohl and the Bundestag which supports him find themselves acquiring merit as good Europeans for having clamoured most keenly for political union, even if most Community members view the possibility with caution, at least along the lines proposed by Germany.

The Federal government is therefore genuinely not suspected of power-seeking, at least for the time being; and if one day Germany finds herself under such a suspicion, the European agreements at Maastricht may perhaps prevent a political interpretation. Such is the calculation of Chancellor Kohl and those in the Federal Republic who advocate integration within the Community. They interpret German history in terms of the *Sonderweg*, the 'special, singular way; singularity', which was Germany's style from the middle of the nineteenth century until 1945: wanderings and mistakes are attributable to Germany's ideological isolation, sheltered from the Enlightenment, and also to the political isolation of her encirclement. For the protagonists of European integration, the unified Republic's international security will prevent any revival of this isolation.

The concept of the *Sonderweg* as an explanation for German history – whether exegesis or myth[27] – is however open to various interpretations. Although the bulk of political and public opinion reads the German past from the nineteenth century until 1945 in terms of the *Sonderweg*, reject-

---

26. One needs only to look, for example, at the anti-European tone of certain articles in the German press, including a liberal newspaper such as the *Süddeutsche Zeitung*.

27. The reality of the *Sonderweg* is currently challenged by German and foreign historians. In contrast the concept of the *Sonderweg* played the role of a positive myth until 1945 and, since then, has played the role of a largely negative myth.

ing it as a political model for the Federal Republic, the practical lessons to be drawn from it sometimes contradict one another. For Chancellor Kohl and his entourage (but also for all those who support him on the right or the left of the political chessboard) European integration is to some extent the German Republic's raison d'être, to paraphrase the Chancellor who, in 1983, described the Atlantic alliance as the justification of the Federal Republic.

The lessons of the past and rejection of the Sonderweg may yet, paradoxically, lead to a rehabilitation of singularity, if not in name at least as an idea. Thus, because the Germans know the meaning of war better than anyone, they would have a specific duty to preach peace, obscuring by the very process the fact that democratic values are sometimes defenced by force of arms. This is the meaning of the debate during the Gulf War which, at least during the Allied attack on Iraq, set the supporters of peace at any price against the heralds of a democratic universality, even if it has to be defended sword in hand. The militant defenders reproached the former for their urgent wish for peace, attributing their empathy for bombarded Iraq to the resentment of a conquered Germany recalling Dresden and Berlin in flames. The unique nature of the war (but not the unique nature of Auschwitz!) would seem to lead to a present-day uniqueness and the *Sonderweg* concept would quietly regain its place in a current of German thought. The universalists denounce this development and are exhorting their nation, perhaps for the first time in German history, to support democratic values everywhere unequivocally.

The notion of *Sonderweg* also surfaces in geopolitics or cultural geography. Divided, West Germany turned to the West and the Enlightenment. With the re-emergence of internal German or Central European ties and currents during the 1980s the concept of Central Europe, of *Mitteleuropa*, made a marked reappearance in West German political writing, representing the search for an identity which, although not expressly anti-Western, is nonetheless heavy with ideological connotations. Would not the reunification of Germany and of Europe lead some in the Federal Republic to pursue this quest by other routes?

Even if reunification does not mean the creation of a new state whose legal obligations and political identity would have to be redefined, it nonetheless raises once more the question of Germany's ideological and political integration into the West. It re-establishes Germany at the heart of the continent; but the post-reunification Federal Republic is slightly different from the Republic created in 1949, without being exactly the same as the Germanies of the nineteenth and twentieth centuries. The Germany of 1949 was created as a system, a democracy closed in practice to national reality; the new Republic is a nation-state where identity is shared between state and nation. Surely the two shifts – geopolitical and ideological-cultural – will require a redefinition of German identity in terms which, if not anti-Western, are at least different from those of a Western identity?

If we contrast the partisans (the majority) of a Western anchorage with those (the minority) who favour German singularity, an even more confused front line appears to divide the two schools of thought. There are those who see in reunification the constitution of a Western nation-state, the final achievement of a tardy German historical evolution along the lines of Great Britain or France, and those who for more than a decade now have been emphasising the *Kulturnation*, the cultural nation, the nation without a state, or one which is a nation first and then a state, with flexible and shifting cultural frontiers.[28]

The two dimensions – geopolitical and geocultural, or perhaps East-West, on the one hand, and institutional or ideological on the other – do not necessarily support each other, even if the partisans of westernisation tend to favour a nation-state and the advocates of the *Sonderweg* are partisans of a *Kulturnation*.[29] Nevertheless the fact of the nation exists in some places as a politico-cultural influence beyond its frontiers or an affirmation of the nation-state: does not a section of the CDU close to Chancellor Kohl (who preaches the integration of the European Community) claim currently that they are defending the national interests of the Federal Republic? Through a general historical reshuffling it is therefore the German Right which now expects to defend the national identity and interests, while in the preceding decade this was the concern of the Social Democrats.

In future, will national identity and interests coincide with those of Europe? And will this Europe, to which Germany will perhaps contribute more than any other nation, be more Western or more Eastern, more Central European or more German? While the Chancellor does his utmost for the European Community his minister for foreign affairs appears to want to stress the CSCE more than the WEO. Will this Europe also see the triumph of German influence and of different models transmitted by various German actors, or will Germany confirm her existence as a nation-

28. Cf. Ole Waever, 'With Herder and Habermas. Europeanization in the light of German Concepts of State and Nation', Panel on State and Nation, at the second international conference of the International Society for the Study of European Ideas, Comparative History on European Nationalism, *Europe Towards 1992*, 3–8 September 1990, The Catholic University of Leuwen.

29. I have borrowed this 'crossing of dimensions' from Pierre Hassner, who developed it in a speech on *La France, L'Allemagne et la Russie*, at a colloquium organised in Berlin by the Freie Universität, in honour of Richard Löwenthal, 8–9 December 1990.

state? It remains true that German models are fading just as they prove themselves as European models. This may either be because they have become weak (as with federalism in the face of the double challenge of European construction and German reconstruction) or because their success invalidates them (as with the monetary model: even as German rigour compels the recognition of her European partners, the Federal Republic is talking of renouncing the DM).

3 JAPAN AND THE QUEST FOR LEGITIMACY

JEAN-MARIE BOUISSOU

For many reasons, Japan today lies at the heart of the new worldwide problematic. The economy, no less than politics and military questions, is now part of the fabric of international relations, be it in North-South problems or in shaping the future course of China or Eastern Europe. Here the full weight of the Japanese economy and the influence of Tokyo in international organisations such as the IMF make her a major deciding factor. The persistent gap between Japan's rate of growth and that of her partners, the unfailing profits from her colossal foreign investments and the cumulative effects of her technological advance make the increase in her power an essential element in forming the future international system; this is more than a hypothesis, it is an inescapable certainty for the coming decade, at the end of which Japan's GNP may well exceed that of the United States.

To Western eyes, however, the expansion of Japanese economic power is tainted with illegitimacy because it lacks any avowed political aim based on universally applicable values. It thus appears to pursue no other purpose than its own existence, no aim except its own development, to which there is no limit. The recurrent denunciation of 'a plot to dominate the world', quoted at the slightest excuse to stigmatise Tokyo's actions, combines these two criticisms.[1]

Now that she is endowed with a high degree of economic power, will Japan attempt to 'create purpose' in order to acquire the legitimacy and authority which would help her to influence the international game? Surely she will rather be 'invested with purpose' from outside, and set up as a supposed 'Japanese model', to be reappropriated by others according to their own strategies, for in the absence of any self-avowed purpose her 'emptiness' leaves her open to the imposition of almost any prefabricated explanation. Or will she continue to expand her material power, without any

---

1. Quoted in black and white in the report of the CIA working group, *Japan 2000* (July 1991) denouncing, for example, 'the construction of an economic power tending to dominate the world'.

ideological justification in the eyes of her partners, at the risk of being denounced increasingly bitterly as a destabiliser of the Western order?

The case of a first-class economic power which is not at the same time a military power is extremely atypical in modern times. Such exceptions as have existed were very rare, short-lived, and affected only very small territories. Are the Japanese and Germans capable of enduring, and on what conditions? The question is all the more pressing because Japan may already be defined as a *militech society*,[2] in the sense that she possesses an industrial and technological base with the potential to turn to the production of sophisticated armaments on a large scale, including nuclear weapons. Furthermore, she is capable of jeopardising the maintenance of arms systems among her partners, to whom she supplies the most advanced technological components.

Japan is also an exception historically, as the only non-white nation with a non-Western culture which efficiently operates a democratic political system and an economy which is generally labelled as 'liberal'. Yet their transplantation into very different cultural and social environments is accompanied by distortions which now allow the American revisionist school to maintain that Japan is neither democratic nor liberal by Western standards.[3]

The ability of the 'market democracy' model to respond to the needs of the South and of Eastern Europe is a pressing question for the future of the world order. Although very different in themselves, both groups present striking similarities to Japan: a very limited or non-existent tradition of democracy, the need to develop from nothing or from an obsolete base, the significance of foreign models and the partial or total absence of independent economic actors capable of generating development by their own efforts. Such conditions create a leading role for political action. Although it dominates the current world ideological scene, the correlation between democracy, the market and development has never truly proved itself in such a context nor in the very short space of time that pressing need dictates. Only the Japanese version has achieved it, since 1868. Such a sequence may be formulated as follows: *state-led* development, moving to a *controlled* market economy and then to a *democracy*, which is somehow *adapted* to the cultural domination of group values. This does not exactly match the ideal model promoted by Washington's hard-core partisans of market democracy.

2. David T. Yamada, 'Rearming Japan? A Militech Society?' in *Current Politics and Economics of Japan* 1 (1), pp. 13–20.

3. Karen van Wolferen, *The Enigma of Japanese Power*, London, Macmillan, 1989. See also CIA, *Japan 2000*, 'A fiction consists in thinking that this nation is a State . . . similar in most respect to ours, and exercising a liberal economy.'

Japan therefore challenges the validity of theories which have led the ideological market since the end of the Cold War. Until now Tokyo has refrained from asserting the difference, clinging instead to the language of dominant Western values (liberalism, human rights, etc.) and denying those adaptations which she has undertaken. But when the development of non-Western nations constitutes a major challenge for the world order, can the significance of Japan's unique experience be concealed indefinitely? Will she not sooner or later proclaim it, as part of a strategy of legitimisation, and question the Western version of liberal democracy?

Finally, Japan's situation is unique in geopolitical terms. In contrast to her Western partners, she is in immediate contact with both of the two major areas of instability marked out by the collapse of the communist system in China and the Soviet Union. At the same time, Japan lies at the heart of the Asia–Pacific zone, where the rhythm of development beats much faster than elsewhere in the world, and will no doubt continue to do so in the short and medium term; yet her power is also projected all around the world and her vital economic interests depend today on multiple and complex relationships on an international scale. Any form of retreat would be incompatible with the maintenance of stability and the standard of living, either in Japan or for many of her partners. And, since 1945, Japan has been engaged in a unique bilateral relationship – both in the gross weight of exchanges and in the degree of interdependence – with the United States, which have now become the hegemonic pole of military and ideological power. These four factors place Japan in a unique and highly complex position *vis-à-vis* the world order. She must simultaneously manage: a world logic which implies exceptionally significant constraints for her; a highly demanding bilateral relationship, which is shot through with growing tensions, with a partner who is simultaneously a superpower and vulnerable; a regional context which may offer her an opportunity to slacken these constraints by building an integrated power-base in her immediate environment that is capable of compensating for Japan's diminutive scale; and the considerable Chinese and Russian uncertainties over which Japan has even less control than the Western powers.

Japan within the Cold War: A Potentially Variable Alignment

As a consequence of her 1945 defeat a multi-level dependence was imposed upon Japan by the United States. At the military level, although Japan started to rearm in the 1950s, her security rested on the global deterrence provided by the US army. At the economic level, Japan's reconstruction and then her growth were dependent on the goodwill of an America which accepted a one-way free exchange that was all the more congenial to her because the surplus of bilateral trade had long been in her favour. At the diplomatic level, in contrast to Germany and her reintegration into Europe, Japan had only Washington to count on to act as her mediator with international organisations. The victors retained the island groups of Bonin and Okinawa, with restitution depending solely on their good will. Finally, the 1945 defeat and the reforms of the occupation created a mixture of admiring submission to and recognition of a conqueror whose leniency came as a heaven-sent surprise. To this should be added the rapid diffusion of the Coca-Cola culture, creating a type of psychological dependence of which the periodical flare-ups of anti-Americanism are merely a reverse aspect. Even the United States' need for a stable and prosperous Japan as a bastion against the communist drive in Asia did not redress the balance of a relationship which at the international level forced Tokyo into an unconditional alignment with Washington.

Circumstances changed at the beginning of the 1970s: Japan now had a place in all the international organisations and recovered Bonin and then Okinawa (1972). The Vietnam War provoked violent disturbances in Japan and the American defeat raised doubts: with Asia apparently irrevocably on the road to communism, Japan risked becoming a regional outlaw in exchange for uncertain protection. The economic growth which finally pushed Japan ahead of Germany in 1968 allowed her to garner growing trade surpluses with the United States from 1965 onwards. An endless series of trade crises began with textiles (1969) and television sets (1970). Following the unilateral denunciation of the Bretton Woods agreements, the temporary interruption of American soya supplies (1973) looked to the Japanese like a form of open blackmail aimed at the security of their food supplies. The era of goodwill was over, the relationship of confidence broken. The news of Richard Nixon's visit to the People's Republic of China (15 July 1975) – arranged without consultation with Tokyo even as Japanese diplomats laboured yet again to prevent Beijing's entry to the United Nations – left Japan exposed, threatened with isolation and forced to operate a humiliating volte-face.[4]

Occurring just after the 'Nixon shocks', the first oil crisis revealed a danger against which American protection was useless: international economic dependence. Japan had to sort out her problems on her own, with the result that from 1973 she began to detach herself for the first time from the United States on a major international issue: the problem of Palestine.

The fashion for the phrase *jishu gaiko* ('autonomous diplomacy'), and the concept of 'all-round diplomacy' (*zenhoi gaiko*) from 1973 onwards,

---

4. On the 'Nixon shocks' see Tatsuro Uchino, *Japan's Postwar Economy*, Tokyo, Kodansha, 1983, pp. 169–88.

reflect this reassessment. Prime Minister Tanaka stole a march on the Americans in China by granting Beijing the official recognition which Nixon had not dared to concede, and then hurried on to Moscow. The great projects for the development of Siberia with the help of Japanese capital appeared to provide an economic basis for this diplomatic readjustment. Tokyo initiated a strategy of regional influence, which was marked by a busy tour by the same Prime Minister Tanaka in 1974. From 1977 onwards Japan planned a massive increase in her official development aid, with two-thirds going to the Asian region. She worked to revive regional forums which had been discarded after the Vietnam débâcle. In 1978 Japan signed a peace treaty with Beijing which included the famous anti-hegemony clause, which was aimed in theory at both the superpowers, and began to pose as a mediating power between the West and the developing nations. In the Middle and Near East Tokyo continued to detach herself from Washington, allowing a PLO office to open and embarking on lively economic cooperation with Khomeini's Iran.

In 1979, however, a special commission set up by Ohira's government defined the concept of 'global security' (*sogo ampo*)[5] as the new framework for Japan's international activity. Because the United States could no longer assure their allies of absolute security, Japan increasingly had to count on herself. But the dangers were no longer limited to armed aggression launched by the communist bloc: 'Any conflict anywhere in the world may be a threat to Japan because she is totally dependent on foreign supplies and markets.'[6] This was reflected by the growing discontent of her Western partners when faced with the expanding imbalance in commercial exchanges. This manifold and multi-directional danger required a global response. Japan had to try to create a favourable international environment by reducing bilateral friction, and also by working to reduce all kinds of tension throughout the world. Significantly, in addition to Foreign Affairs and the Defence Agency, the interministerial Council for Security Problems which met throughout the 1980s covered Finance, Agriculture, Transport, MITI (the Ministry for International Trade and Industry), the Plan (of the long-term Planning Agency) and the Science and Technology Agency.

In an apparent paradox, however, the concept of global security resulted in shifting Japanese diplomacy back to the West, because, as the communist threat subsided, it became clear that the relationship with Japan's traditional allies was deteriorating. Tokyo had to take care not to aggravate it

---

5. See Shinkichi Eto and Yoshinobu Yamamoto, *Comprehensive Security and Japan's Future*, Tokyo, Kodansha, 1991.

6. Masayoshi Ohira's programme for the election of the LDP's president, Tokyo, 1978, typescript.

through hazardous initiatives towards the East, where the markets turned out to be much less profitable than anticipated. Significantly, the new path of Japanese diplomacy coincided with Beijing's unilateral breaking of numerous treaties signed in 1978; and when Tokyo reacted to the invasion of Afghanistan by cutting off all credits to the Soviet Union, the Siberian projects had already been shown to be impracticable.[7] Meanwhile, the profits of Japanese companies in the United States grew enormously (a trade surplus of 7 billion dollars in 1980, 69 billion in 1989) while Tokyo tried to cling to Washington again. Military cooperation was once more the order of the day: after Suzuki (1980–82), who proposed that the Japanese navy should share in sea defence within a thousand-mile radius, Nakasone (1982–7) committed it to regular manoeuvres with the US navy and promoted the Japanese archipelago as an 'unsinkable aircraft carrier' facing the Soviet coastline. Tokyo now spoke up loud and clear for human rights and made no attempt to profit too quickly from the Tiananmen Square tragedy by acting alone in China, although she clearly disapproved of the West's sanctions against Beijing.

On a general level the concept of global security presupposes a more positive response to demands addressed to Japan by her partners, and a greater willingness to accommodate them through internal policies. Thus the report of the commission on national security is inseparable from the famous Maekawa Report (drawn up at the request of the Nakasone government) which advocated a redirection of growth to placate Western criticisms. Together they initiated an official campaign to promote 'internationalisation' (*kokusai-ka*) which grew to full strength under the Nakasone government.[8]

'Foreign pressures' (*gaiatsu*) were clearly used by the government as an excuse to force measures required by the modernisation of the system of production upon some sectors of the Liberal Democratic Party's electorate, notably the peasantry and small shopkeepers. Blatant media publicity over 'internationalisation' was also designed to convince the West of Japan's good intentions, which were slow to produce concrete results. Nevertheless, it did finally have a genuine educational effect on Japanese opinion, which increasingly became inclined to admit the sound basis of international criticism.[9]

7. See Gerald L. Curtis, 'The Tyumen Oil Development Project and Japanese Foreign Policy Decision-Making' in Robert E.Scalapino (ed.), *The Foreign Policy of Modern Japan*, Los Angeles, California University Press, 1977, pp. 146–75.

8. On the methods and consequences of this campaign, see Jean-Marc Bouissou, Guy Faure and Zaki Laïdi, *L'expansion de la puissance japonaise*, Brussels, Complexe, 1992.

9. See Eric Seizelet, 'L'opinion publique japonaise et la politique étrangère', *Le Trimestre du monde*, Winter 1990, p. 108: '44.7 per cent of Japanese admit the accuracy of American claims and 85 per cent of them consider it is right to respond positively' in a poll of March 1990.

Each of these three phases was matched by a specific Japanese style of integration. From 1945 to 1970 Japan was content to exploit the overriding politico-ideological logic which the Cold War imposed on each bloc. She exchanged the passive fidelity which the Western camp demanded of her and her strategic position for an unparalleled preferential economic treatment, while still occasionally looking outwards to re-establish discreet trading links with China and the Soviet Union.

With détente, Japan threw herself into an occasionally spectacular series of 'all-round' diplomatic moves, but they were always linked to parallel moves on the economic level – the negotiation of major Chinese and Soviet contracts, investments and delocalisation with her Asian neighbours [10] The policy was confined to marking out and legitimising the new areas open to business, or to assuring their security. Where this was unnecessary (Africa, South America, etc.), Japanese diplomacy continued to cling passively to Washington. Japan's active political reappearance on the world scene operated in broad terms within limits fixed by Western solidarity (for example, Tokyo's pro-Palestine stance set her apart from Washington but was still in line with many West European powers) and remained closely linked to economic logic.

During the 1980s this economic logic won total autonomy. Henceforward it ruled the development of the bilateral relationship with the United States, which keeps deteriorating through repeated commercial crises, hard-fought negotiations and feverish surges of opinion on both sides, although its politico-military foundation remains mostly unchanged. Faced with growing tensions abroad provoked by the 'Japanese economic invasion', the bureaucracy of the Foreign Affairs Ministry is following in the wake of big business. Diplomacy has to defuse crises as they occur (often taking a stand with foreign partners to encourage moderation among economic operators), with mixed success. At the same time, diplomats are attempting to upgrade their status for the future by taking advantage of the current debate on Japan's role in the world and by launching a reform plan designed to extend the Foreign Affairs Ministry's powers of action.[11] Under attack from economic logic, the politico-ideological element, which is managed by diplomats and the government, is now attempting a revival; for this particular purpose it puts itself forward as the only force able to cope with the main challenge confronting contemporary Japan: the legitimisation of her power.

---

10. See Nobutoshi Akao (ed.), *Japan's Economic Security. Resources as a Factor in Foreign Policy*, Tokyo, Tokyo University Press, 1989.

11. *Asahi Daily News*, 10 November 1991.

Collective Attitudes as a Factor Inhibiting the Promotion of a Worldwide Purpose for Japanese Power

Japan's traditional inability to give the expansion of her power a purpose which is acceptable in the eyes of the world is linked to three sets of internal constraints. Some are rooted in the national collective psychology, others are functional and arise from the organisation of the decision-making process, and yet others are derived from a public opinion traumatised by history and subject to contradictory currents.

Because they have been used for too many ready-made simplistic popularisations, the culturalist explanations applied to Japan have lost much of their credibility. They remain operative, however, only if one takes 'Japanese-ness' for what it is: *a language manipulated* by power, a set of mental attitudes forged and cultivated in specific historical circumstances, mostly from the sixteenth century onwards, which ensure that their value is only relative.

The kernel of this collective stock response is the proposition which postulates an irreducible difference between the Japanese and the rest of the world, a trait which they share with many other island nations. But, taken to its logical conclusion during the 250 enclosed years of the rule of the Tokugawa Shoguns and systematically cultivated in schools and the vast specialised literature of the *nihonjinron*,[12] it nourished an unrivalled capacity for closing ranks against the outside world whatever the level of internal discontent. This reflex remains very active even among the modern intelligentsia, as can be seen through analysis of editorials in *Asahi*, the traditional supporter of pacifist and liberal opposition to conservative power. Ferociously critical on domestic policy, when it comes to foreign affairs *Asahi* puts the highest value on maintaining national consensus even at the cost of blurring its own beliefs.[13] This feeling of difference is strengthened by the myth of a pure Japanese race (*tanitsu minzoku*), born and grown from the native soil of the four islands and drawing its strength from this purity. The pejorative remarks against cosmopolitan nations which regularly escape the lips of certain senior politicians – including Prime Ministers – bear witness to the vigour of this fantasy even among the governing élite.[14]

12. *Nihonjinron*: a school of thought and literature specialising in the exploration of Japanese uniqueness in contrast to all other nations. See Ross Mouer and Yoshio Sugimoto, *Images of Japanese Society*, London, KPI, 1986.

13. Jean-Marie Bouissou, 'Deux quotidiens face à la crise du Golfe: le *Asahi* et *Le Monde*', colloquium of the Fondation nationale des sciences politiques, Paris, 25 March 1991 (typescript).

14. The most famous is no doubt the phrase of Prime Minister Nakasone (1982–87): 'The invasion of the United States by Blacks, Puerto Ricans and Mexicans has had the effect of lowering the average intellectual standard and the performance of the country.' Quoted by the CIA, *Japan 2000*, p. 23.

This feeling sustains a marked insensitivity towards non-Japanese people, with whom many Japanese are not inclined to display any active solidarity. In this context it is worth noting that Japan contributes less than 2.5 per cent of the funds collected from individuals for humanitarian causes in OECD countries[15] and that the government's policy of increasing official development aid is approved by less than one citizen in five.[16] Another example is the striking contrast between the prolonged and costly efforts undertaken to locate the Japanese orphans left behind in Chinese families during the débâcle of 1945 and return them to the land of their ancestors, and the refusal to provide space in the Hiroshima Peace Park for a monument to Korean victims of the atom bomb. (This space, at least, will now be provided.) While everything is done to bring home the nation's scattered elements, equal efforts are made to exclude foreign corpses from the highest symbolic events of its contemporary history. No less significant was the decision to open the labour market to South Americans of Japanese ancestry while closing it to Asian immigrants, a move based on the supremacy of a racial right which has been accepted in the past (or is still accepted) by the great Western nations, yet which nonetheless contradicts the principles of equality between individuals which form the basis of human rights.

This assumption of difference must lead the Japanese to question, more or less openly, the universality of the value-system on which Westerners base their international policies and which proposes that liberty, democracy and the rights of man and of nations are of universal value and applicable everywhere under any circumstances. The Japanese value-system tends to be more pragmatic. It ultimately gives precedence to the particular over the universal and it sees the possibilities offered to individual development as conditional upon the group (in this case, the national group), its stability, its material prosperity and the affirmation of its power. As a result, Japan lacks skill in legitimising her undertakings with reference to internationally dominant values, and is even less skilful at promoting her own values, since they are seen as distinct and wholly specific to Japan. Tokyo has never managed to promote a missionary type of foreign policy, of which the powerful potential for legitimisation has been shown once again by the Gulf War. It also has the capacity to confer on the 'ideal-bearing' nations an authority which allows them to manipulate world opinion to their advantage (we are reminded of Maoist China), and constitutes an element of power that is liable to persist even after military or economic decline. But Japan's only attempt of this type, posing as a 'freedom fighter' bent on liberating the Asiatic peoples from the white colonial yoke, was too clumsy and too late to

15. 'Tiers-Monde. Les Japonais arrivent', *Croissance*, 33, December 1990, p. 13.
16. Poll of the Prime Ministerial Services, January 1989.

be credible. Thus, since her return to the world scene at the end of the nineteenth century, Japan has appeared to be motivated only by concern for her national interests and by a wish for pure power.[17]

At a strategic level Japan sees international relationships fundamentally as a zero-sum game in which everything won by one party is necessarily lost by the other. There too, the radical distinction made between 'them' and 'us' makes it very difficult for Tokyo's élite to perceive the world scene not as an arena for the open confrontation of brute strength but as an area dominated by relationships of interdependence regulated by shared principles and legal norms, where gains have to be balanced out in the end for the common good.

Paradoxically, the assumption of her radical difference allows Japan to bend without any effort of conscience to constraints and changes when the balance of forces goes against her (1853, 1945), for nothing which she is forced to accept can obliterate the irreducible uniqueness which she sees as her very essence, her intangible 'national soul' (*kokutai*). Conversely, when circumstances favour her Japan tends to act as a solitary predator on the world scene, as during the 1875–1941 period, or from the mid-1960s until the present day.

In international negotiations Japan has gone to absurd lengths to stress her difference, and she continues to do so, going so far during commercial negotiations as to invoke a supposed uniqueness of Japanese blood groups and intestinal structure, or of Japanese soil and snow.[18] But this is a double-edged weapon, for her negotiators cannot claim special treatment for their country while simultaneously complaining of possible discrimination. Tokyo is uneasy at the growth of the American revisionist school which aims to exclude Japan from the current liberal interplay between industrial democracies, on the pretext that she does not share the same values. Her lobbyists put forward an opposing argument, insisting on the growing 'internationalisation' of Japanese society and the 'interdependence' between her economy and those of her partners, which will undoubtedly lead to progressive adjustment. A substantial effort of public relations has been undertaken to present Japan as a country which genuinely shares the values of the Western camp.[19] Yet this has to be done today because in the past Japan has stubbornly presented herself as an entity whose radical uniqueness constitutes her very essence.

Chronic fear of the external environment is also congenital in a nation to

17. This explanation seems essential for the CIA 'The concept of national power is not very well understood outside Japan [but] it conditions all relationships of this country with others.' CIA, *Japan 2000*, p. 13.

18. Ibid., pp. 27–8.

19. See Pat Choate, *Agents of Influence. How Japan's Lobbyists in the United States Manipulate America's Political and Economic System*, New York, Knopf, 1991.

whom threats have always come from outside. This fear is inseparable from the fear of living in a small, exposed and overpopulated country that is threatened by natural disasters, lacks natural resources and is at the mercy of vulnerable lines of communication. Having no concept of international solidarity, Japan does not expect it for herself. Furthermore, she feels that she is a victim of racial prejudice, and historical experience appears to prove that her successes only bring her jealousy. Despite détente, this complex that 'the world is dangerous and hateful' is displayed even now in opinion polls which persist in rating the situation surrounding the archipelago as 'worrying', several years after the end of the Cold War.[20] Even economic triumph cannot eliminate this feeling of chronic precariousness. In a poll of January 1991 more than one Japanese in three still thought that the country would no longer be a major economic power in the next century.[21]

The prime objective of Japan's foreign policy must therefore be to ensure her security. In this respect, her reaction to the irruption of Western powers in her immediate vicinity – the radical closing-off decreed at the beginning of the seventeenth century – betrays a fundamentally defensive attitude intended above all to minimise risk. After 1853 this strategy could no longer be maintained. Japan was compelled to respond to the threat of colonisation by modernisation. But this created a new set of dependences (market needs, primary materials, secure communications) which was soon perceived as a new threat, forcing her to move her lines of defence beyond her own shores. She is therefore gradually projecting her power ever closer to the thresholds of Australia and India. Yet even so her policy remains reactive, evolving in response to other powers' moves rather than corresponding to a carefully planned strategy for long-term expansion. At first one notes alternating sequences of precipitate advances and retreats (1895, 1920) and then, after 1930, a growing lack of balance between Japan's means and the successive objectives which she set. This attitude arose partly from feelings of racial superiority and a lack of experience at the international level which prevented her leaders from carefully weighing the balance of forces. But, above all, Japan launched counter-measures against the reactions that she provoked[22] and that she perceived as so many new threats, to which she reacted with an impulse rooted in an acute feeling of vulnerability. This led her to seek control over an increasingly broad area.

---

20. Seizelet, 'L'opinion publique japonaise': 'In December 1989 two-thirds of Japanese still described the situation around the archipelago as 'worrying' and only 12.7 per cent saw it as improved.'

21. *Asahi Daily News* poll, 3 January 1991.

22. For a detailed analysis see Bouissou, Faure and Laïdi, *L'Expansion*.

The 1945 defeat and the communist thrust in her immediate neighbourhood forced unconditional acceptance of US protection on Japan, although the price was an internal dependence much greater than in the post-1853 period. The equation of Japanese security was modified. The nation would henceforward pursue a triple objective: to assure her international security in the new context of confrontation between the blocs by ensuring the maintenance of the American shield; to assure her security within the Western bloc by transforming her unilateral dependence on the United States into a balanced relationship of interdependence; and to regain progressively some influence over her non-communist neighbours (the only basis on which Japan could hope to build one day in order to escape the preceding constraints).

Without any military means or ideological instrument comparable to that supplied to Germany by the European ideal, the only means by which Japan could manipulate the international environment was the economy, as underlined in 1957 in her first diplomatic Blue Book. Today it is clear that the balance has been restored. The United States and Europe need Japanese capital funds, components and technologies so much that they can no longer credibly threaten her; and they present a disunited front to her economic offensive.

Japan has re-established a high degree of security, but in so doing she has created a new situation in which her lines of defence have extended worldwide, as has her economy. The variables which command her security are therefore increasingly numerous and difficult to manage. Willy-nilly, in future Japan must lean towards controlling, or at least surveying carefully, the world environment as a whole. This is the true basis of the concept of 'global security', which seeks to include even natural disasters. The equation of national security is couched in singularly extended terms, but it is always to be found at the heart of Japanese foreign policy, with its four practical consequences: the concern to gather the greatest amount of information possible before taking any action; the concern to minimise risks by taking action only where the national interest requires it; a constant wish to seriate problems and adversaries; and the exercise of an essentially reactive external policy.

Perception of the international environment, like that of society as a whole, is mostly shaped in Japanese eyes along vertical lines. The sociologist Chie Nakan, prone to hasty generalisations and non-scientific methodology though she is, has documented rather well this tendency to think of the world along hierarchical (vertical) axes and not along the horizontal axes which prevail in Western societies and bring together those who place themselves on the same social level and share the same functions.[23] Japan is

23. Chie Nakane, *Japanese Society*, London, Weidenfeld & Nicolson, 1970.

famous for a sort of classification syndrome: Todai-Keio-Waseda (the universities), Seibu-Isetan-Mitsukoshi (the department stores), etc. The international application of this vision is aided by the difficulty for most Japanese of feeling regional, racial or ideological solidarity with outsiders. Furthermore, in 1945 the chance of history allowed the United States, which stood at the summit of the absolute hierarchy of powers, to assert in addition their leadership of the Western camp – the horizontal structure which Japan had just been forced to join. Vertical classification by brute force coincided with horizontal classification by politico-ideological solidarity. The one legitimised the other and the nation found itself in a classic situation, the inescapable rite of passage to which every Japanese has to submit many times during his life: as the tyro, the new arrival in a group of seniors, and thus naturally at the foot of the ladder. Dependence, certainly, but nothing unfamiliar.

The result of this vision is that progress along the vertical axis constitutes a major international objective in itself. To improve one's rank, to overtake foreign powers one after another, these are legitimate aims, consistent with the manner in which society as a whole functions and independent of any concrete benefit which the citizen may acquire. Even if today increasing numbers of people question the inconsistency between the status of Japan as number two in the world economy and the reality of a standard of living inferior to that of most other industrialised nations, the shared national obsession of 'a climb up through the ranks' has undeniably contributed powerfully to the Japanese miracle.

This tendency to structure the international order along vertical axes is reinforced by Japan's evolution in an extremely inegalitarian and clearly hierarchical environment, ranging from the 'little dragons' to the fourth-class nations (Vietnam, Laos, Cambodia, Burma), via the intermediate grade of Thailand or Indonesia. This characteristic also partly explains Tokyo's inability to get rid of the moral debt left with Japan by the Second World War. Unlike Germany, Japan is called on for more excuses and reparations every time her Prime Minister visits a formerly occupied country. In the context of the Confucian culture common to most nations in her region, her ill grace in submission is rooted in the feeling that it detracts from her status, although the lower members of the hierarchy have no other hold on her (in the absence of any horizontal solidarity) than to recall unceasingly that she owes 'a debt which nothing can ever erase'.

Furthermore, the Japanese attach so much importance to their rank in the world hierarchy because they overestimate its functional effectiveness. In their minds, simply by having reached the top of the economic ladder, Japan should *ipso facto* have acquired the legitimate authority which would in turn further enhance her security. Yet, conversely, she has become the butt of multiple criticisms. After a lapse into indignation during which the neo-nationalist fire burst into flame (with Shintaro Ishihara and others pouring oil on it),[24] most of the governing élite and the media acknowledged the gap in perception which divides Japan and the Western powers about what 'power' and 'authority' mean on the world scene. They initiated a debate on Japan's international role for which the Gulf crisis was a powerful stimulant. At the same time, this crisis revealed a second constraint which prevents Japan from asserting herself on the world stage by profiting from the dramatic circumstances covered by the media, in contrast with lesser powers such as France. This is the inability of her political system to produce bold and clear decisions when needed, decisions which are capable of making sense in the eyes of international public opinion.

Internal Constraints on the External Game: The Process of Decision-Making and Public Opinion

This dysfunctioning is the result at a general level of the consensual tradition; more precisely, the way in which the executive leader is designated deprives him of all personal legitimacy. A further factor is the nature of a government formed on the basis of unstable alliances between rival factions and the interdependence between political power and a bureaucracy which is both highly autonomous and very jealous of its sphere of jurisdiction. As soon as Japan becomes involved in an international problem a large number of actors are ready to intervene in the decision without any one of them being strong enough to act decisively. The Prime Minister must obtain the agreement of factional leaders and even more of their mentors, who are usually former presidents of the Council for whom foreign policy may well be at least a hobby, if not their private domain, now that they are out of the race for power. At the bureaucratic level, the Minister of Foreign Affairs has a poor power base and an inadequate organisation (lack of staff, rivalry between departments), and is often accused of servility towards American interests.[25] He is watched closely by the Ministry of Finance and the MITI, because commercial relationships weigh heavily on external questions, and also by lesser luminaries such as Education, which did not hesitate to provoke repeated crises with Beijing and Seoul on the ultrasensitive point of the censorship of school textbooks. Finally, the Liberal Democrat Party (LDP) authorities intervene *ex officio* if legislative or financial measures have to be approved or a treaty ratified: nothing appears before Parliament until it has first been approved by the Policy Action Research Council and

24. Shintaro Ishihara, *Le Japon sans complexe*, Paris, Dunod, 1991.
25. See Reinhard Drifte, *Japan's Foreign Policy*, London, Routledge, 1990, pp. 21–2.

the Executive Committee of the LDP, where all lobbies can intercede via their elected representatives.[26]

Internal political considerations thus interfere heavily in decision-making and no matter how urgent the situation there will always be a period of sorting-out and negotiation, frequently even of confrontation, between the various actors. Finally, most decisions will be reached through compromise. Added to the reactive nature of Japanese diplomacy, these constraints accumulate to produce delayed half-measures in moments of crisis. Such measures often have to be modified through successive stages, as a result of reactions from Japan's partners, and this causes considerable harm to her national image.

The permanent concern to minimise risks runs on similar lines. The process of examining and appreciating a situation tends to drag out. The most welcome solutions are those which avoid engaging Japan and which maintain the international equilibrium unchanged. But when it is impossible to maintain the *status quo* and the situation becomes threatening for Japan because she is not clear about her commitments, the decision-makers tend to panic because in the end they have to make bold choices, which runs counter to their long-nurtured instinct.[27]

Over recent years, two new factors have further complicated the decision-making process. Because of the opposition's victory in the 1989 elections for the Upper House the LDP now has to obtain the agreement of the centrist parties (at least of the Komeito, the 'Clean Government' party) on all decisions, including foreign policy. Furthermore, international affairs are having an increasing media impact and now involve the immediate interests of a broad electorate, from farmers threatened by the dismantling of protectionism to urban consumers affected by the American-promoted policy to open the way for more supermarkets. The politicians traditionally shunned international responsibilities because they were time-consuming, subject to polemics and of no electoral value. But many LDP heavyweights are now seeking to build their careers on the world stage. This strategy was inaugurated by Yasuhiro Nakasone in the highly media-publicised setting of the 'Ron–Yasu relationship' with President Reagan. It was taken up again by Prime Minister Kaifu (1989–91) and before him by the party leader Shintaro Abe who monopolised Foreign Affairs for four years (1983–6), disregarding the rules on the annual rotation of portfolios. An interview with

26. For a detailed example see John E. Endicott, 'The 1975–1976 Debate over the Ratification of the Non-Proliferation Treaty in Japan', *Asian Survey* 17 (3), 1977, pp. 275–92.

27. See Michael E. Blaker, 'Probe, Push and Panic. The Japanese Tactical Style in International Negotiations', in Scalapino (ed.), *Foreign Policy*.

the American president became an essential rite of passage for any potential Prime Minister, with the government unable to exercise more than minimal control over their statements.

The decision-making process may thus be driven by a range of actors, depending on the circumstances. Unsuccessful efforts to mediate in Cambodia – a complex affair with little publicity appeal – were mostly left to Foreign Affairs. The thaw with North Korea, very sensitive politically because of Japanese public opinion's hatred for both Koreans and communists, was dealt with by specialised pressure groups within the LDP and some businesses in close collaboration with the socialists. Chinese affairs were long managed by political emissaries, former Prime Ministers or opposition leaders from the Japan Socialist Party and the Komeito, which played an important part in recognising the People's Republic of China.[28] And during the Gulf crisis Takako Doi, president of the Socialist Party, succeeded the former Prime Minister Nakasone as Japanese ambassador to Baghdad. In such circumstances the management of foreign policy is burdened with interventions of varying motivation. It is very difficult for such procedures to create a clear purpose.

The Gulf crisis illustrates this well. During the first phase of the crisis Japan cautiously committed herself to a contribution of a billion dollars, which was immediately scorned by the Americans as wholly inadequate. It was then quadrupled, under pressure, thus forfeiting any potential political credit. At the same time the Kaifu government attempted to exploit the situation for its own sake by presenting a bill to create a 'peace-keeping body' which would have allowed elements of the Self-Defence Forces (SDF) to operate outside national territory. In breaking one of the fundamental taboos restraining the use of Japanese forces the Prime Minister should have strengthened his position within the LDP enough to gain re-election in 1991. But Kaifu had to act mostly alone because none of his rivals bothered to strengthen his hand,[29] and the bill was killed off in the Diet in November 1990. In Washington's eyes the proposal was irrelevant to the crisis. Its failure further undermined Japan's credibility and left her in a very weak position *vis-à-vis* the West when it came to open war. Japan could not refuse a further contribution of 9 billion dollars, which made her the principal financial backer (apart from the Arab nations) in a war in which she never had any say. In addition to Kaifu, his Finance Minister Hashimoto and the LDP leaders each tried to steal the show by being the

28. See Haruhiro Fukui, 'Tanaka Goes to Peking. A Case Study in Foreign Policy-Making' in Theodor J.Pempel (ed.), *Policy Making in Contemporary Japan*, Ithaca, Cornell University Press, 1977, pp. 60–102.

29. 78 per cent of opinions were against it in an *Asahi* poll of 6 November 1990.

first publicly to announce the Japanese contribution.[30] As a result, Japan's financial participation in the conflict appeared as an unconditional and unprincipled capitulation to Washington, lowering Tokyo still further in international opinion.

Although the decision-making process does not seem to be very efficient when faced with an open crisis, the same is not true for the development and implementation of long-term policies. The decision-making process is very effective in bringing about settlements between vested interests and at balancing the short-term views of politicians with the long-term visions of the administration. It gives a say to economic agents and assumes that a broad consensus is forged at the decision-making level, thus permitting a wide mobilisation of resources and the establishment of long-term plans for execution (enhanced by political stability) which are measures of effectiveness. One example is the sudden appearance of Japan among the leading dispensers of development aid (ODA), which came as a surprise to Western commentators but was the result of a deliberate policy pursued since 1977.

The case of ODA is also quite significant because of the fact that public opinion was largely kept out of the process. Despite its major financial implications, the effort to increase ODA was not the subject of a national debate. As far as possible, it was dealt with inside the ministries concerned, and their fear that it should leak out was evident in the vigilance with which they insisted on surveying all NGO-type movements and keeping them under supervision. One consequence is the great reserve concerning this effort expressed in public opinion polls, and the total absence of public involvement already mentioned. But the deliberate pursuit of action at the bureaucratic level is the best way for decision-makers to get round the obstacle of a chronically divided, indecisive and inhibited public opinion.

Even more than social problems, foreign policy and security questions have presented post-war Japan with her most traumatic national crises particularly in 1960 and 1968–72. Today's opposition parties are no longer capable of proposing an economic and social programme significantly different from that which the LDP has been operating successfully for several decades. Only foreign policy and the related debate about the SDF remain as a tool for mobilising opinion. Furthermore, some of the most pressing economic and social problems, such as the future of the peasants and small shopkeepers, are the result of the pressures exerted on Japan by her foreign partners. They appear largely to be a by-product of external relations and the media dramatise them with striking headlines about 'last-chance negotiations' on every occasion.

30. See the Japanese press of 21–25 January 1991.

Opinion polls show the Japanese above all to be indecisive. Simultaneously, they approve by crushing majorities both of Article 9 of the constitution (the pillar of the neutralist policy and pacifism promoted by the Left) and the Security Treaty which forms the cornerstone of the policy of alignment with Washington promoted by the LDP. They are inclined to think that the SDF have reached a satisfactory level of capability, but nevertheless tend passively to accept the *fait accompli* every time the LDP increases this capability, as it regularly did during the 1980s. Finally, they refuse to acknowledge that these are, genuinely, armed forces, and fantasise about sending them on purely civilian missions.[31]

Public opinion has made Shintaro Ishihara a star, and his book *The Japan that Can Say No* a bestseller. At the same time, however, a majority tends to accept Western criticism with surprising humility. Although they were qualified as 'unilateral' or 'arbitrary' by a majority of Japanese in 1987, by March 1990 the sound basis for such criticisms was already acknowledged by 44.7 per cent of those responding to polls.[32] In a 1991 poll 66 per cent confessed that Japan had become 'arrogant' in her self-enrichment, 76 per cent that she was wasting natural resources at the expense of humanity, 50 per cent that she was 'insular and racist' and lacked solidarity over refugees, and 44 per cent concluded that these were the reasons why her partners lacked confidence in her.[33]

Periodically, public opinion suffers from a bout of anti-American fever, but America is still at the top of the popular cultural market and regularly reaches the top rating in polls as the best-liked country. The Japanese simultaneously feel proud of the results obtained by Japan and afraid that they will not last. At the same time, they desire to play an appropriate international role, and experience a vague feeling of guilt at not doing so,[34] while refusing to grant themselves the means to put this desire into effect. Pacifist themes command a majority, but the tide of opinion in favour of strengthening the army is better organised and weighs more heavily with the decision-makers. Finally, public opinion is very sensitive to orchestrated campaigns, as has recently been seen in the reversal between the autumn of 1990 and the spring of 1991 on the question of SDF missions outside national territory.[35]

The government's traditional answer to these contradictions has been to proceed very gradually and to avoid debating ideas, preferring a policy of

31. See Defense Agency, *Defense of Japan – 1989*, Tokyo, 1990.

32. Seizelet, 'L'Opinion publique japonaise', p. 108.

33. *Asahi* poll, 3 January 1991.

34. 56 per cent of those questioned approved the principle of a supplementary contribution to support the war effort in the Gulf if the allies asked for it. (*Asahi*, 27 February 1991).

35. A move from 78 per cent of opinions against (*Asahi*, 6 November 1990) to 62 per cent in favour at the dispatch of mine-sweepers to the Gulf (*Asahi*, 16 April 1991).

fait accompli. Thus it is that the problem of the constitutionality of the armed forces has never been decided by the Supreme Court. At the time of the Gulf crisis the decisive step of sending troops on a mission outside Japan was finally accomplished by a simple decree in April 1991, when the Kaifu government dispatched minesweepers to the Gulf. This style of decision-making made a definite advance possible, but it did nothing to clarify the meaning and the objectives of Tokyo's intended future international activity.

Hypotheses for Japan in the Loosened World Order

Japan has now achieved her major post-war objectives. She is near the summit in the hierarchy of nations. Her relationship of dependence on the United States has become balanced. Her economic power on the world scale remains sensitive to specific pressures, but in overall terms it is protected from brutal dispossession and capable of evading most of the barriers with which she is threatened. Japan has developed a range of measures against any break in her supplies (diversification of suppliers, stockpiling, consumer economies, substitution) which combine with her capacity for retaliation to protect her from economic blackmail. She has achieved the maximum degree of security to which a tiny archipelago can aspire. Only a major conflagration causing lasting disturbance to worldwide communications could still constitute a threat, and she can still count on American support for protection against such an eventuality.

But just as Japan is achieving this vital goal, the end of the system of blocs against which she had defined her security policy requires her to reconsider it, in the context of a loosened world order with changing axes and different types of conflict. A major pole of power is developing in Europe, a zone which has always lain largely outside the field of Japanese strategy. In addition, there are uncertainties in the public mind and pressure from Washington to increase the price of American protection, which have been taken up by the West as a whole to summon Japan to assume 'international responsibilities' matching her wealth.

This rhetoric does not mean that Japan's partners genuinely wish to see her intervene in the politico-ideological field, still less in the military domain, in any way which would let her return to being an entirely independent major power once more. At the very moment when the United States have got rid of communism they have no wish to see a competing ideological model assert itself, sustained by an impressively dynamic economy. The United States are aware that Japan now represents a danger at this level and that 'Japanese concepts could replace western concepts, for they persist in spreading', while to them 'there is a total discrepancy between

Japanese and Western thought concerning the use of power and the values which sustain it'.[36] Washington therefore cannot leave the field open to autonomous Japanese political activity and would like to define the 'responsibilities' which Japan should assume: to adjust her economic policies to US interests, to take over the maintenance of American bases on Japanese territory, to supply technology for military purposes and to put her finances at the service of undertakings initiated by the West, under the umbrella of the United Nations where Tokyo has almost no say. Behind the calls to assume 'her responsibilities' one can see the concern that Japan's international activity should continue to match policies defined by others, i.e. that she cannot create purpose by herself, nor acquire any legitimacy beyond that conferred on her by the United States.

As James Baker reaffirmed in Tokyo on 12 November 1991, 'Relations between the United States and Japan constitute the most important bilateral partnership in the world, without exception.'[37] In effect, no hypothesis on the future of the world order can be formulated without first taking into account this relationship between the world's two leading economic powers under the protection of a military force which no longer has any rival.

Japan still maintains a third of her trade with the United States. She derives about 40 per cent of her commercial surplus from them and a large part of Japanese direct investment overseas, although both are diminishing markedly. But this interdependence has reached the point at which a threat to close the American market is no longer credible and where Japan can even weather measures designed specifically to damage her interests.[38] Furthermore, Japan is currently putting on an impressive demonstration of her capacity to redirect her economic driving-force towards Europe and the Asian region, where her exports overtook in value those to the United States for the first time in 1991. As for the economy, Japan would manage more easily without America than vice versa, so great is the US need for Japanese technology and capital.

Today, therefore, only two of the elements still remain on which Japanese dependence on the victors was based in 1945. A certain psychological dependence persists, which is linked to the acculturation of large sections of the population on the American model and to the disarray of the political élites faced with the perspective of a world deprived of American leadership. Still, this dependence is diminishing, since Tokyo has responded to criticisms by firmly inviting America to correct the blatant gaps in her

36. CIA, *Japan 2000*, p. 6 and p. 14.

37. Quoted in *Libération*, 12 November 1991.

38. For actual examples, see Choate, *Agents of Influence*, and Dominique Nora, *L'étreinte du samuraï*, Paris, Calmann-Lévy, 1991.

own economic and social system, which is increasingly presented to public opinion as the example of what not to do. In these circumstances the military domain remains the only one where Japan is genuinely dependent. She cannot attain complete international autonomy without breaking away, i.e. without questioning the Security Treaty and the future of the Self-Defence Forces.

As the communist threat disintegrates the departure of American forces is more conceivable, because the budgetary deficit leads Washington to reconsider their deployment overseas. Although the United States' preference no doubt remains in favour of retaining their military presence in Japan (provided that Tokyo assumes the full cost) it is probable that, if all fails, Washington would be content with technical co-ordination between the two armies, together with harbour stop-over rights and the assurance of continuing to supply part of the Japanese forces' equipment. After all, the Security Treaty can be renounced by one or other party with a year's warning in advance. Even if the former Soviet Union and China still possess formidable armed forces, Japan no longer faces any credible military threat whatsoever. The collapse of the communist bloc has eliminated any possibility of aggression from that quarter. Whatever the economic tensions and the territorial mini-conflicts which may bring Japan into conflict with some of the over-armed secondary regional powers (Korea, Taiwan), none has the capacity to attack Japan, or even her air or sea lines, without the active support of a major power, which today is inconceivable. This does not exclude the threatening possibility of adventurist military régimes emerging in former communist countries, or a challenge launched by a reunified Korea, over-armed, endowed with nuclear capacity and stirring up the lively anti-Japanese feeling that is prevalent in the Asian region. But the current absence of any short-term threat gives Tokyo an opportunity to reconsider the means by which Japan's security may be guaranteed.

This does not necessarily mean that Japan would wish to break the dependence established by the Security Treaty and Article 9 of the constitution, if only because, without the solidarity to which this dependence ties *both* parties her relationship with the West would be reduced to economic competition exacerbated by the racial factor, which already looks to some like a struggle to the death.[39] Any initiative towards escape from military dependence therefore risks placing Japan in a situation which history has taught her to fear above all: isolation in the face of the white powers. Furthermore, Asian nations would certainly contest such a move vigorously, for in their eyes the Treaty constitutes their sole guarantee against a massive Japanese rearmament.

39. CIA *Japan 2000* 'It is time for the United States to take the measures necessary for their survival as a world power.' (p. 54).

Nonetheless, major rearrangements in the world military order cannot definitively be excluded from consideration. Such rearrangements may be occasioned by the emergence of an independent European defence policy or the United States' material inability to maintain their forces at their current strength. In this respect, Japan now possesses the technical potential for independent defence against any conventional aggression and for exercising nuclear deterrence. Her armaments industry already supplies nearly all her needs;[40] she is also capable of damaging the West's arms industry (although nobody can guess how much) by putting an embargo on certain high-technology components and by launching an export drive on the world arms market. The equipment programme for Japanese forces in 1991–5 aims to supply the nation with an 'enlarged self-defence high-tech system' capable of detecting attacking aircraft or missiles up to two thousand kilometres away, of controlling far-distant sea and air space and of successfully resisting any airborne or amphibious attack on national territory.[41] It aims clearly to establish a 'fortress Japan' which is capable of resisting any conventional attack long enough, perhaps, in case of mortal danger, to achieve the (brief) respite necessary to assemble the nuclear weapons for which she already possesses all the materials and know-how.

To protect the whole nexus of communications necessary to her survival, Japan would also need the capacity to observe the world from a network of satellites and to dispatch military forces towards distant theatres of operation. No doubt she could eventually muster the resources to do this, but it is doubtful whether the political conditions necessary for pursuing the effort over two or three decades can be met. Internally, neither the current state of public opinion nor the balance of forces in the Diet permit it. Externally, the West and Japan's Asian neighbours would most probably not draw back from an open test of power (politically speaking) to prevent it. The most likely hypothesis is therefore that Japan will remain incapable of attaining full military autonomy and of ensuring her security independently. Furthermore, considering that the Japanese economy is now extended all around the world, and considering the geographical characteristics of the archipelago, one may think that Japan is quite simply indefensible by military means. Even a nuclear force would not play a deterrent role, so much does the country's configuration make her annihilation in a single blow inevitable.

It would therefore make little sense for Japan to wish to be released from

---

40. Japan is already 100 per cent autonomous in tanks, artillery, light weapons and ammunition; 92 per cent in shipping; 75 per cent in aircraft; and 55 per cent in missiles. Source, Defense Agency, *Defense of Japan*.

41. General Henri Eyraud, 'Politique de défense du Japon', *Le Trimestre du monde*, Winter 1990, p. 54.

the Security Treaty. Whatever the world order which may emerge, her security will remain based on four inseparable elements. Firstly, the acquisition of a *regional military power* capable of providing independent protection against any threat from its immediate surroundings. Next, and primarily, the maintenance and *growth of her economic, technical and financial superiority*; this is Japan's only means of protection on the world scale, and trade surpluses thus form part of the 'global security' which she is seeking. This means that it would be unrealistic to expect them (or the tensions that they produce) to disappear. To avoid a degeneration into open confrontation, which would cast her in the rôle of accused on the world stage, Tokyo will have to embark on a *systematic strategy of influence* aimed at legitimising her success, reducing hostility towards her and creating a clientèle among developing nations or newly industrialised countries which would grant her greater authority within the international organisations. Finally, *the constant observation of the environment*, the gathering and management of as much information as possible (in which Japan already largely outranks the West), influences the effective implementation of these strategies.

As the collapse of communism has created the conditions for a reshaping of the ideological configuration of the world, Japan could put herself forward as a new type of 'civilian power', preparatory to confirmation of the economy as the fundamental principle of control in international relations. In a world rid of the significance of universalising political models, her technological and financial power and her historical experience would confer on her a status of 'Master of Development'. Without even openly promoting a specific value-system, this would result from the organisational models set in action by the technical advisers she sends abroad, the Asian trainees going through the Japan International Cooperation Agency's programme, and the managers of her factories overseas. Thus Japan could gradually be 'invested with purpose' as a *de facto* alternative to the Western model. As the only non-white power in the circle of international decision-makers, Japan naturally appears there as the representative of developing or newly industrialised nations which are capable of furthering her claim to a permanent seat on the Security Council. But at the same time she must offer pledges to the Westerners who control the United Nations by endlessly reasserting her support for classical liberalism and human rights, and catch them in the trap of their own values by outclassing them in this field of the 'common good of all humanity', upon which their own legitimacy rests. Japan would thus legitimise her growing national power (primarily in the eyes of developing nations) while avoiding open ideological confrontation with the Western powers.

The immediate interests of the large Japanese companies obviously make

such steps inadvisable. Resisting debt rescheduling, exporting their pollution, over-exploiting oceans and tropical forests or evading the
Consultative Group Coordinating Committee (COCOM), by all possible
means they put the logic of their profit ahead of governmental exhortations
to behave like 'good world citizens'. But, in the past, the Japanese power
system has shown how it can reconcile the tendency of economic actors to
maximise their profits with the needs of a clearly defined national strategy.
This is a game at which Japan totally outclasses the Western democracies
and she could succeed again in operating a 'campaign of legitimisation' for
which the outlines have already been well sketched in.

These include, firstly, a characteristic concern to gather the greatest possible quantity of information in advance. In the United States a study conducted between 1982 and 1984 by Japanese located and listed 30,000
decision-makers and personalities, and was intended to serve as the basis
for a systematic strategy of influence.[42] The new stake was clearly perceived
in 1988 by the government and by the Federation of Economic
Organisation (Keidanren), which established respectively an *ad hoc* commission on 'cultural diplomacy' and a permanent committee for international cultural exchanges.[43] Material means were released which matched
the importance of the issue at stake: among the seven nations which invested the greatest amounts in lobbying in the United States, Japan on her own
would spend as much as the other six put together.[44]

Development aid in all its forms is an essential pillar of the strategy for
legitimisation. For several years Japan has led the world in terms of overall
financial transfers to the Third World. In media terms her most impressive
success was in 1989 when she became the world's leading dispenser of
ODA. Ranked by the percentage of her GNP (0.31 per cent), Japan still lies
only twelfth in the world, but she plans to double this in value by 1994. She
has also grasped the importance of visible activity at a practical level and
NGOs are proliferating at the instigation of various ministries anxious to be
represented in this very high-profile area of activity,[45] in addition to government organisations. The political impact of ODA is inescapable,
whether in Tokyo or elsewhere, as can be seen in the United States' effort to
regain the lead after 1990 by entering in their accounts a reduction of 1.2
billion dollars granted to Egypt for her military debt.

42. CIA, *Japan 2000*, p. 31.
43. Drifte, *Foreign Policy*, p. 25.
44. James Fallows, 'The Great Japanese Misunderstanding', *The New York Review*, 8
November 1990, p. 35.
45. In 1990, 270 NGOs were noted as working for development aid, of which the majority
created since 1988 are more or less directly attached to a ministry which subsidises and 'advis-
es them'. *Le Trimestre du Monde*, Winter 1990, p. 81.

Japanese ODA primarily obeys an economic strategy.[46] Indonesia, an essential supplier of raw materials, is her leading beneficiary. But Tokyo has also used her to retain contact with Teheran, Hanoi and San Salvador, without it being possible to specify whether she was acting as intermediary on Washington's behalf or playing the political game on her own account. Japan is also the major supplier of ODA for small marginalised nations such as Burma, Jamaica or Paraguay, which might constitute embryos of a UN clientèle. Finally, in affirming her intention to link ODA to the level of its beneficiaries' democratisation and military expenditure, the Kaifu government (1989–91) clearly sought to improve its image in Western capitals.

Tokyo has also seized hold of the ecological theme, sometimes through micro-activities, such as the dispatch of 57 experts to save birds harmed by oil pollution during the Gulf War;[47] sometimes through massive contributions: 2.3 billion dollars over three years promised at the Paris summit (1989); sometimes through solemn declarations such as the adoption of an Environment Charter for the Earth by the Keidanren, or grandiose plans principally aimed at publicity, such as the green barrier dreamed up by the Agriculture Ministry to halt the advance of the Sahel Desert.[48]

Japan has also realised that political 'plus-value' can be gained by a nation such as France on the stage of great international dramas through humanitarian organisations like Médecins Sans Frontières. Tokyo has sent three aid teams to Kurdistan and created disaster relief teams endowed with substantial funds.[49] It is no coincidence that the two UN agencies managed by Japan are the World Health Organisation and the High Commission for Refugees. These efforts have received little media attention and there still remains much for Japan to do to win a minimum of ecological credibility; but she is trying hard. Aided by her unmatched wealth and proven efficiency in matters of depollution and energy economy, she may soon be able to effect a breakthrough in this area of the common good which still appears to be a closed Western playground. Furthermore, Japanese companies may very well reap big profits from environmental business, and economic logic may fit well with political logic.

The beginnings of a systematic strategy can also be seen in Japan's ostentatious efforts to establish herself as an intermediary between North and

46. See Dennis T. Yasumoto, *The Manner of Giving. Strategic Aid and Japanese Foreign Policy*, New York, Lexington Books, 1986.

47. Yukio Sato (Director General of Analysis, Research and Forecasting to the Japanese Foreign Affairs ministry), 'Le nouveau courant de la diplomatie japonaise. A la recherche d'une identité japonaise au sein de la communauté internationale', in *Politique Internationale* (forthcoming).

48. *Croissance*, 33, December 1990, p. 14.

49. Sato, 'Le nouveau courant'.

South, a task which Prime Minister Nakasone allocated to her as a 'moral duty' in a speech on the fortieth anniversary of the United Nations. In the same vein, Kiichi Miyazawa has pleaded before James Baker for 'an expanded role for the small nations within the UN'.[50] Tokyo has proclaimed itself the representative of the whole of Asia in G7 (the Group of Seven advanced nations) since Williamsburg (1983) and consults the nations of ASEAN (the Alliance of South East Asian Nations) and Korea before every summit. At GATT Japan tries to join hands with developing nations against the protectionist threats issuing from the European Community and the North American free-trade zone. Even if Japan is not in practice particularly generous towards the South, she is working hard to create an image that she is.

At a political level, Japan is seeking to establish herself in the only appropriate niche for a 'civilian power': mediation. She had no success with the Iran–Iraq War, or with Cambodia or Korea, but diplomatic expertise comes with practice. Since the voting of the Peace-Keeping Operations Law (June 1992), Tokyo is also ready to share in blue beret missions. This would allow the Rising Sun flag to fly at the hot spots of the globe as a symbol of Japanese willingness to share political responsibilities assigned to the great powers through morally irreproachable efforts for maintaining peace. Also in keeping with this ostentatious concern for the world's peace and stability is the demand for observer status at the CSCE (Conference on Security and Co-operation in Europe).

This strategy for legitimisation may encounter many obstacles. In general terms, one may doubt whether the economy can prevail as principal co-ordinator of the world order in the face of a violent and multiple revival of ideological politics (nationalisms, fundamentalisms) which could make Japanese strategy appear irrelevant. Japanese government may also fail to control the brutal logic of economic actors, or the growth of a provocative neo-nationalism. The image of a predatory and arrogant Japan would then prevail, and the growth of antagonisms could provoke the European Community and the North American area to close ranks: both have the capacity to sustain most of their economies and their power on the resources available on their own territories, and the military means to acquire those that they lack. Japan has not, and if she felt threatened, she would have no choice but to attempt to revive the Sphere of Co-prosperity strategy through economic and political influence.

Helen Milner and Jean-Louis Margolin discuss this hypothesis elsewhere in this book and it is therefore unnecessary to dwell upon it here. One can discern an Asian strategy at work in Japan since the 1960s, the results of

50. Quoted respectively by *Le Trimestre du monde*, Winter 1990, p. 62, and *Libération*, 12 November 1991.

which are apparent in terms of development, influence and regional coop-eration. It is true that the loosening of China (see the chapter by Jean-Luc Domenach in this book) and American disengagement leave the field open to a new leadership in Asia. The need to develop a system of collective secu-rity, which is rendered more pressing by the threat of a nuclear Korea and by Chinese moves in the South China Sea, may provide an opportunity to create a permanent forum for political cooperation. But the obstacles to genuine regional integration are formidable: the gulf between differing lev-els of development; the heterogeneous nature of the political systems; the persistence of territorial and guerrilla disputes; the strategy of secondary powers to hold Tokyo in check by manipulating the United States and Europe; the centrifugal effect of the projection of the 'four little dragons' in the global economic field; and finally the emergence of synergies outside Japanese control, beginning with the Chinese triangle linking Taiwan, Hong Kong and the coastal zones of Korea.

4   THE MIDDLE EAST AFTER COLD WAR AND GULF WAR

ELIZABETH PICARD

The Gulf War was the first international event after the fall of the Berlin Wall. To some it seemed like a new form of global intervention, a direct result of the end of bipolarity, which was marked by a UN attempt to regulate international relations and by general hopes for democratic progress. Yet the war was less the result of upheavals in the world order than the 'analyser of purpose', revealing powerful Middle East currents following the Soviet collapse. It is indeed doubtful now whether it was the war between Iraq and the international coalition that brought the region to this decisive turning point, the 'irreversible' changes precipitately acclaimed in some quarters, either through optimism or, more frequently, through pessimism. But it was undoubtedly significant, the moment when the differences and contradictions between the world system and state-based systems, as well as the burgeoning regional dynamics, could be grasped in full.[1]

Despite the complexity of developments in the Middle East (and it may be too soon to analyse them in full) we will attempt to evaluate the effects of the end of bipolarity, through the processes of loosening, diversification of power and the globalising tendency of world time. More precisely, we aim to focus on the link between two realities: a Middle East developing its asymmetric rapport between North and South (an entity, in the words of Bruno Etienne, representing a new definition of the boundary between civilisation and barbarity)[2] and a Middle East enclosed in its own time-scale and regional subsystem, distanced from the new universal purpose known as 'market democracy' by its economic functioning, culture and ideology.

---

1. For an attempt at an analysis of the three orders of factors and stakes articulated in this war, cf. E. Picard and A. Roussillon, 'Entre *linkage* et *leadership*: la recomposition des équilibres arabes dans la crise du Golfe', in preparation, *L'Annuaire de l'Afrique du Nord 1990*, Aix-en-Provence, IREMAM, 1992.

2. In *Le Trimestre du monde*, 4, 1990, p.15.

During the Gulf crisis the full logic of the Iraqi approach, which was based on the denunciation of an American conspiracy to gain control over Arab oil, focused on power relationships between the various categories of producer and between producers and consumers. Were these relationships affected by the standardisation of East European economies and the reduction in Soviet oil production? And would the triumphant law of the market-place apply to revenue-dominated economies? If not, what type of integration and above all which hierarchies would emerge triumphant in the Middle East? The question is even more pressing in geopolitical terms: the Soviet disengagement has provoked desperate revisions as well as fresh regional ambitions and a new role for the American superpower. Both economic and strategic aspects can probably be compared with other parts of the South, supporting the hypothesis of world 'loosening'. Next, an assessment of those areas open to the universal purpose promoted by the Cold War victors, with emphasis on the forms of resistance created by a locally produced purpose, will make it possible to indicate some of the routes taken by social actors. Comparison with reorientation (or disorientation) elsewhere in the international system will be equally relevant.

The 'Useful Zone' and its Margins

The collapse of communism has confusing ideological implications for Central and Eastern Europe: a return to religious fundamentalism? greater xenophobia? social splintering? None of these is yet apparent in geostrategic terms, mainly because German reunification is another major ingredient of European upheaval. But in the economic field they undoubtedly mark the triumph of the market and extraversion, with no state anywhere in the world claiming to resist this hegemonic purpose. Few Middle Eastern states, however, possess a socio-economic structure susceptible to this orientation. Iran may be cited, as it emerges from a state of isolation with a sort of bazaar frenzy or, somewhat marginal to our own zone, the successive attempts by Algerian governments to respond to their internal crisis. Turkey is the most relevant of all and deserves examination, set against the experience of the 'socialist' Arab republics.

Ankara had agreed to implement the substantial structural adjustments demanded by the World Bank some years before the changes in Eastern Europe, at a time when Turkey hoped to join the European Community; the wish for Turkish 'westernisation' was strong among Turkey's leaders, whose overriding desire was to see their debt rescheduled by the international financial organisations. Under pressure the successive governments of Ecevit and Demirel (1977–80), the military governments of 1980–83, and above all the governments of Turgut Özal, converted an economy based on replacing imports with home-produced goods into one aimed at industrial exports.[3] The concept of conversion to the private sector economy is not wholly relevant, however, because although it underwent a remarkable expansion during the decade the private sector remains a modest investor, preferring real estate to industry and remaining wary, for example, of the vast hydro-agricultural project in South-East Anatolia.

The dissolution of the Soviet empire, the liberation of its European neighbours (limited in Bulgaria, chaotic in Romania) and the emergence of Turkish-culture entities (Azerbaijan, Turkmenistan, Uzbekistan, Kirghizia and Kazakhstan) on the southern fringes of the Soviet area provide Turkey with an opportunity to relaunch her policy of industrial exports. Whether in the free-exchange zone of nations bordering the Black Sea (set up in January 1992), or in the Turkish-speaking region of nearly 150 million consumers, from Cyprus to Sinkiang Turkish entrepreneurs are offering their European partners joint ventures to which they bring their *savoir-faire* (the market to be won is one of low demand) and above all their cultural affinity. Ankara hopes for increased prosperity from this new *Ostpolitik*, as well as recognition of her partnership by the EC nations (a hope shared by all the country's political actors) and Turkey's unequivocal integration with the North.

Integration into Europe is still the principal aim. Everything else is simply a means to this end, so that we must question the credibility of *European* opportunities offered to Turkey by changes in the East. When Ankara agreed to accept the humiliating terms of structural adjustment ten years earlier Turkey was already looking towards the European Community. Even then, the European and American response had been to direct Turkish economic ambitions elsewhere, towards the oil-exporting Arab nations where financial resources had just increased tenfold following the two oil crises of 1973 and 1979. The first half of the 1980s was the golden age of Turkish–Arab cooperation.[4] The Arab nations supplied oil to Turkey, who in turn exported manufactured goods and even greater quantities of food products. Tens of thousands of Turkish workers settled in Libya and several hundred Turkish businesses won substantial contracts in the Gulf countries, with a total value of 18 billion dollars in fifteen years. The project for a 'peace pipe-line' to carry the waters of the rivers Seyhan and Ceyhan to Oman emerged from the Center for Strategic and

3. Industrial products represented 36 per cent of exports in 1980 and 75 per cent in 1985, according to C. Kirkpatrick and Z. Onis, 'Turkey', in P. Mosley, J. Harrigan and J. Toye (eds.), *Aid and Power. The World Bank and Policy-Based Lending*, vol.2, Case Studies, London and New York, Routledge, 1991, p. 16. By 1989 this proportion had dropped to 72 per cent.

4. H. Akdar, 'Turkey's Export Expansion in the Middle East, 1980–1985', *The Middle East Journal*, 41 (4), Autumn 1987, pp. 553–67.

International Studies (CSIS) in Washington.[5] Above all, Iraq's growing demands, as she sought to sustain her level of internal consumption despite the war with Iran, helped to make the Middle East the destination for 55 per cent of all Turkish exports.

The net value of trade between Turkey and Middle Eastern countries declined after 1986; half of the expatriates returned from Libya and nearly one-third from Saudi Arabia, where Iraq's debt had risen to more than 2 billion dollars[6] (in recent years the region has represented no more than 30 per cent of Turkish exports).[7] This reduction, which is relevant to a consideration of Middle Eastern integration into the modern economy, stems from two structural reasons. The first relates to the globalisation of local economies, because the resources of most Middle Eastern nations are related to oil-wells (dependent, both directly and 'politically', on oil) and, correspondingly, because of the difficulties for the cartel of exporting nations (OPEC) in controlling the oil market when – as since 1984 – it is dominated by buyers. According to world consumption forecasts, demand may increase and reverse this situation during the first decade of the twenty-first century. Meanwhile, the revenues of the rich oil states have diminished appreciably – a point I shall return to later – and their receptiveness to Turkish exports remains limited, as it is closely affected by their oil extraction, as was seen during the Gulf crisis. The second structural reason relates to the persistence of local time-scales in the Middle East (I shall return to this too, in the final section). The hopes founded on a common (Ottoman) past and a shared (Islamic) culture, the concept of a proximity, even a unity, of broad purpose between Turkey and the Arab East, have largely been disappointed during these years of cooperation. They have been replaced by cynical opportunism at best or to rancour with racial connotations at worst, with the Turks being roundly accused of being neither *genuinely* modern nor Western. Yet it remains true that Turkey's Middle Eastern experience during the 1980s may presage Ankara's emerging aspirations and illusions in the light of the changes in the former Soviet Union's southern republics.

The contrasting experience of the Arab republics illustrates the limits of Turkish integration. In February 1990 an article in the Iraqi daily newspaper *al-Thawra* claimed that the 'Iraqi model' of economic and administrative revolution had inspired Gorbachev to apply it to the Soviet Union. The statement leaves room for doubt, but since the middle of the 1970s the

5. J. Kolars, 'The Hydro-Electric Imperative of Turkey's Search for Energy', *The Middle East Journal*, 40 (1), Winter 1986, pp. 53–67.

6. *Mideast Market*, 16 (8), 17 April 1989, p. 16.

7. P. Robins, *Turkey and the Middle East*, London, Pinter, 1991, pp. 109–11.

authoritarian Arab republics – Egypt, Iraq and Syria – have undoubtedly learnt from the collapse of the socialist model of development and their uncomfortable cooperation with the Soviet Union.[8] In Egypt and Iraq the *infitah*, i.e. the opening-up to external markets and the encouragement of the private sector, coincided with the quadrupling of oil incomes following the first oil 'shock' in 1973.[9] The developmentalist state utopia was sustained longer in Syria, for complex reasons connected with the pluralist structure of society and the weakness of oil revenues;[10] but with wholehearted cynicism leaders were already protecting a flourishing private sector on the fringes of the public sector, under the direct patronage of the military system and with free-economy nations as privileged partners.

The functioning of these Arab republics affected by 'openness' has little in common with the market economy. True, the businessmen of Aleppo and Damascus communicate by fax with their partners in Rio, Palermo and Lagos, their incomes work for them on the Zurich stock-exchange and they wear Cardin ties (made in Turkey?), but their activities consist more often of buying and selling than of converting and producing. Their logic is less one of accumulation than one of power, so much do political functions overlap with economic positions. Their activities are full of hidden ramifications where the illicit wins over the legal, and are burdened with unavoidable hangers-on.[11] As a result, the effectiveness of privatisation and deregulation is reduced by the resistance of public sector beneficiaries, from the parasitical bourgeoisie to the crypto-unemployed in public office.[12] No 'Marshall Plan' type of aid programme for the Middle East, which was mentioned during the Gulf crisis, could get round this blockage. Apart from the current Turkish leadership, there is scarcely a local régime capable of a legitimising discourse for structural change that is more radical than simple 'openness'. Rather than seeing the economies of these nations, or that of Iran at the end of the Gulf crisis, as existing *outside* world time (since they are capable of responding effectively and remain in touch with international networks) it could be said that they are living

8. E. Picard, 'The Ba'thist Regimes of Syria and Iraq and the Soviet Union', in Z. Laïdi (ed.), *The Third World and the Soviet Union*, London, Zed Press, 1988, pp. 39–57.

9. R. Hinnebusch, *Egyptian Politics under Sadat. The Post-Populist Development of an Authoritarian Modernizing State*, Cambridge, Cambridge University Press, 1985; R. Springborg, 'Infitah, Agrarian Transformation and Elite Consolidation in Contemporary Iraq', *The Middle East Journal*, 40 (1), Winter 1986, pp. 35–53.

10. F. Lawson, 'Political-economic Trends in Ba'thi Syria. A Reinterpretation', *Orient*, 29 (4), 1988, pp. 579–94.

11. Y. Sadowski, 'Cadres, Guns and Money. The Eighth Regional Congress of the Syrian Ba'th', *Middle East Report*, 134, July-August 1985, pp. 4–8.

12. Interview with Nabil Mohareb, counsellor of the Misr Iran bank development, p. 10–14, in D. Butter, 'Special Report. Egypt', *Middle East Economic Digest*, 7 June 1991.

alongside it. Alternatively, the reverse may be true: the immense grey area of the 'alongsides' covering the globe today belongs to a powerful depolarised and deregulated world order which the World Bank cannot apprehend through its dollar accountancy.

In such circumstances the attempts of international financial organisations to make over-indebted nations such as Turkey, Egypt or Jordan (or even Algeria) improve their internal and external balances, preparatory to allowing them back into the international economy on a level footing, are always out of step with local functioning. Indeed, they help to consolidate the merchant élites of these nations and to strengthen their autonomy; it is left to local authorities to deal with problems of unemployment, inflation and growing inequalities.[13] Is Egypt a marginal case or an example? She gained immediate financial advantages from the upheavals in Eastern Europe and the Gulf crisis: a 50 per cent reduction in the service of her debt, granted by the Paris Club and the IMF; remission of her 7 billion dollar military debt to the United States; remission of her civil debt to the Gulf Cooperation Council (GCC), another 7 billion dollars (billions which Egypt would in any case never have been able to pay). At the same time the creation of a 'social fund for transition towards the market economy'[14] will have the effect of maintaining inflation above 30 per cent, with a zero growth-rate in 1991–2.

There is, however, no reason to think that the indebted nations of the Middle East have suffered from decisions among the northern powers in favour of Eastern Europe; it seems more likely that the emerging world configuration entailed the irrevocable marginalisation of these nations (like that of many others in sub-Saharan Africa). The international community sees the region in the light of two complementary premises: (1) the distinction between useful zones and marginal zones;[15] and (2) the determination to sustain the minimal level of cooperation that will eliminate the migrant risk.

13. Kirkpatrick, Onis, 'Turkey' in *Aid and Power*, p. 34.

14. In particular the reduction within twelve months of the budget deficit from 20 per cent to 10 per cent of the GNP – at the cost, naturally, of a lowering of subsidies for staple products. Cf. D. Butter, 'Special Report: Egypt' p. 14–18. This is without taking into account that for more than a decade the experts have been specifying a 'modernisation' for Egyptian agriculture which is rendering Egypt more dependent for food products and raising the cost of basic supplies. Cf. T. Mitchell, 'America's Egypt. Discourse of the Development Industry', *Middle East Report*, 169, March–April 1991, p. 18–36.

15. The Tunisian economist Chedly Ayari thus makes the distinction between a new 'fertile crescent' consisting of the nations of the GCC and their Arab allies (Egypt, Syria and perhaps Morocco) which 'might well rise to being a community of economic cooperation under the auspices of a strategic and military Arab–Euro-American alliance' and an 'arid crescent', a 'group of states too disparate to create a community'. CERES (collected work), *La guerre du Golfe et l'avenir des Arabes, débats et réflexions*, Tunis, Editions du CERES, 1991.

(1) On the one hand, the Gulf crisis was a test-case for the division of the Middle East, in the world order, between useful zones – in general terms, the oil-exporting areas – and marginal zones (simultaneously poor and heavily populated). No ethical or legal formula can disguise the fact that between them Iraq and Kuwait supply 20 per cent of the world's oil exports, or that Saudi Arabia and the other GCC nations required prompt protection from Saddam Hussein's ambitions, for they represent 30 per cent of these exports. On the other hand, these useful zones do not include either the territories occupied by Israel since 1967 – despite some twenty resolutions of the Security Council – or ruined Lebanon; and it is worth observing that the proportion of oil extracted in the Kurdish region (Kirkuk) in Iraq has dropped steadily since 1967 in comparison with the southern Shiite Arab regions (60 per cent of current extraction, and possessing colossal reserves).

At an economic level the treatment by the industrialised nations, in particular the members of G7, of the 'useful' Middle East zones (essentially the GCC nations, and Iran, Libya and Algeria to a marginal extent) consists of confirming their close financial integration with the North. The local leaders, whose cartel meets in Vienna and who know that their oil contributes to the industrialised nations' prosperity, are in agreement with this. Kuwait is not only that small territory that was transformed within a few months into a vast unproductive dustbin polluted by gas from burning wells, it is also the superb seat of the Kuwait Investment Organization (KIO) at the heart of Kuwait City and a powerful source of finance valued at 200 billion dollars in 1989, only 7 per cent of which is invested in the Arab world.[16] The future direction of the post-Cold War era in the Middle East was therefore at stake, with the three poles of the industrialised world – the United States, the European Community and Japan – competing for control of a region where 26 per cent of the world's oil is extracted, a proportion which may rise to 38 per cent by the year 2005.[17] In return for their lightning reaction to the invasion of Kuwait (responding positively to the Saudi demand for help even before it had been formulated), the United States have secured their 'protectorate' over the kingdom and its satellites and with it their access to its oil and the security of a policy of moderate prices, without any international negotiation. They even succeeded in getting their military campaign paid for by Germany and Japan, in proportion to these nations' oil consumption, an indication of the crucial importance of the energy factor in the conflict. Finally, they secured a mortgage for several years on the region's oil income by substantially dominating the

16. S. Sobh, 'Des économies davantage fragilisées', *Arabies*, 45, September 1990, p. 21–3.
17. *Le Monde*, 25 June 1991.

market for reconstruction and protection in the countries affected.[18] It will be seen that this control exercised by the United States over the world oil market is not entirely separate from their control of solutions to the Israeli–Arab conflict.

(2) On the other hand, the frontier between North and South divides the Middle East area itself, and the tightening of American control inhibits the establishment of a policy of harmonisation and economic cooperation. Organisations such as the Kuwait Fund for Arab Economic Development (KFAED) or the Islamic Development Bank in Jeddah prefer a less restricting policy, with the rich countries subsidising the poorer ones. The Gulf crisis even supplied Saudi Arabia with a ready-made pretext for the unceremonious expulsion of nearly a million Yemeni workers suddenly deprived of residence permits, while in Kuwait more than 200,000 Palestinians became suspect. This protectionist immigration policy, which prefers a European or South Asian[19] workforce to one from 'brother' Arab nations, also applies to Egyptians. More than 1 million Egyptian emigrants, now once more unemployed in their own nation, have lost income assessed at several billion dollars annually, and in addition Egypt has won only the crumbs of the Kuwait reconstruction market as her reward for taking part in the international coalition against Iraq.

A New Strategic Deal

The case of Egypt reveals the latent contradictions between two orders of priority, economic and strategic, in the emerging hierarchies of the Middle East. For although Egypt is a heavy financial burden shared between the great industrialised nations and the rich Gulf nations, her demographic power and her human and military potential make her, if not a regional power, at least an actor worthy of attention. With the move from the economic to the geopolitical field, the poles of power have changed and their relationship with the world system is less stable. In this domain the Gulf crisis operated as an analyser of the changes which emerged in the Middle East after the Cold War, the stalemate created by the coalition victory over Iraq, and the current rebuilding of Kuwait. Two specific questions arise: security and leadership, both of which concern the general problems of the loosening of the world order and the construction of regional hegemonies.

For ten years, from 1979 to 1989, the rivalry between the two world systems sustained a fragile equilibrium in the Middle East, founded on multi-

18. Ibid.

19. Or even Ukrainian, according to the echoes in the corridors of the General Assembly of the United Nations in September 1991.

polarity and complementarity: distancing from Egypt after the Camp David Agreement; Syrian–Israeli rivalry in the Lebanon; mutual destruction between Iran and Iraq; falling oil incomes; and the resort to Islamic mobilisation by régimes of dubious legitimacy. This was far from the radical division which saw the confrontation of Nasser's 'progressives' and King Feisal's 'conservatives' during the 1960s. At least during more or less serious crises (the Iranian revolution and the invasion of Afghanistan in 1979, the 1982 Israeli war in Lebanon, the growth in terrorism and attacks on tankers in the Gulf in 1987–8), the two great powers succeeded in preventing the spread of instability to other areas. Despite her weakened diplomatic and economic influence, the Soviet Union helped to perpetuate this equilibrium by continuing to send arms to Iraq[20] and Syria, and above all by continuing to claim a seat on equal terms with the United States in peace negotiations.[21] This extended to the Palestine question, which lost its Israeli-Arab dimension with the birth of the *Intifada* (1987) and the beginning of dialogue between the PLO and the United States. In a Middle Eastern space simultaneously splintered and subject to influence, no state was capable of setting itself up as a regional pole combining economic power and military potential with a purpose acceptable to its rivals and above all to its own people: Arabia was a financial colossus with feet of clay, with no GCC protection from either Iran or Iraq; Egypt was bogged down in grave social problems; Iran was unable to export her revolution except to southern Lebanon; and Syria and Libya's loud claims and protestations did little to conceal the extent of their 'damage potential'.

If the devaluation of the Soviet model neither surprised nor embarrassed her allies in the Middle East, the signs of her loss of power – the retreat from Afghanistan, the ethnic disturbances in the Caucasus, the dissolution of the Warsaw Pact, etc. – caused anxious questioning. This was not limited to the Arab communist parties, historically linked to Moscow conservatives, or 'progressive' régimes such as the People's Democratic Republic of Yemen which succeeded in achieving a straightforward conversion to the market, pluralism and even Islamic piety, between January 1986 (the overthrow of Ali Muhammed) and November 1989 (the agreement for union with Sanaa). The whole region was clearly in a state of disarray at the collapse of a neatly structured world. Examples are Turkey, whose entry to the European Community was refused in December 1989 and who in addition lost her role as guardian

20. According to the *Financial Times*, 7 August 1990, the Iraqi military debt to the Soviet Union had grown to 20.3 billion dollars. The accumulated Syrian debt since 1970 is generally assessed at 15 billion dollars.
21. E. Karsh, *The Soviet Union and Syria. The Asad Years*, London, Routledge, 1988.

of NATO's eastern front, or Syria when the Soviet Union indicated clearly that she would no longer finance her search for 'strategic parity' with Israel.[22] The Soviet Union's altered status was felt as a radical break with the traditional system of dual confrontation: United States and Israel facing the Soviet Union and Arab nations. This change became evident principally through the development, long delayed by Moscow, of the Israeli–Soviet relationship: commercial missions proliferated, direct air links for new Jewish immigrants were re-established (thanks to the Shultz–Shevardnadze agreement of October 1989), and 'consular' relations were opened early in 1991. A new step was taken at the Bourget show that spring when Moscow proposed the sale of advanced equipment to the Israeli army. Up to October 1991 the Soviet Union continued to make the reopening of diplomatic relations with Jerusalem dependent on Israel's acceptance of Security Council resolutions on the Occupied Territories, but the normalisation of her relations with the Jewish state challenged the balance of deterrence which had controlled the Middle East unofficially for some ten years. This balance had been Soviet–Israeli rather than Soviet–American: Israel's destruction of the Iraqi *Tammuz* nuclear reactor in June 1981 had been a clear indication that she expected to retain her position as the region's only nuclear power. In return, however, it was implicitly understood that the Soviet umbrella would protect the Arab nations, particularly those linked with Moscow by a defence treaty (Iraq since 1972 and Syria since 1980).[23]

Iraq was the one state in the region which tried to learn from the new deal brought about by the Soviet changes and to reassemble a disjointed Arab world under her leadership. Considerably weakened by eight years of war with Iran, Iraq would nevertheless like to combine her economic potential (as the third oil producer in the region, behind Saudi Arabia and Iran), her military power (even if she did not have the 'world's fourth army', as was stated by the Pentagon on the eve of the 'Desert Storm' offensive) and the mobilising capacity of the Ba'ath nationalist discourse which since 1983 has been largely impregnated with Islam to compete with the Shi ites. Ambitious to realise his 'regional ambitions', Saddam Hussein stressed the 'serious consequences for the Arabs and for pan-Arab security' of the 'void'

22. From the progressive warnings (cf. H. Cobban, *The Superpowers and the Syrian-Israeli Conflict. Beyond Crisis Management?*, Washington, CSIS, 1991, pp. 120–21) to the declaration of Alexandre Zotov, Soviet ambassador to Damascus, in the *Washington Post,* 20 November 1989.

23. An indication of the functioning of this Soviet umbrella had been given at the time of the first launch of *Jericho II*, a 1,500-km range missile, by the Israeli army. Moscow had protested then against this Israeli advance. Cf. 'Soviet Cautions Israel Against a New Missile', *New York Times*, 29 July 1987.

left by the Soviet Union, before calling on his partners in the Council for Arab Cooperation to close ranks in the face of the 'new danger'.[24]

The new Iraqi strategy had secondary implications: financial blackmail of its partners in OAPEC (the Organisation of Arab Petroleum Exporting Countries); aid for anti-Syrian factions in Lebanon; and the establishment of a clientèle of nations ranging from Sudan to Mauritania. Primarily, however, it established the terms of a new balance of deterrence in the Middle East confronting Israel, which is why the famous 'link' between the fates of Kuwait and Palestine, as defined by Saddam Hussein in his speech of 12 August 1990, reflected a global vision of the region between the Mediterranean and the Gulf rather than a mere legal quibble. Iraq had just extended the range of her Scud-B missiles bought from the Soviet Union (December 1989), the Western press had revealed Baghdad's purchase of components capable of being used to manufacture atom bombs (February 1990) and, openly defying Jerusalem, Saddam announced his possession of the binary chemical weapon which he threatened to use on Israel at the slightest aggression against Iraq.[25] In this new regional configuration made possible (at least Saddam believed so) by the loosening of the world order, the Near East was dominated by Israel and the Gulf region by Iraq. Deterrence by the major power (the United States) over the lesser (Iraq) had no place here.

The clear intention, and achievement, of 'Desert Storm' and 'Desert Shield' was to destroy this ambition and demonstrate unequivocally that it was unacceptable in American eyes, even though the other objectives of Washington and the international coalition (principally the restoration of Kuwaiti sovereignty) must not be neglected. The United States had specified their 'vital interests' in the Middle East at the time of the second Cold War, more precisely by the formulation of the Carter Doctrine (1980). These were, on the one hand, Israel's security, and on the other, the defence of their oil supplies and the protection of the Gulf monarchies' financial holdings, the essential factor of American world supremacy.[26] In 1977 the United States had set up a Rapid Deployment Joint Task Force for protection against the Soviet Union (and, soon, revolutionary Iran), followed in 1983 by CENTCOM. Far from weakening US interest in the Middle East, the disappearance of the Soviet menace strengthened it. They

24. *FBIS Daily Report. Near East and South Asia*, 27 February 1990. Much of this report would be worth quoting.

25. Speech by Saddam Hussein to the general command of the Iraqi armed forces, 1 April 1990, translated into English by FBIS, 4 April 1990.

26. A. Cordesman, *The Gulf and the Search for Strategic Stability, Saudi Arabia, the Military Balance in the Gulf, and Trends in the Arab-Israeli Military Balance*, Boulder, Westview Press, 1984.

could no longer count on the earlier international stability maintained by the rivalry between the two Great Powers, nor could they continue to tolerate the development of autonomous regional dynamics and the emergence of Iraq as a new dominant power at the heart of the Arab world.

With the destruction of this bipolarity, America's new concept of the post-crisis system of security implies a return to a multipolar system which would allow her to maintain a military presence in the Middle East. More than in any other part of the world, therefore, the United States behave like an intrusive and exclusive power. Several factors make them intrusive. Henceforward their military presence will be permanent,[27] at least at sea and in bases in Egypt, Israel and Turkey, in the latter case in the form of a 'rapid reaction force'. In the last resort the decision is theirs to intervene for humanitarian purposes to help one specific group (the Iraqi Kurds) and not another (the Iraqi Shiites) when it suits their interests; it was they who established the criterion of legitimacy for their local allies, a criterion unrelated to sound finance (Israel and Egypt are both disastrously indebted nations), to respect for the law (Syria was still listed among terrorist-linked states at the end of 1991), or to democracy (a principle rejected by Saudi Arabia). They are exclusive because Washington has no wish to share the role with the other members of the Security Council and because appeals to the Soviet Union (whether from Iraq or elsewhere) to continue behaving like a great power in the region have proved vain.

The first question raised by the new Middle Eastern configuration, which is simultaneously splintered and under the influence of the world superpower, is that of compatibility between, on the one hand, regional security (which is nonetheless global: the Mediterranean is a small inland sea and Moscow is within range of the Intermediate Range Ballistic Missiles (IRBMs) which Israel will soon possess) and, on the other, a selective policy of rearmament. An early American reaction during the crisis was to secure the most urgent requirements and to improve the equipment of the GCC nation-states, which was weak, despite the 18 billion dollars spent on the defence of their 18 million inhabitants in 1989.[28] This was undertaken partly by delivering them fresh arms and partly by selling them equipment brought in for the campaign against Iraq, for another 18 billion dollars. At the same time Israel was promised fresh supplies to preserve her strategic superiority, seen as essential to her survival in a hostile environment. This policy became more delicate when Turkey, whose army

27. Denied and then confirmed in turns, it was announced as such by James Baker at the beginning of September 1990. Dick Cheney justified it by the 'feeling of security and confidence [which it created] among the friendly and allied nations in the area'.

28. According to IISS, *The Military Balance 1990–1991*, London IISS, 1991, p. 125.

had remained ready to open a second front against Iraq, made insistent demands on NATO to modernise her equipment. It was then frankly embarrassing to learn that the Soviet Union was about to deliver Sukhois to 'allied' Syria, and Czechoslovakia a dozen T72s. There was a lesson to be learned from the Islamic Revolution's overthrow of the Shah and the metamorphosis of Iraq from reasonable client state to bankrupt dictatorship in the space of a few months (during which, admittedly, the whole world was concentrating on the Berlin Wall): relations with the region's states remained fundamentally unstable and weapons risked being turned overnight against those who had delivered them.

Another American view sees the Missile Technology Control Regime accords of 1987 as inadequate, despite their contribution in 1990 when Argentina, Egypt and Iraq abandoned the 'Condor II' programme. On the basis of the Baker–Bessmertnykh agreement of January 1991 'for a common approach to the search for peace in the Middle East', the United States demanded the banning of all arms exports to the 'zone of violence', from Marrakesh to Bangladesh.[29] Immediately after the war George Bush's administration made it a priority in negotiations on the 'moralisation' of the arms trade between the five members of the Security Council. According to Washington (promoted to the role of policeman for the region) no external danger now threatens the Middle East, where arms imports can only feed interstate and domestic conflicts and the American presence should be enough to guarantee its security. One could hardly emphasise more effectively the inability of the nations in the area to control their international environment.

In the current world context – intense arms trade competition in the North, and multilateral cooperation in the South for the production of high-level military technologies – the arms control project in the Middle East appears utopian. Neither the United States nor the new states of the CIS are willing to abstain from such a profitable business in a period of economic recession. Furthermore, the American line of argument disregards the growing proportion of domestic strife and internal conflict in the violence which is appearing in this area.[30] Moreover, this argument suffers from a major drawback which is seized upon with criticism and distrust, even by those seen by Washington as its closest allies: consideration

29. E. Luttwak, 'Stop Arming the Third World', *New York Times*, 4 November 1990. See also the final communiqué of the meeting of the five Security Council members in Paris, 9 July 1991, which demanded the elimination of SS missiles, the banning of chemical weapons and the 'control by the IAEA of nuclear activities'.

30. E. Picard, 'Society and State in the Arab World: Towards a New Role of the Security Forces', in R. Brynen, B. Korany and P. Noble (eds), *The New Face of National Security. Dilemmas of Security and Development*, London, Macmillan, in preparation.

of the ABC equipment and the missiles envisaged by the Bush project of Enhanced Proliferation Control Initiative (EPCI, February 1991) excludes the 200-odd nuclear warheads held by Israel, as if that nation belonged to a different region, one of democratic rationality, or as if her nuclear power was part of her American protector's inventory. To the other nations in the area, however, geopolitics have placed Israel firmly at the heart of the Near East: if Israel is excused the constraints that the North would like to impose on others, demands for limitation affecting other states in the region will no longer appear legitimate. In response to reproaches that she is cooperating with North Korea to extend the range of her Scud-Bs, Mubarak's Egypt repeated her appeal to the United Nations for a Middle East 'free from nuclear weapons'.[31] Everything appears to indicate that the 'lesson' which the allied forces wished to give Iraq has been learned, but that its intended message has been distorted: what has been retained is that only control of a powerful weapon of deterrence can provide protection from annihilation by the superpower. The war will therefore have served only to delay nuclear competition in the region (Iran is negotiating keenly with France and Germany and cooperating with China, Algeria is cooperating with China and is welcoming Russian scientists) while at the same time increasing the risks of Israeli recourse to the bomb in any future conflict.[32] In this way, the end of bipolarity will have taken the Middle East into the paradox of a strategic space which is dominated but less controllable.

A second question posed by the fresh Middle Eastern configuration also revives the debate on security and proliferation: that of the leadership around which balanced regional relationships can be reorganised, to achieve a resolution of international tensions and to slow down the armaments race. Faced with the long-term weakening of Iraq – a matter of satisfaction but also of serious concern for the oil monarchies – the United States tried to encourage the creation of a collective military structure endowed with an armed force, including the Six of the GCC and Egypt and Syria, the two Middle East Arab states which shared in the multinational force. For two reasons these nations have made little progress in the establishment of a 'new Arab order'[33] since their first meeting on 6 March 1991; the economic cooperation demanded by Cairo and Damascus[34] in return for their military presence in the Gulf is of no inter-

31. *International Herald Tribune*, 5 July 1991.

32. R. E. Harkavy, 'After the Gulf War: The Future of Israeli Nuclear Strategy', *The Washington Quarterly*, 14 (3), Summer 1991, pp. 161–79.

33. L. Freedman, 'The Gulf War and the New Arab Order', *Survival*, 23 (3), May-June, pp. 195–209.

34. This is not confused with *aid* – a 7 billion dollar debt written off for the former, an 'exceptional' grant of 2 billion dollars for the latter.

est to their royal partners, and patronage from the United States, while supporting her Arab allies, tends to undermine their legitimacy by emphasising their weakness and submission to a code which may be universal but is nonetheless alien.

In contrast, the collapse of Soviet patronage has liberated Israel and Turkey, the United States' two non-Arab allies in the area – the former to a lesser extent as she loses the advantage, so persuasive in Reagan's time, of being a 'strategic trump card' in the face of a communist threat. Turkey, however, is now in a position to declare her claims to a hegemonic role in the Middle East. Iran, her rival, has so far neither recovered from the war with Iraq nor firmly reintegrated herself into the world concert of nations, although with the passing of the Khomeini era she may surprise us with her liveliness in catching up with world time. In the meantime, Turkey holds the lead with several strong cards: her army of 800,000 men is one of the largest in NATO, she welcomes the reaction force created by the United States and will take part in it, she controls 80 per cent of the Asian Middle East's water resources, and she is rich in manpower, which favours her integration into the three regions which she shares (in particular the Soviet area where she trades gas for manufactured products).[35] This integration is demonstrated by the regular growth of foreign investment in the country since 1983.

Furthermore, driven by her European aspirations and the demands of her partners, Turkey is making progress along the route to democracy The authoritarian Kemalist state has accepted compromises with society, which is increasingly being reintegrated into the political game through growing market independence and cultural liberalisation; this includes compromise with the Islamic forces which know how to play the card of modernity much more skilfully than their Arab counterparts. It also, however, means finding a new compromise over Turkish national identity on a multicultural basis. Asserting with lucidity and boldness that the days of the Ottoman empire are finally and conclusively over, Turgut Özal commented[36] that Turkey was gaining an opportunity in the 'greenfield site' of the Middle East since the collapse of the bipolar order. It remains to be seen whether Ankara is capable of channelling or producing a purpose strong enough to win regional adherence and to allow Turkey to realise her potential.

35. All these facts have been supplied by S. Vaner in an address to the *Ordre mondial relâché* group, 27 June 1991.

36. Quoted in *Cumhuriet*, 31 January 1991.

World Time and Regional Mishaps

The points discussed above are inseparable from the question of how Middle Eastern states and cultures can be integrated into the single world time which has been expanding inexorably since the end of the bipolar world. In outline, this can be reduced to four major problems: (1) grafting on the universal model of the nation-state; (2) the coherence and effectiveness of the Islamic alternative; (3) the importance of democratic aspirations within these two models; (4) finally, the fragility of states torn between contrasting temporalities.

(1) The economic collapse and crisis of legitimacy in the people's democracies challenge the essence of the statist model created in the Middle East after the dissolution of the Ottoman empire. While the British, French and Italian colonial episodes lasted for at least a quarter of a century, it must be recognised that in decolonised nations such as Turkey and Iran (nations already independent in the aftermath of the First World War) the Western model known as the 'nation-state' was also dominated by the fascist and Stalinist models. This model entailed nationalism denying the ethnic, religious or class divisions of society, authoritarian modernisation implying secularisation 'from above', nationalisation of the economy and social redistribution. Turkey was instrumental in transmitting these models, which were adopted by the Arab republican regimes, Nasserist or Ba'athist in particular, with a time-lag corresponding to the colonial era.[37] With the collapse of communism these models are once more being challenged throughout the Middle East, through promotion of the legal entity of the state which threatens the ruling élites, whether traditional or modern, with a loss of legitimacy and power. Henceforward the king is naked, and defence of the 'nationalist' and 'developmentalist' state led by Hafiz al-Assad in Syria or the FLN in Algeria may be interpreted as the struggle for survival of a régime. In Iraq, meanwhile, Saddam Hussein has pushed the reinforcement of his state as far as dictatorship, in a security-minded logic which has led him into systematic attacks on his own society.[38] It is no small paradox that the world forces (Western nations, international institutions) which hastened the fall of Eastern Europe's authoritarian régimes contributed to his survival long after the war, for the sake of a much-vaunted 'regional stability', in their intense concern to preserve the status quo rather than see the Middle East enter a zone of turbulence: immediately

37. E. Picard, 'La modernisation autoritaire par les nationalistes arabes, écho et test de l'expérience kémaliste', in S. Vaner (ed.), *Modernisation autoritaire en Turquie et en Iran*, Paris, L'Harmattan, 1991.

38. S. al-Khalil, *Repubic of Fear: Saddam's Iraq*, Berkeley, University of California Press, 1989.

after his capitulation in March 1991 Saddam's army was granted the time, and freedom to manoeuvre, to crush the Shiite and Kurdish rebellions.

(2) The Middle East is a world region[39] where an Islamic 'counter-model' has been developed and proposed in opposition to the universalist model of market democracy. Islam, which may be analysed as a regional version of world purpose, is in a mobilising phase, as can be seen in the Saudi influence on Arabic media throughout the world, or in recent events in Algeria. What remains uncertain is whether it is still in an ascendant phase. The crisis of the Marxist–Leninist utopia leaves the field open to transcendental utopias and favours the 'revenge of God'; but it entails criticism of all types of faith and a distaste for globalising doctrines. To this can be added Islam's inability to offer a doctrine which is not commentary, exegesis and interpretation of its ancient texts, or to produce fresh intellectual thought matching its social and political ambitions.[40] Thus Iran's plan under Khomeini to export its revolution was thwarted, even in the Shiite regions of the Middle East, by the specificity of the Iraqi, Lebanese or Azeri 'national times', and perhaps even more by the persuasive power of the world time.

The question which faces Islam is truly that of its effectiveness, of its capacity to respond to both the demands of the international system and the expectations of local cultures. In constitutional and judicial terms, the nations which see themselves as Islamic only achieve this at the price of compromise and uncomfortable contortions: Iran, which attempted to resist, paid for her resistance with a period of isolation lasting several years; Saudi Arabia disconnected its internal from its external functioning, ignoring the growing proportion of her subjects involved with the interface of the two systems. It is virtually only the opposition Islamists who can still promote the 'pure' Islamic state. In the economic domain the Islamists' inability to propose an alternative to capitalism and market laws, to elaborate a system combining individual liberty and solidarity within Muslim society, is illustrated by the blighted hopes of the 'Islamic banks'. These institutions, the Saudi banks in particular, are often capitalist-style establishments differing only in a terminology borrowed from the religious repertoire. Having thus failed to invent a different economic system, are the Islamists willing and able to legitimise the current move from centralised redistribution economies to a liberal and productive economic system? Can there be an Islamist (i.e. not simply Middle Eastern) modality that is adaptable to the world economy, and responsive to the universal aims of

39. Not the only one. Is not Japan's eagerness not to offer itself as a model 'exemplary'?
40. O. Carré, *L'utopie islamique dans l'Orient arabe*, Paris, Presses de la Fondation nationale des sciences politiques, 1991.

satisfying material needs without contradicting its particular ideological system? This leads us to the problem of the coincidence between economic liberalism and democratic liberties, a coincidence which is rarely verified and which is outside any causal relationship.

(3) Furthermore, it seems unlikely that the fall of Eastern Europe's dictatorial régimes caused more than a ripple of democracy in the Middle East in 1990–91. Rather than finding expression in the expansion of the progressive Syrian National Front from five to seven parties in March 1990, in President Assad's promise to moderate (but not to withdraw) the emergency law in force since 1963, or again in the Iraqi Revolutionary Command Council's authorisation of foreign travel in January 1990, the 'Ceausescu syndrome' has instead given many Middle Eastern régimes an opportunity to display their self-satisfaction and prove how effectively they exercise control over their peoples. As dictatorships everywhere else – and particularly in Africa – assessed this 'Ceausescu syndrome', the traditional monarchies and authoritarian republics of the Middle East absorbed the renewed challenge and democratic demands and transformed them into 'bureaustroika'.[41] At the same time the fall of the people's democracies sowed division and disarray within local communist parties[42] torn between their Marxist faith and the wind of *perestroika*. The progressive parties of the Arab world had to face up to the contradiction between their plans and their participation in power, and for the first time for several decades opened a debate, often confused but ultimately open, on the economic and strategic orientations of hitherto untouchable régimes. Certainly the two significant examples of the return to mixed party politics – in Jordan and in Algeria – predated this: from April to December 1991 in Jordan, from October 1988 to June 1990 in Algeria, where the first defeat of a governing Arab régime in a free election was greeted as a democratic victory.[43] But the comparison with current moves in the East European countries at least has the merit of identifying some of the contradictions of the claim to democracy in the Middle East, and of illustrating its importance.

One must first note the Western world's reticence, even its negative stance, as much among governments as among liberal intellectuals, concerning the move to pluralism when it allowed Islamist parties onto the political stage. The hostility towards the Iraqi Shiites, the ill humour of

41. Isam al-Khafaji, 'Who's Afraid of Bureaustroika?', *Middle East Report*, November-December 1990, pp. 30–4.

42. P. Robins, 'Middle East I. Arabs Eye Eastern Europe Warily', *The World Today*, August-September 1990, pp. 157–60.

43. As for the election of a Consultative Assembly in Kuwait in June 1990, it marked a step backwards for democracy with regard to the parliamentary system.

Western chancelleries when the Muslim Brotherhood entered the Jordanian government, the warnings of former French '*porteurs de valise*' at the rise to power of the FIS (Front Islamique du Salut – Islamic Salvation Front) in Algeria – all these show that the world had adapted reasonably well to the authoritarian régimes of the Middle East, whether monarchical or republican, and above all that Islam was perceived as an obstacle to democratic liberalisation. Without entering into an already well-aired debate,[44] it should be noted that the achievements of the Islamic state, like the Saudi experience, justify such an assessment; but today the question is posed rather in terms of the integration of Islamic organisations into pluralist political systems. Thereafter, acknowledgement of the gap between Islam's inclusive globalising discourse and its pragmatic and diversified practices should be combined with assessing the gap separating world time from local times. This will enable observers to appreciate the vagaries of democracy as a concept in Middle Eastern cultures. An illustration of this complex combination is given by the 'Islamic engineers' who surround Turgut Özal in Turkey:[45] trained in modern technocracy at American universities, fully integrated into world networks, champions of ultra-liberal economics, true Muslims and often members of a mystical brotherhood, they take their religious ethic to the point of integrating it into the programme of the Motherland Party (ANAP), in the setting of a republican, pluralist and resolutely European Turkey.

Islam aside,[46] it remains for us to question the meaning of the transition to democracy in these Middle Eastern states. They have a marginal manufacturing sector but no domestic market, their leaders have spent decades in paralysing the institutions of civilian society and marginalising its organisations and expression, and their opponents are unenthusiastic about sharing the unpopularity of measures such as higher taxes as the price of gaining the status of political interlocutors. Even the Jordanian experience of legislation, integration of traditional opposition parties into the state, and abrogation of martial law, can be seen as an attempt to win back the opposition leaders by a régime whose popularity has been reduced. By releasing only a few crumbs of his power and introducing populist rather than democratic measures, and by keeping the army as his most reliable support, King Hussein's aim was above all to consolidate his throne.

44. See for example *The Middle East Journal*, Summer 1991, 45, (3), pp. 407–41.

45. N. Göle, 'Ingénieurs musulmans et étudiantes voilées: entre le totalitarisme et l'individualisme', in G. Kepel and Y. Richard (eds), *Intellectuels et militants de l'islam contemporain*, Paris, Le Seuil, 1990, pp. 167–92.

46. Even if so many commentaries in the West have been prompt to designate Islam as the chief obstacle to democratisation in the Middle East; for example, the editorial in *Le Monde*, 18 January 1990.

The participation of a narrow fringe of society in claims to democracy, if not in its construction, raises few illusions as to the importance of the 'other side' of Middle Eastern societies.[47] Today in Egypt less than 10 per cent of the population use their right to vote, a figure that should be seen in relation to the immense proportion living on the margins of public services (water, electricity, education) but not always protected from their constraints (conscription), and who at the same time live outside the market economy. The current process of economic liberalisation has the effect, here and everywhere in the Middle East, of expanding these marginal categories, including even the graduates and salaried intellectuals who are oppressed by inflation. Yet there is one global field from which these groups of people are not excluded, that of information: it gets through to the most remote villages connected to a satellite dish. The immediacy of social acculturation makes their frustration and claims even more urgent in the world arena, creating the paradox that their unstoppable entry into politics – a positive step in itself – takes place chiefly by means of protest, rebellion or mob culture.

(4) Final problem: as well as delegitimising authoritarian nationalist régimes ('conservative' or 'progressive') as a dominant discourse of the post-Cold War era, the discourse of law and rights (human or minority rights, etc.) also allows the religious, ethnic and regional groups of the Middle East assembled by history in the same territorial state (a term to be preferred to 'nation-state') to display their lack of consensus on common rules and on fundamental aspects of the state's social, political and economic organisation. Virtually since the Second World War, the dominance of the superpowers had ensured the perpetuation of the state system from outside and, furthermore, its international and regional legitimacy. The scrupulously maintained fiction of the integrity and sovereignty of Lebanon, maintained despite its progressive internal collapse since 1975, illustrates this consensus, which is shared equally by the United Nations whose pressure created FINUL in 1978 and by the Arab League which backed the Taëf agreement in 1989. But with the end of the bipolar world, the arbitrary partitions imposed on the ruins of the three empires – Russian, Austro-Hungarian and Ottoman[48] – collapsed simultaneously; and the fetish of nation-state communities, 'imagined'[49] at the end of the nine-

47. M. Camau, 'Trois questions à propos de la démocratisation dans le monde arabe', *Egypte/Monde arabe*, 4, 1990, pp. 25–47.

48. See G. Corm, *L'Europe et l'Orient de la balkanisation à la libanisation, histoire d'une modernité inaccomplie*, Paris, La Découverte, 1989.

49. P. Anderson, *Imagined communities. Reflections on the Origin and Spread of Nationalism*, London, Verso, 1983.

teenth century and the beginning of the twentieth century by the power of nationalist ideology, collapsed in pieces.

In the Middle East the social fragmentation experienced as states suffer setbacks in securing integration is undeniable. There are many examples: 'political communitarianism' in Lebanon, the revolt of the Sunni Muslim majority in Syria against the 'Alawi state',[50] the double revolt in Iraq since March 1991, of the Kurds in the north and the Shiites in the south; and the war led by the PPK Marxist Kurdish militants in south-east Turkey since 1984 against the army and its local militias. The evolution of Palestinian society after three years of *intifada* in the Occupied Territories, simultaneously turned inwards to the preoccupations of survival and marked by a drift towards internal confrontations, shows the strong temptation everywhere to retreat to basic solidarities. The collapse of the Soviet Union will have had the effect of devaluing the political activities of the 'modern' parties of the 1950s and 1960s (with all their manipulations, pretended overturnings of social divisions and mystic ideologies, it is true, but also with their progressive utopia and their dynamism).

At the same time the atomisation of society is balanced by the emergence of transnational actors, by the revival of networks, clientèles, groups of interests and of 'primary' solidarity,[51] whose vigour is the more remarkable because they are wholly in step with the pattern of world time. The case of the Aleppines, which I have had occasion to study, illustrates the dynamics at work not only on the Middle East's Mediterranean front but probably in their new Caucasian dimension, which has been helped by the lifting of the iron curtain. Since Aleppo lost its territories in the Gaziantep and Mardin areas (in what is now Turkey) after the division of the Ottoman empire, these lands have gradually lost their economic and emotional value, particularly because the great families, who were once both the symbol and the driving force in maintaining the privileged relationship with the separated regions, have been progressively marginalised in the construction of the Syrian state. However, the Christians of Aleppo have retained from the Ottoman period the custom of living, studying and travelling between Aleppo (Syria), Alexandretta (Turkey) and Beirut (Lebanon). The Kurds, meanwhile, have become the masters of a flourishing trade in goods, gold, arms and drugs which extends beyond the Middle East. These examples of minorities are simply indications of the existence of trading, religious and political networks throughout all the communities, inherited from the social history of Aleppo with their roots deep in

50. M. Seurat, *L'Etat de Barbarie*, Paris, Le Seuil, 1989.

51. O. Roy, 'Le double code afghan. Marxisme et tribalisme', *Revue française de science politique*, 36 (6) December 1986, pp. 846–61.

the memory of the openness and dynamism of the recent past, the imperial era. Today, to escape from the extraordinarily bureaucratic functioning of their country, the businessmen of Aleppo have redeployed their activities all round the Mediterranean basin, particularly in Turkey, because she offers the advantages of a legal system that is highly favourable to foreign investments, but above all because in Turkey they can enjoy *personal* facilities and connections. Let us take as an example one particular Sunni industrialist, with a Christian wife, whose son is a student in California and who, with his Jewish associate, benefits from the intercession of an Alawite officer to obtain the necessary permits for the purchase of Carrara marble to decorate hotels for Saudi holidaymakers, which he is building in the Antalya region.

In the mobilisation of transnational identities, that of ethnic identity (the least 'artificial' of all identities) is today the most effective in the Middle East. It can be seen in the renewed negotiations over areas of sovereignty of four nations (Turkey, Iran, Syria and Iraq) as a result of the Kurdish claim for autonomy in Iraq. This mobilisation, which strengthens Turkish hopes of developing a new Turkish-speaking zone of influence in central Asia, a market now open to Europe, is undoubtedly aided by the breakdown of the Soviet state as power and as model, because of the paradoxical bond of principle between the nation-state model and cultural pluralism.[52] But can it, in the Middle East or elsewhere, create political innovation and avoid the dangers of the neo-nationalism towards which so many of today's liberated ethnic claims are veering?

It may be suggested that the answer depends principally on the connections between three spheres – economic, strategic and socio-political – and their sensitivity to the dominant world order. At the end of our sketch, the Middle East appears as a zone that is particularly resistant to market democracy: modes of recovery and of diversion (certainly extremely inventive) appear beneath the discourse of openness and economic liberalisation, which leave the bulk of the region largely outside economic creation and production while still permitting a fringe of the population to benefit from it. At the same time, the democratic discourse there is almost exclusively one of claims; access to politics for groups hitherto enclosed within the sole legitimacy of the authoritarian 'nation' – state brings new exclusions, so long have pluralist practices been repressed. On the other hand the new post-Cold War strategic dynamics have quickly, and effectively, become established in the Middle East. In this respect the end of the bipolar era has done little to reduce conflictual intensity in a region where

52. J. Leca, 'A propos de *l'Europe et l'Orient*', *Maghreb-Machrek*, 126, October–November–December 1989, p. 124.

the overall system remains linked to Arab–Israeli confrontation and fragile negotiations, and to North–South confrontation through the search for control of oil. It could even be suggested that it has aggravated tensions, because at the same time as the Gulf War was resolved by a stronger American military dominance in the region, it incited local actors to redouble the arms race. Impermeability to market democracy and the conflictual structuration of the regional system go together, for they are linked by many logics – international and internal – in respect of nations and cultures. In this sense it is premature to speak of a 'new world order' in the Middle East.

5

THE EVOLUTION OF THE INTERNATIONAL TRADE RÉGIME: A THREE-BLOC TRADING SYSTEM?*

HELEN MILNER

The international trade system is at a crucial turning point. After the Second World War, the United States took the lead in setting up a multilateral system, governed by a set of rules embodied in the General Agreement on Tariffs and Trade (GATT). This system, which did not operate fully until the late 1950s, enabled world trade to flourish. It helped to mitigate trade conflicts among countries and reduced tariff barriers to very low levels. The GATT system functioned on the basis of three central principles: liberalisation, multilateralism and reciprocity. The first implied that the system was intended to reduce barriers to trade. The second meant that the system's rules were applied without discrimination to every country in the GATT.[1] Discriminatory actions which gave preference to one country's trade over another's were outlawed. Reciprocity meant that nations traded concessions in a balanced fashion; equal sacrifice was to be made by all. Since the first GATT negotiations in 1947, seven rounds of trade liberalisation through multilateral and reciprocal barrier reductions have been completed successfully. The eighth round, the Uruguay Round, is currently in trouble. If it fails, the GATT system may be irreparably damaged.

A number of scholars have been predicting the demise of the GATT. The problem in their eyes is that the world is disintegrating into three hostile trade blocs: North America led by the United States, Asia led by Japan, and the European Community (EC) led by Germany. The rise of these blocs reflects for many the decline of American hegemony and the creation of a more multipolar international system. A multipolar world may create the conditions that foster the development of such economic blocs around each polar power. In this environment, it is feared that these blocs will

* I would like to thank David Baldwin, Zaki Laïdi, Ed Mansfield, Tim McKeown, Robert Keohane and Susan Strange for their comments.

1. See J. Ruggie, 'Multilateralism', *International Organization*, 46 (3), Summer 1992, pp. 561–99, for further discussion of the concept of multilateralism.

become exclusive, promoting trade within each area and discriminating against trade with outsiders. According to one scholar, 'In the 1980s, the world economy is coalescing along three axes. Debt, monetary and trade matters as well as security concerns will surely pull the regions of the world further apart but should not cause a complete break.'[2] This move would mark an end to the multilateral GATT system. It might reduce world trade and could ignite political conflict among the three blocs. As two economic analysts noted in their annual review of the system for *Foreign Affairs*, 'A major risk of failed multilateral trade talks is the impetus it will provide toward regionalism and protectionism.'[3] Multipolarity may go hand in hand with the end of multilateralism in trade.

In part, the GATT's problems today reflect the development of such blocs. The European Community is battling with the United States, joined by Canada, over the issue of agricultural trade. Part of the US response to this battle and to the creation of a larger European space after 1992 has been to push ahead with its own trading bloc to match the European Community. It agreed on a Free Trade Area (FTA) with Canada in 1988 and has recently concluded a tripartite accord involving Mexico and Canada for a large North American FTA (NAFTA).[4] Concerned with being left behind by these two blocs, Asian countries have started discussing an Asian FTA. These political developments could threaten the core principles of the GATT: liberalisation on a multilateral basis. They could entail the rise of exclusive, regional trading blocs, each dominated by a single country. Increased conflict among the blocs could also result.

This chapter attempts to assess the current prospects for the international trading system. The implicit model used by scholars to make predictions about the growth of regionalism and one of its possible consequences, conflict, has two steps. One is that political events – primarily, the decline of US hegemony and the emergence of a multipolar world – are leading to policies that foster regional trade blocs. The second step is that these regional trade blocs will be both a source of and a reflection of increasing conflict in this multipolar world. This chapter asks first whether multilateralism is dead and regionalism rising. To address this, it examines data on the changing trade flows in the system to see if regionalism of trade is already occurring. Next it looks at the possible political con-

2. Robert Gilpin, *The Political Economy of International Relations*, Princeton, Princeton University Press, 1987, p. 397.

3. C. Michael Aho and Bruce Stokes, 'The Year the World Economy Turned', *Foreign Affairs*, 70 (1), 1990–91, p. 169.

4. This accord must still be ratified by the three countries before it comes into force. Ratification may be very difficult. For procedural information, see the *New York Times*, 3 August, 1992, A–1 and D–4.

sequences of changing trade flows among countries. How are trade and conflict among nations connected? Finally, it discusses how political developments might alter these economic data in the years to come. Have political developments been responsible for growing regionalism and are they likely to enhance regionalism in the future? This addresses both steps in the argument about future regional blocs and international relations.

Economic Data on Trade Flows, 1958–89

Do data on trade flows confirm the growth of three regional trade blocs? The answer is complicated, but in many cases the data do *not* support the idea of growing blocs. In terms of absolute figures intra-regional trade (as a percentage of total regional trade) has grown in all three cases. Over the past thirty years it has grown by 25 per cent for North America and Asia, accounting in 1989 for a quarter of North American trade and two-fifths of Asian trade. For the European Community, the change was even more spectacular. Internal trade grew by almost 100 per cent, amounting to nearly two-thirds of all EC trade.

But the data also suggest another development. The largest increases in trade flows over the thirty years are for North American trade with Asia and EC trade with Asia. Indeed, Asia's percentage of trade with North America and the European Community and North America's percentage of trade with Asia and the European Community have grown faster than their internal trade. These figures suggest that trade flows *among* the blocs are healthy and growing. Inter-regional trade for North America and Asia has been catching up with intra-regional flows from 1958 to 1989.

This does not seem to be the case for the European Community. Intra-regional trade dominates inter-regional. The European Community is becoming an increasingly exclusive bloc. Its trade with North America actually declined over the thirty-year period, and its Asian trade remains at a very low level. This growth of regional trade is not surprising. It reflects in part the deliberate political efforts of the nations to create a single European market; the European Community's mission was to eliminate barriers to trade among European nations, while maintaining a common external tariff. The data suggest that the countries have succeeded in creating a common market. The 1992 project to further reduce barriers will probably contribute to greater increases in intra-regional trade. This will be especially true if the GATT round fails and its common external trade barriers are not lowered.

But the European Community cannot take all the credit for growing intra-European trade. Historically, Europe has been a large, self-contained trading area. In the nineteenth and early twentieth centuries its internal trade (as a percentage of world trade) was greater than in the late 1980s. The data strongly suggest that extensive intra-European trade has long been a historical fact. In comparison, North American and Asian trade have been more externally oriented. The data show that European countries are just now returning to the historically high levels of intra-European trade that existed before the two World Wars. The wars and colonial experiences of the Europeans between 1913 and 1958 distorted their trade from its traditional European context. In contrast, regionalism in North America and Asia has not been strong historically. Before the World Wars, North America traded mostly with Europe, and Asia had strong trade ties with North America. The growth of intra-regional trade for these two areas would be a new phenomenon.

European integration is returning to earlier, historical levels, which suggests that it is driven by more than just the creation of the EC. This view is corroborated by data about the European Free Trade Area (EFTA) countries. Despite being discriminated against by the European Community, these countries are as economically integrated with the European Community as the EC countries are with themselves. Indeed, EFTA trade flows much more to the European Community (between 50 and 60 per cent of EFTA trade) than it does among the EFTA countries themselves (about 14 per cent of EFTA trade).[5] Geographic proximity, cultural similarity and political association may all play a role in fostering intra-European trade.[6]

One interesting question about the future will be the effect of the demise of the Soviet trading bloc, known as COMECON, on the international tradingstem. Since its inception in 1949, COMECON has drawn the trade of its members into an ever-tightening regional network. While in 1938 only 10 per cent of East European exports went to the Soviet bloc and 68 per cent to Western Europe, by 1953 trade flows had been reversed: with 64 per cent of East European exports going to the Soviet bloc and only 14 per cent to Western Europe.[7] By 1958 between 50 and 90 per cent of East– Central European states' trade was with the Soviet bloc.[8] Until 1989 these intra-regional ties remained very strong. This regional

5. Nicholas Schmitt, 'New International Trade Theories and Europe 1992', *Journal of Common Market Studies*, 29 (1), September 1990, table 1, p. 60.

6. Karl Deutsch came to similar conclusions much earlier, although he cast doubt on the role of geography. See his 'Toward an Inventory of Basic Trends and Patterns in Comparative and International Politics', *APSR*, 54 (1), March 1960, p. 48.

7. J. E. Spero, *The Politics of International Economic Relations*, 4th edn, New York, St Martin's Press, 1990, p. 307.

8. See IMF, *Direction of Trade*, annual, 1958–62. Percentage of country's total trade to 'Soviet Europe' for 1958: East Germany, 85 per cent; Hungary, 60 per cent; Poland, 51 per cent.

bloc represented a major change for Eastern Europe; its evolution arose from the political efforts of the Soviet Union to create an opposing bloc to the West and from the efforts of the United States to embargo the East. The demise of the Soviet bloc, beginning in 1989 and formalised in 1991, is likely to lead to the reorientation of East European trade. Even if they are not admitted to the EC, the Eastern countries should see their trade with the EC grow rapidly. This suggests that over time the European region now associated with the European Community (and EFTA) may expand to include Europe from the Atlantic to the Urals. This would be an enormous trading bloc, but one that has deep historical roots.

Of all the regions, Asia seems to be the least developed as a bloc.[9] But it is certainly the fastest growing economic area. If the key event at the end of the nineteenth century was the decline of European trade as a percentage of total world trade and the rise of North American trade, the key now is the decline of North America's share and the rise of Asia's.[10] Asia's share of world trade is today larger than North America's. In large part this is due to the rapid industrialisation and export-orientation of Japan and the Asian NICs. While Asia has a high absolute level of intra-regional trade (42 per cent), it has maintained strong, growing ties with the rest of the world, especially the United States. In 1989 Japan's proportions of trade with the United States and with the rest of Asia were almost equal, much as they were in 1958. Similarly, while the rest of Asia's trade with Japan has greatly increased, its proportion of trade with the United States is still larger than that with Japan. Its rate of increase in trade with the United States is greater than with other Asian nations. Indeed, Japan still does more trade with the United States than with Asia, and the rest of Asia still does more trade with the United States than it does with Japan.[11] For individual countries in Asia, the United States is usually their largest trading partner, although Japan has risen to become almost as large in some cases.[12]

9. Asia here means Japan and the rest of Asia, including India, China, South-East Asia, and North-East Asia. When Japan is not included, it will be specified as the rest of Asia.

10. For historical data, see Lamartine Yates, *Forty Years of Foreign Trade*, New York, Macmillan, 1959, pp. 32–3, or A. G. Kenwood and A. L. Lougheed, *The Growth of the International Economy, 1820–1980*, London, Allen & Unwin, 1983, pp. 90–5 and pp. 223–5, table 7; Derek Aldcroft, *From Versailles to Wall Street*, Berkeley, University of California Press, 1981, p. 309, table 19. For recent data see IMF, *Direction of Trade*, annual 1990.

11. Some have suggested that this may well be changing. Japan's heavy direct foreign investment and large aid flows to the rest of Asia may precipitate a shift in its trade to that area. See, for instance, Leonard Silk, 'A Japanese Shift Away from the United States', *New York Times*, 27 September 1991, C-2. This is confirmed for trade and financial flows by Jeffery Frankel, 'Is Japan Creating a Yen bloc in East Asia and the Pacific?', manuscript, April 1992.

12. According to the IMF, *Direction of Trade*, annual, 1990, statistics, the largest trading partners for a sample of Asian countries are in 1989 as follows: for South Korea, the United States; for Singapore, the United States; for Malaysia, Japan; for Thailand, Japan; for India, the Soviet Union.

Unlike in Europe, where each country's trade is heavily concentrated on European partners, in Asia trade is often split three ways: about equal proportions to the United States, to Japan, and to the other Asian countries. Asia is much less of a regional bloc, given its strong ties with North America, than is the European Community. These data suggest that a *Pacific*-wide trade area might make the most sense economically in the future.

The costs to Asian economies of forming an exclusive Asian trade bloc are impossible to estimate with the present data, but they could be enormous. Creating an FTA involves eliminating trade barriers among countries in the area, and may or may not involve raising barriers to external trade. Increasing barriers to external trade would obviously reduce that trade, contribute to more inefficient trade intra-regionally and could provoke retaliation, thus severely disrupting all external trade. Just eliminating internal trade barriers, however, may not necessarily improve the region's welfare. If the trade that results is on balance the displacement of inter-regional trade by internal flows, then the FTA is trade-diverting and could have negative overall welfare consequences. On the other hand, if trade is created by ending domestic production in favour of imports from other regional partners, then the FTA could be welfare-enhancing. Both these effects are likely to arise in any FTA; the issue is whether trade creation outweighs trade diversion. Creation of an Asian FTA would affect the sizeable percentage of trade that Asian countries conduct with inter-regional partners, especially the United States. The most preferred course of action for most Asian countries would seem to be the maintenance of a global, multilateral trading system. Indeed, for them a Pacific trade area may make more sense than an Asian zone, for two reasons. An Asian trade area would be dominated by Japan, a country that other Asian states are suspicious of for historical reasons. Firstly, a Pacific trade area would enable the Asian countries to partition their trade between the United States and Japan, thus reducing their dependence. Secondly, an Asian trade bloc would still not be large enough to rival the European Community; growth of the European Community, which is very likely, will only increase this disparity. A Pacific trade area, on the other hand, would match the European Community in terms of its share of global production and world trade. Such a Pacific trade area may, however, be politically impossible given the tensions between the United States and Japan.

North America, including the United States, Canada, and Mexico, is also not showing clear economic signs of increasing regionalism, although the recent NAFTA accord, if and when it is implemented, may change this. Intra-regional trade has declined over the past thirty years. For the three countries, trade with their regional partners also shows the smallest increases over the 1958–89 period. Interestingly, North American trade with Asia is booming. By 1989, the North American region was almost as tightly integrated with Asia (29 per cent) as with itself (35 per cent). For each of the three countries, the largest increases in their trade have been with Asia. The rapid growth of United States trade with Asia meant that by 1989 it conducted more of its trade with Asia than with North America. Canadian and Mexican trade with Asia have also grown rapidly, although they started at low levels. Asia's strong ties with North America are reciprocated by North America's strong links with Asia. An attempt to create an exclusive North American bloc could then be economically costly, especially for the United States.

There is a notable asymmetry within the North American bloc. Mexico and Canada are extremely dependent on the United States, with whom they conduct nearly two-thirds of their trade. In contrast, the United States carry on only a quarter of their trade with them. In this way, the North American region is unlike the other two. While Germany looms large in the European Community and Japan in Asia, the other countries in the two regions tend to be much less dominated by them than are Canada and Mexico by the United States. The asymmetries in North America are far greater than in the other two regions. As Albert Hirschman argued long ago, a country whose trade is concentrated heavily on one other country risks being dependent on and hence politically dominated by that country.[13] This suggests that Canada and Mexico should have mixed reactions to a North American FTA. While they may gain more trade with the United States, they will surely augment their dependence on them in the process. Again, for them the appeal of a Pacific trade area which included Asia, might be greater. It would allow them to diversify their trade and, for Mexico at least, to improve its balance of trade. The concern, of course, is that freer trade with Asia will stimulate Canadian and Mexican raw material and agricultural exports while battering their manufacturing sectors. It is political considerations, not solely economic ones, that will determine countries' preferences for trade blocs, a point I shall return to later.

In concluding our analysis of the economic data, three points deserve attention. Firstly, Europe does seem to be forming a more exclusive bloc. Propelled in part by the European Community, the European continent is moving towards a large trade bloc that is relatively independent of other regions. A large European Economic Space (EES), involving the current

13. Albert Hirschman, *National Power and the Structure of Foreign Trade*, Berkeley, University of California Press, 1980 (reprint, original edn 1945).

European Community, EFTA, and parts of Eastern Europe, may develop as a tightly integrated economic unit in the future. Secondly, Asia has grown phenomenally in economic stature. It is now the second largest trading zone after the European Community. Asia has the largest population of the three regions, but it also has the most variation in terms of political systems, language, culture, and level of economic development. Its potential is only matched by its problems. Thirdly, neither North America nor Asia form as exclusive a bloc as the European Community. Asia and North America have strong, increasing trade ties with each other. Inter-regional trade is accelerating faster than intra-regional trade for these two. An exclusive zone in North America or Asia could cost both regions a great deal.

Politics and Trade Patterns

The relationship between politics and trade patterns is multifaceted. Two questions at least need addressing. What consequences do trade patterns have for international politics? And what political factors – international and domestic – have caused, or could cause in the future, significant changes in these trade flows? The first question has several different aspects. One is the relationship between trade and conflict, a debate with a long history. The issue is whether closer trade relations between countries lead to greater conflict or cooperation. On the one hand, increasing trade between two countries raises the costs of cutting those relations in the event of political or military tension. Countries' economies come to depend on their exports to or imports from the other. Domestic groups develop an interest in this trade; these may be exporters, importers, or financial institutions supporting this trade. High levels of trade can in these ways create costs for the countries, making it harder for them to contemplate conflict that affects this trade. This seems to be the model upon which the European Community was built, and perhaps explains the relative lack of conflict in intra-European Community relations today.

On the other hand, significant trade ties between two nations may lead to constant friction as the nations are forced to deal with each other more and more. This is especially likely if the trade is unbalanced. If one state is running a sizeable and constant trade deficit (or surplus) with the other, this may enhance conflict, as trade is perceived as 'unfair'. Japanese–American relations in the late 1930s and the 1980s seem to fit this argument. Empirical analyses of these two hypotheses have provided mixed conclusions. As one recent study concluded, 'The arguments of both schools of thought are thus confirmed when applied narrowly to trade: costly trade produces an increase in conflict while beneficial trade produces a decline in conflict.'[14] At present it seems difficult to sort out which of the two hypotheses performs better; it is likely that they depend on other conditions in the system. Trade probably does affect relations between states, but in a complex fashion.

What do these two arguments suggest given the trade patterns we have describe? If we applied the first argument – that increasing trade reduces conflict – what would it predict? Three predictions seem apparent. Since trade between Asia and North America is sizeable and rapidly growing, conflict between these two regions should decline.[15] The European Community, in contrast, as it grows more exclusive, should find itself in greater conflict with Asia and North America. But as trade flows within the European Community grow, the European states should experience less conflict among themselves. Applying the second argument leads to reversed conclusions. Conflict should decline between the European Community and its external partners, and grow within the European Community as well as between Asia and North America. If large, persistent trade imbalances are taken into account, then Asia becomes the clear target of the other regions' wrath. Asia's large trade surplus with both the United States and European Community may have the effect of driving them together in opposition to Asian penetration of their markets. On the whole, it is likely that trade does affect political relations although in a complex way. Other factors, however, also influence the relationship between countries, making it more difficult to assess the impact of trade flows.

Trade patterns may be important for understanding more than the political relations between nations or regions. Trade flows are often used to estimate the power resources of a country relative to others. A number of different aspects of trade can serve as measures of a nation's or region's (potential) capacity to exert international influence. One of these is the country's percentage of total world trade. Britain in the latter part of the nineteenth century and America in much of the twentieth century were considered 'hegemons', in part because they controlled a much greater share of world trade than any other country. Controlling a greater percentage of trade suggested that the country's economy was more efficient or technologically advanced than those of other countries. If control of world trade is relevant, then the United States have suffered a loss in relative power resources in the post-war period. Japan has experienced the greatest growth in its percentage, narrowing its relative disadvantage with both

14. Mark Gasiorwski, 'Economic Interdependence and International Conflict', *International Studies Quarterly*, 30 (1), 1986, p. 36.

15. Decline relative to what is unclear. Should conflict be lower than in their previous relations, or lower than in their relations with other countries?

the United States and Germany. The United States, however, are still the dominant force according to this simple statistic. In regional terms, as noted before, the European Community continues to control the largest percentage of world trade. This is in part due to the fact that the European Community has doubled its membership since 1958. But Asia's share has been rapidly increasing, suggesting its rise in influence.

Control of overall levels of trade may not be a good indicator of international influence. As Hirschman argued years ago, a country's 'dependence' on trade may be a better indicator of its relative influence. If country A depends more heavily on country B in its trade than does B on its trade with A, B may have leverage over A. The costs of severing the relationship should be higher for A, *ceteris paribus*. Countries with their trade heavily concentrated on one other country are often in a position of dependence.[16] In examining the data with this in mind, three points are notable. Of the three leading economies in each region, Germany and then the United States seem the least dependent. Germany sends only 13 per cent of its total trade to its leading partner, France, and less than a third to its top three partners. The United States send a fifth of their trade to their leading partner, Canada, and two-fifths to their top three. But of these top three, two are Canada and Mexico, who depend even more heavily on the United States. Japan seems quite dependent on its trade with the United States; just under a third of its trade is with the United States. It is interesting to note that this percentage has not changed over the past thirty years. Like the United States, it conducts just over two-fifths of its trade with its top three partners. These figures suggest that of the big three regional economies Japan is the most dependent.

As a second point, on a regional basis the European Community is the least dependent on external trade. While the European Community conducts about 40 per cent of its trade with external countries, Asia and North America conduct 60 to 65 per cent of their trade externally. Asia and North America are each other's primary trading partners, each sending one-third of its trade to the other. One probably should speak of mutual dependence in such a case.

Thirdly, relations of intra-regional dependence are significant. As noted above, the North American area is unique. Canada and Mexico depend much more on the United States than vice versa. This asymmetry is more marked than in the other regions. United States domination of a North American bloc would be more far-reaching than German or Japanese dom-

16. He also maintains that countries which export or import a single product to or from one country will be highly vulnerable. See his *National Power and the Structure of Foreign Trade*.

ination of their regions. The implication of the NAFTA agreement could have widespread ramifications. Canada and Mexico would gain increased access to the large and wealthy United States market, and this access would supposedly be more secure than in the present system. But the countries would almost certainly be increasing their already high economic and political dependence on the United States. They would be fostering the further concentration of their trade, rather than its diversification. This may make more sense, however, for two reasons: the prospect of being excluded from European and Asian markets combined with that of rising protectionism against their products in the United States. As one observer summed it up, 'Ensuring against protection in [their] principal market seemed wiser than pursuing the chimera of trade diversification.'[17] For Mexico, the NAFTA agreement may provide an additional benefit. Such an agreement may help institutionalise its own domestic economic reforms and promote a move toward a more democratic system. The international agreement may have profound domestic effects.

For the United States, interest in the NAFTA agreement for from several reasons. Fear of being excluded from European and Asian markets is certainly one. Helping to ensure access to Canadian and Mexican raw materials, especially energy products, is another. Promoting economic and political liberalisation in Mexico may be a third. Most importantly, though, the NAFTA accord may promote United States economic competitiveness through the economies of scale and specialisation of production it would allow. 'A North American production-sharing alliance will help United States industries gain competitiveness in a world where multipolar geo-economic rivalry is supplanting bipolar geostrategic conflict '[18] Even though NAFTA may enhance America's dependence on Mexico and Canada, it may be a relatively inexpensive way to promote a number of other national goals.

Trade patterns may also indicate a potential to exercise influence through a country's balance of trade.[19] The mercantilists first suggested this. They claimed that countries should run a trade surplus, exporting more than they imported, since this would result in a net inflow of gold, which could then be used to finance more production and larger armies. While this idea has been challenged by modern economic theory, many still believe that a trade surplus is desirable and a sign of potential power.

17. M. Delal Baer, 'North American Free Trade', *Foreign Affairs*, 70 (4), Autumn 1991, p. 134.

18. Ibid., p. 140.

19. The balance of payments, which is different from the balance of trade, may reveal more about a country's position.

Or, at least, the running of a persistent trade deficit is seen as a symbol of weakness for an economy. Japan's growing and continuing trade surplus and America's deepening deficit have led to predictions of the eclipse of American hegemony by Japan, not to mention the political friction they have caused. The relationship between surpluses and power (or deficits and weakness) may be more complicated. Britain throughout much of its hegemonic reign ran a trade deficit. Moreover, the Soviet Union often ran a deficit with its East European COMECON partners, and few suggested that this was a sign of Soviet weakness. Also, as noted before, Japan's high concentration of trade with the United States, combined with its surpluses may make it extremely vulnerable to United States pressure.[20] Bilateral balances of trade may be poor indicators of influence; the key will be how costly it is for a state to alter its pattern of trade, whether this refers to its imports or its exports. A surplus country which exports mainly to one country (or exports one commodity) may face just as high costs by shifting by its trade as does a deficit country which depends heavily on imports from one country (or of one commodity).

Trade flows may then tell us something about international politics. They may suggest the extent of conflict likely in a relationship, or they may indicate the direction of influence that states possess relative to one another. Trade flows do not provide unambiguous information about world politics; what they suggest depends much on the intuitive model people carry in their heads about how trade affects political relations. Here the data cannot definitively answer many questions; they are only suggestive. They neglect the consideration of capital flows, the composition of trade flows, and trade with large parts of the Third World (i.e., Africa, South America, and the Middle East).

The second large issue is the role of politics in the shaping of trade flows. This is important for understanding the future of the trade system, i.e. whether political factors promoting regionalism will indeed actually lead to regional blocs. This question has several aspects. Firstly, how important is politics rather than other factors, such as geography, cultural similarity, or economic variables, in influencing trade flows? Secondly, how important is public policy rather than other political factors, such as the climate of bilateral relations or the similarity of political institutions, in affecting how trade flows among countries? Thirdly, what is the relative weight of international political factors versus domestic ones in shaping trade patterns? There is no simple answer to any of these questions. Each,

---

20. For an argument along these lines, see H. Milner, 'American Debt, Deficits, and Power', manuscript, 1991.

however, deserves attention because they are crucial to understanding the way people think about the future of the trade system. Many political scientists assume that public policy has a crucial effect on trade flows. In contrast, many economists seem to believe that trade responds above all to shifts in economic variables, e.g. comparative advantage, technology, exchange rates, price levels – which, depending on the economist, they realise can be more or less affected by public policies. If trade responds most to economic fundamentals, then we should not be concerned about the current policy initiatives to increase regionalism (i.e. the 1992 programme in Europe, the NAFTA agreement, or the Asian trading zone idea).

Some evidence that policy matters less than is often thought is included in a recent article by Timothy McKeown.[21] He shows that despite the GATT, American hegemony, and liberal trade policies in the post-war period, the level of openness and regionalism had not changed significantly by the late 1960s from what it was before the Second World War, given the changes in economic fundamentals (i.e. incomes) that had occurred. More openness was evident from the beginning of the 1970s, however. As he notes, scholars have sometimes been fixated more on policy instruments than on outcomes. Actual trade flows may not respond immediately or dramatically to public policies.

Can the data examined here shed light on this issue? They can do so only vaguely since they do not examine policy and other influences on trade systematically. The data do suggest a role for public policy, but a limited one. Comparing the European Community with the other regions, one notices it has increased its internal trade most rapidly and dramatically. This coincides with its political attempt to create a common market. This coincidence suggests causality, but as we noted before, Europe has historically had high levels of internal trade, long before the European Community appeared. Other studies of the effects of an FTA on actual trade flows provide mixed results; in many cases, the FTA had no effect or the opposite effect on trade than was expected.[22] Without the historic ties, cultural similarities, and general atmosphere of good political relations, the European Community might not have had much effect on trade flows. COMECON is another interesting example of 'success'. Through its policies (including armed intervention), the Soviet Union was able to redirect East European (and other) countries' trade.[23] This is an extreme case, one

---

21. Timothy McKeown, 'A Liberal Trade Order?', *International Studies Quarterly*, 35 (2), June 1991, pp. 151–72.

22. See, for example, Josef Brada and Jose Mendez, 'Regional Economic Integration and the Volume of Intra-Regional Trade', *Kyklos*, 36, fasc. 4, 1983, pp. 589–603; Norman Athen, 'The Effect of the EEC and EFTA on European Trade', *American Economic Review*, 63 (5), December 1973, pp. 881–92.

23. Cuba and Mongolia are two other countries.

not likely to be repeated. The issue is whether the NAFTA agreement, or an Asian one, or a Pacific one would actually have a significant effect on trade flows. Given the lack of historic ties, the radical cultural, economic, and political differences, and the climate of suspicion between many of these countries, policy may be less effective in these two regions than in Europe.

A broader issue is whether trade 'follows the flag'. Does the general tenor of relationships between countries affect the volume of trade? Including more than just policy, this issue focuses on the atmosphere or character of relations between countries as the explanation for their trade flows. This argument also reverses the causality discussed above about how trade affects the level of conflict or cooperation among states. While the answer to this question is likely to be complicated, one recent empirical study shows that trade does follow the flag: cooperative relations between all types of states lead to growing trade; hostile ones reduce trade flows.[24] The broad nature of international relations among states may influence their trade strongly, perhaps more so than the policies themselves. For instance, the United States may lift all trade restrictions on the Eastern bloc only to find that its trade there does not increase because traders do not foresee increasing cooperation between the United States and these countries. The demise of communism may not spell the end of superpower rivalry, as some realists have often contended. This argument also suggests that trade and international relations stand in a relationship of mutual causality. Greater trade flows between the United States and Japan may have led to a more conflictual relationship, which in turn may lead to reductions in those trade flows. If this occurs, conflict between them may also return to lower levels. This interactive relationship, of course, makes it much more difficult to predict future events.

Another interactive relationship is related to a point discussed above about how trade flows may indicate power potential. Trade flows can be used as measures of the capabilities of states to influence the international system. But the international distribution of such capabilities may also influence trade flows, according to the hegemonic stability theory. In this theory, the concentration of power in a single hegemon is associated with the rise of free trade and multilateralism. While many attacks have been made on this theory, it still informs much of current thinking. The rise of regionalism in trade is usually associated with the decline of a hegemon, whether Britain in the 1930s or the United States today. In this view, the shift in world trade away from United States control is one element in declining United States power, which in turn will lead us to further moves

24. Brian Pollins, 'Does Trade Follow the Flag?', *APSR*, 83 (2), June 1989.

away from a multilateral trade system.[25] Regionalism then serves as both a measure and a consequence of growing multipolarity. Actual evidence to support this argument is scanty. The best data available, which stop at 1968, indicate that regionalism, during the peak of US hegemony, remained at levels similar to those in the inter-war period when the United States supposedly did not exercise hegemony.[26] American hegemony, according to these data, does not seem to have significantly affected the extent of regionalism in world trade.

These data may not tell us about the future. The loss of hegemony by the United States or the end of bipolar competition between the United States and Soviet Union could lead to political efforts to increase regionalism. Why should this be the case? Why should the new international political environment lead countries to prefer regional trade to multilateralism? The logic underlying this may reflect several political calculations. One is that in the new multipolar world a state's security may be best ensured by regional affiliations, rather than global ones. In the past the United States provided a security blanket for the European Community and much of Asia. With the loss of United States pre-eminence and the decline of the Soviet threat, countries may either not be able to rely on the United States and/or they may develop new enemies against which the United States will not provide a shield. Instead, relying on neighbours who share one's problems may appear to provide more security; and trade may then follow the flag. This argument is not without its problems. Geopolitical neighbours often tend to be a state's most feared enemies, and increasing trade may exacerbate conflict and insecurity rather than the reverse. It is in any case curious that countries should view the increase of their trade dependence on a certain set of neighbours, who already control the lion's share of their trade, as promoting their security. If they fear their neighbours, it would be wiser to diversify their already concentrated trade.

Concerns over 'economic security', may have more to do with it. If imports from far-off countries are causing domestic difficulties and threatening one's industries, it may be appealing to try to switch one's trade to less competitive regional neighbours. This seems a plausible explanation

25. In an interesting article, Ed Mansfield shows that the absolute level of trade flows is positively related to both high levels of inequality among states (hegemony) and very low levels of inequality. See his 'The Concentration of Capabilities and International Trade', *International Organization*, 46 (3), Summer 1992, pp. 730–64.

26. See I. Richard Savage and Karl Deutsch, 'A Statistical Model of the Gross Analysis of Transaction Flows', *Econometrica*, 28 (3), July 1960, pp. 551–72; Richard Chadwick and Karl Deutsch, 'International Trade and Economic Integration', *Comparative Political Studies*, 6 (1), April 1973, pp. 84–109; Stephen Krasner, 'State Power and the Structure of International Trade', *World Politics*, 28, April 1976, pp. 317–47.

for recent regional policies in both the European Community and the United States. Import pressures from Asia may be the target of both, suggesting that on balance trade diversion, not creation, may be the result. 'Economic security' here means avoiding competitive (Asian) imports. This is likely to prove a short-sighted policy. Such regional policies will only increase American and European dependence on their neighbours, so making them more vulnerable to them. Also if the blocs turn out to be protectionist, then Europe's and America's long-run competitiveness and potential power will be further eroded. It is especially hard to see how regionalism will promote 'economic security' if increasing trade leads to growing conflict. In this case, regional policies will augment a country's dependence on those neighbouring countries it is increasingly likely to come into conflict with. This may not be a recipe for improving a state's security.

American attempts to build a regional bloc in the NAFTA accord and Asian discussions to do so may reflect a defensive orientation. For them, regionalism may be the only answer to the European Community. The European Community now controls two-fifths of world trade. America alone controls only 15 per cent, and Japan 8 per cent. If control over world trade is a source of power, especially in negotiations over trade, then Japan and the United States by combining with their neighbours, may be able to exert more influence relative to the European Community.[27] According to this argument, a Pacific trade area would, however, make more sense.

In a similar vein, regional agreements may have a tactical utility. The threat of NAFTA or an Asian FTA may be wielded to exert leverage over the European Community and others for several reasons. The threat in the United States case may be used to push for European, Japanese or Third World acceptance of American terms in the GATT Uruguay Round. It may be used to pressure the European Community to keep its market open after the 1992 process is completed. It may be used to force Japan and the Asian NICs to do something about their trade surpluses with the United States. It may in effect be a macroeconomic version of strategic trade policy, which the United States has used before to justify policy in certain sectors. Asia's discussions of an FTA may be a defensive reaction to this: indeed, for the Asian countries an open, multilateral trading system would seem to be their most preferred outcome. Given their rapidly rising trade

27. This depends heavily on the assumption that in combining with their regional partners they do not lose as much influence as they gain. For Japan and the United States, who dominate their regions, this may be a valid assumption. For smaller countries it may not. But these countries may worry more about controlling their regional superpowers than about negotiating with the European Community. And an FTA may provide them with some control over or input into the policies of the United States or Japan.

with North America and Europe, the costs of an exclusive regional system would be quite high. In the future, it may be Asia more than the United States that provides support for the multilateral GATT system. If the desired outcome of both the United States and Asian countries is really a more multilateral, liberal trading system, then the regional policies may be tactical expedients. If, however, they fail as threats and have to be implemented, then all sides may be worse off. The fact, though, that the United States feel they have to make explicit threats to get their way may itself reflect declining American power and/or growing hostility in relations among the advanced industrial countries.

Conclusions

This chapter has tried to analyse whether the international trading system is likely to break into three regional trade blocs and what the possible consequences of this could be. The first part examined the data on regional trade flows. In general, it suggested that only in the case of the EC was regionalism growing importantly. For Asia and North America, inter-regional trade is as important as intra-regional trade. The European Community is much less dependent on inter-regional trade than the other two areas, but this has been true historically. The trade flows suggest that a Pacific trade area would make more economic sense than an exclusive Asian or North American one; it would also be more politically desirable if the goal of regional policies is to control a share of world trade large enough to match Europe's. As of 1992, it still seems difficult to speak of three regional blocs; only the European Community may qualify.

One of the assertions made about the regionalisation of trade is that it will be associated with more international conflict. The assumption is that increasing intra-regional ties will exacerbate (or cause) inter-regional conflict. This depends on the further assumption that increasing trade ties promote friendly relations and decreasing ties induce conflict. As the second section argued, it is unclear what effect trade flows have on relations among countries. It might turn out that increasing intra-regional trade exacerbates conflict within the region, and leads to relative improvement in relations with countries outside the area. For example, the NAFTA agreement, while increasing trade flows among the three countries, could heighten tensions among them, leaving the United States more dependent on Canada and Mexico but also in a less secure and more conflict-ridden regional arrangement. The effect of trade flows on international relations is neither simple nor always direct; it is likely to be complex and to interact with other factors.

The effects of international politics on trade flows also merit further attention. It is often assumed that countries' policies must have a substantial effect on trade patterns, and thus that the regional policies of the European Community and recently of the United States will lead to the growing regionalisation of trade. But policies may not be effective. Trade flows are influenced by other factors, from the general political environment to economic fundamentals in the market. Regional policies, in the absence of other favourable conditions may have only minor effects on the direction of trade. Political leaders may understand this. They may have no desire to bear the costs of reorienting their country's trade. Regional policies may be threats designed to change other states' behaviour. These policies and their declarations may be designed more as symbols.

Secondly, the decline of United States hegemony may not automatically be associated with growing regional blocs. The logic connecting these needs to be spelled out. Must multipolarity lead to regionalisation? Why should countries choose to reorient their trade? What goals are they trying to achieve, or what costs are they trying to avoid, by increasing intra-regional trade? How would regionalism enhance their security or prosperity? Answers to these questions do not appear to be well thought out. If regionalism for the European Community and North American markets means protection from competitive Asian imports (i.e. net trade diversion), then it will only reduce their efficiency further and lead to losses in their world market share, which may erode their international influence. This is not a recipe for enhanced prosperity. If regionalism in Asia and North America is viewed as a political response to the European Community, then it seems that a more effective policy would be a Pacific trade area. This would at least match the European Community in its share of world trade. If regionalism is meant to enhance countries' security, it also seems a curious approach. If one's security is threatened by too extensive trade with extra-regional states, then how will increasing one's already concentrated intra-regional trade improve the situation? It will make the state even more dependent on its neighbours while heightening the likelihood of conflict with them. This is not a recipe for enhanced security. Diversification is the strategy that almost all economists recommend for reducing overall risk. States may, of course, adopt policies for less than rational reasons. But the erection of exclusive economic blocs, particularly in Asia and North America, could have very significant costs for all the states involved; it might lower both their rates of growth and their sense of security. The costs of such attempts to reorient trade should be examined carefully before choosing such a course of action.

6

THE LOOSENING OF CHINA

JEAN-LUC DOMENACH

The Chinese are familiar with the concept of 'loosening' (*fang*): for centuries it has floated like a spectre over their history. The Confucian tradition sees politics essentially as a constraint upon society,which would fall into weakness and wilful disorder without guidance and control. Loosening is therefore the negative pole of politics. For the intelligent mandarin it can also be a sort of cynical retreat, allowing the operative powers to gather strength while distracting the attention of malcontents. The Leninist tactics of 'consolidation', such as the NEP (New Economic Policy) are easily adaptable to Chinese political culture. In this latter case loosening becomes a constraining factor.

Contemporary Chinese history offers interesting examples of these two variants of 'loosening'. What scandalised the fathers of Chinese nationalism was the nation's general laxity before the imperialist thrust; indeed Sun Yat-sen compared Chinese society to sand.[1] The communists were able to capture nationalism because they won the legitimate right to designate the Kuomintang's foreign policy as lax. The war enabled them to achieve power and systematically transform the sands of society into hard cutting rock. It was not long, however, before economic and political errors crept in: the rock wore away at the edges and then split. Provoked by the Maoist policy of mobilisation, the fragmentation of the régime accelerated during the Cultural Revolution. In 1978, faced with imminent catastrophe, Deng Xiaoping chose to ease the party's domination as well as the nation's seclusion – 'openness' was presented formally as 'openness and loosening' (*kaifang*) – while still promising to take back concessions as soon as possible.

Inspired no doubt as much by the immemorial pretensions of Chinese governing élites as by the NEP, Deng then displayed a double blindness. He closed his eyes first to the effects of the fundamental transformations imposed by communist power on Chinese society. Unlike Soviet society, it did not disintegrate under repression but was consolidated and com-

1. Jean Chesneaux, *Sun Yat-Sen*, Paris, Club français du livre, (Portraits de l'histoire), 1959.

pressed: once the pressure of power was relaxed, the individuals fixed in the stone began to move once more.[2] New social dynamics emerged, legitimised by traditions, particularly family ones, which power was unable to destroy, even within the cells of the former totalitarian grid. These dynamics tend to escape politics. And Deng was also blind to the capacity of the Chinese Communist Party (CCP) to withstand external changes. Recognising the significance of international economic competition and the full measure of the capitalist world's success, he still thought that the balance of strength could be controlled internally by repression and externally by the power of the Soviet pole, to which Beijing drew closer during the 1980s. He was wrong both because power was held by his police and not by society and because the Soviet camp collapsed in 1989.

Today, many Chinese believe that their country is simply entering on a fresh phase of disorder and negativity from which a new strong dynasty will inevitably emerge, a feeling shared by several different groups of Sinologists. Some are obsessed with the antiquity of imperial history and the vitality of its cultural norms; others with the power, particularly military and police power, of the state established by the communists; others again with the pragmatism of the Beijing régime's current economic policy, a pragmatism in which they perceive the CCP's willingness to listen to those whom they had first refused to hear. The debate lacks neither significance nor originality. It is concerned not so much with change in the balance of forces as with the nature and breadth of the internal changes which this has created, or rather with the combinations and connections between the two phenomena.

Our hypothesis is that this time the loosening of the country is going much further than cautious observers realise, because of the crisis in the communist régime and even more because of the vigour of the world climate. From now on, as well as indicating the CCP's diminishing domination it is substantially changing the very texture of the Chinese political fabric. The loosening of China is particularly marked because it is relatively old, is responding to a decline in the nation's strategic role, and is influenced by a social crisis of unprecedented proportions. In the case of China the concept of loosening refers not only to a historical episode of disorder but probably also to a new political disposition and a change in the very meaning of Chinese politics.

2. A study of repression in China after 1949 shows that the quantifiable numbers of victims, whether killed or imprisoned, were proportionately lower than in the Soviet Union because they were sociologically different (the gulag population is essentially rural in the Soviet Union, urban in China), i.e. because the Chinese communist powers preferred mobilisation to elimination. Cf. Jean-Luc Domenach, *Chine. L'archipel oublié*, Paris, Fayard, 1992.

The Chinese 'Advance'

This new process should first be placed in its historical context. The initial 'loosening' of Chinese policy precedes that of international politics, i.e. the appearance around 1989 of a 'complex and loosened mono-ideological system' (Zaki Laïdi) on the world scale. Throughout the 1970s Chinese time was clearly different from world time, being behind at first (at the beginning of the decade) and later ahead. As the hostility between the two Great Powers faded and their co-existence began, the China of the final years of the Cultural Revolution embarked on a 'class struggle' which she sought once more to extend abroad. But in thus becoming more rigid the CCP exhausted its revolutionary model and the cracks in its structure widened. The crisis then moved faster than in Brezhnev's conservative and paralysed Soviet Union, as from 1976–8 onwards Mao's successors abruptly changed direction. In order to survive they decided to relax both their own power and the nation's seclusion, a move which placed China at the head of the reform of communist systems.

This advance can therefore be explained first by internal factors. The Cultural Revolution was both the highest point of Maoist ambition and the trap into which it fell: it prevented the system from becoming fossilised and forced the communist leaders into a rescue manoeuvre, which meant relaxing their political domination. From the outset the manoeuvre was turned towards economic modernisation and matched by openness to the outside world. These two characteristics can largely be explained by the influence of the external environment: not so much international power relationships (for Mao Tse-tung and Zhou Enlai had adapted to them skilfully with their invention of the 'strategic triangle' at the beginning of the decade), as the attraction of neighbouring economies. If China loosened earlier it was largely because her regional environment was already 'ahead'. Japan's economic triumph became established in the 1960s and the success of the neighbouring NICs (South Korea, Taiwan, Hong Kong, Singapore) in the following decade. Through the medium of overseas-based Chinese and news received within the country the towns heard of the triumph of market democracy, i.e. of capitalism and thus of democracy. The content of this news was economic at first and political only subsequently, vaguely and by derivation. Political democracy was not distinguished from its supposed economic effects[3] and

3. Popular aspirations were thus much more economic in China than in the Soviet Union and the former people's democracies of Eastern Europe. Among the Chinese dissidents can be found violent criticism of totalitarian monopolies of communist power, but no fundamental reflection on the circumstances of the move to democracy. Cf. the book of Jean-Philippe Béja, Michel Bonnin and Alain Payraube, *Le tremblement de terre de Pékin*, Paris, Gallimard, 1991, which brings together many documents of Chinese dissidents.

such news lacked any strategic content. In effect, Japan and her emulators minimised the danger – which was none the less genuine – of the Soviet thrust in the region. They disdained to respond with proportionate measures of defence, particularly through alliance with Beijing: despite her treaty of friendship with Tokyo in 1978, China never managed to win an explicit anti-Soviet alignment from Japan's diplomats, still less from ASEAN.

Eastern Asia at the end of the 1970s thus offered a curious combination of political phenomena, some 'classic' and others 'new'. On one side, a whole set of diplomatic–strategic relationships was forming round the problems of Indochina, bringing the East–West conflict into the region: alliances, counter-alliances, negotiations, wars. Other regional conflicts (Korea, Taiwan), however, became self-contained or quietened, the United States adopted a lower regional profile, and the essentially military thrust of the Soviet Union was increasingly counterbalanced by the dazzling economic prosperity of her capitalist enemies. In general terms the military–strategic elements declined under the influence of economic changes (progress for some, relative or more confirmed decline for others), leaving room for more varied and more complex relationships: commercial links, currents of migration, exchanges of symbols and images. The region remained strongly polarised but without a single leader. Actors of very different character and internal orientation were juxtaposed as their degree of openness to the world market developed rapidly.

The Great Loosening

At the end of the 1980s a second loosening was to operate in China. This was much more sharply marked than its predecessor and, although still organised, went much further than the simple easing of political controls. This loosening springs from the development of earlier elements, but also from the changed international order.

The continually growing prosperity of the NICs now exercises a massive attraction for nations in the area. Not all yield to it, but all are affected. Some still resist, but for how long? China herself is now open to it. Originally conceived as buffers, her 'special economic zones' and coastal provinces now operate priority economic relationships with Taiwan and Hong Kong. Before they are possibly (for the former) and undoubtedly (for the latter) reintegrated with the continent, these two territories are exercising an extraordinary economic, social and cultural influence on their neighbouring Chinese provinces. Hong Kong and Taiwan currency circulates there and Canton follows the rhythm of its neighbouring colony. This zone forms a true 'corridor of prosperity', a second, maritime, China that is partially liberated from the shackles of the empire. The nation's economic and psychological map has thus been simultaneously extended and fragmented. Maritime China is mapping out a socially attractive and politically dangerous future. The desert China of central Asia moves more slowly, however, and sometimes appears fixed in the past. Between these two Chinas the destiny of the nation is at stake in immense zones longing for progress and desperate at the obstacles which impede it. As was the case before the 'liberation' of 1949, modernisation is making irregular progress according to the lie of the land, routes of communication and social networks. There is nothing inevitable about this progress, it is regularly threatened by new forms of resistance or economic setbacks, or accelerated by fresh investments and images; and however specific its transformations and however subtle its acclimatisation to Chinese social rituals, these advances into modernity are seen as inescapably Western. Despite all its efforts communism has failed to appropriate the concept of modernity: in China the watches may be made in Japan, Taiwan or Korea, but intellectually they are set on San Francisco time. More strongly even than ten years ago and in an almost brutal style, the whole of cultivated China believes wholeheartedly in the victory of market democracy. There is even a sort of derisive hatred for anyone, anywhere in the world, who persists in ignoring the evidence that during the Gulf War the population of Beijing backed the Western nations in the same enthusiastic and hostile way as sports club supporters.

The collapse of the East European régimes in 1989 added the defeat of communism to the victory of capitalism and, like foreign analysts, the urban populace sees these events as considerably weakening the political legitimacy of Beijing. The defeat of the 'soft' as well as of the 'hard' régimes, the defeat of the communists of the GDR as well as those of Hungary, discredited both the repressive obstinacy of the CCP and the hypothesis of reformist compromise, which had already been checked by the crisis of spring 1989. After vacillating between two 'solutions', each as unrealistic as the other (turning back or continuous reform) the coalition in power now finds itself identified with the camp of defeated East Europeans and various ambitious tyrannies (Kim Il Sung and Fidel Castro), always mistrusted by the mandarins of Tiananmen Square.[4] After the hopes raised in Beijing by the *putsch* of August 1991, the dissolution of the Soviet Union added ridicule to error for, in their isolation, the Chinese managers had ended by investing heavily in the political counterbalance that Soviet Union diplomacy still represented.

4. *Beijing Information* of 19 August 1991 still naively published (pp. 8–9) a eulogy of Cuban policies which concluded: 'a new chapter in Sino-Cuban relationships is currently developing'.

The international collapse of communism aggravated the ideological crisis within the Chinese régime, with the Chinese leadership now openly forced to disguise a short-sighted empiricism behind increasingly hollow speeches. Nonetheless, communism's ideological crisis constitutes a grave danger for its democratic enemies, for it forces them to assume an ideological power beyond their capabilities. The idea of democracy is certainly nothing new for China, but today it faces more substantial obstacles than in former times: the obstacles accumulated by forty years of totalitarian domination and civic incapacity are added to others inherited from the old political culture.[5] Sustained by the triumph of capitalism, the democratic concept is inescapable and even overwhelming but, as in a traditional willow pattern picture, its obscurer features in the foothills of Chinese political scenery conceal the landscape. The crisis of communist ideology leads in effect to a more general loosening which affects all of China's political ideologies. As with other former communist régimes, the crisis of civic and public spirit created by decades of 'ordinary totalitarianism' weakens the very bedrock of any democratic policy.

The End of the 'Strategic Triangle'

Another familiar effect of the 1989 world changes is the devaluation of Beijing's strategic role. As is well known, Chinese diplomacy made full use of the competition between the two camps to raise the price of her own options. This was possible because at that time China fully satisfied all the recognised norms of power: space (her immense size), time ('older than history' according to General de Gaulle, she was supposed to have the future on her side), strong in numbers and in symbolism (communist but also nationalist). The emergence of Japan and the NICs helped to undermine these criteria; and the collapse of the bipolar game deprived China of her best strategic card. China can no longer use the concept of the 'strategic triangle' to impose the image of a 'third Great Power', destined by her past, her culture and her size to figure more substantially in the future. Her international prestige is in decline. She has only one real card left: her permanent seat in the Security Council.

These arguments should be considered in greater detail.[6] China's relative decline in the world is irrefutable but difficult to assess precisely. It was shown up by the Gulf War, but so also were its limits. Although Beijing

<hr>

5. See my article, 'Chine, la longue marche vers la démocratie', *Pouvoirs*, 52, 1990, pp. 55–64.

6. There is a good discussion of the evolution of Chinese diplomacy and Sino-American relations in Michel Oksenberg's article, 'The China problem', *Foreign Affairs*, Summer 1991, pp. 1–16.

was barely consulted by the more important actors, the Chinese vote carried weight in the Security Council, as was proper for a large nation, weakened but independent, respected but unpredictable.

More generally, the evolution of Chinese foreign policy since June 1989 offers cause for hesitation. Beijing has been seen to display a new weakness on important points: for example in accepting the spiriting away of the dissident Fang Lizhi from his shelter in the American embassy in Beijing; and in accepting, in June 1991, the very contract for the sale of French frigates to Taiwan which she had resisted in the winter of 1989. In other ways Chinese diplomacy has notched up a series of brilliant successes, possibly showing greater skill, indeed, than at any time since the 'Western campaign' led by Zhou Enlai at the beginning of the 1970s. She broke the political isolation with which she was threatened after the Tiananmen Square massacre and restarted the flow of Western aid, an achievement which should not be overlooked.

One theory is that the link between China's isolation and her diplomatic successes is logical and not contradictory, because the same international evolution which weakened her has strengthened those factors which made her strategically attractive at the beginning of the 1970s: her indecision and unpredictability. The Beijing government is reaping the fruits of China's size and geopolitical situation, as well as those of her failures and even of her crimes. As before, her leaders can add to their own importance by playing on the ambiguity of their policy. Faced with criticisms inspired by their repressive practices, their discourse could be summarised as follows: 'You say that we pursue our opponents? (1) It is not true, because they are not opponents but criminals, agitators stirring up disorder; and (2) take care; we may be forced to do more.' This carries weight. The Beijing government is simultaneously criticised and supported. It is vacillating? Lean on it. The nation is breaking up? Help to maintain its unity. Their policies threaten Western allies? Appease them.

The West's attitude to China has more to it than simply laziness and cowardice. The position adopted not only by Japan (normally disinclined to take risks) but also by the other nations of Chinese Asia gives cause for thought.[7] After 1989 they chose, in effect, to preserve a murderous régime because it was in their interests to see her both weakened and preserved. This diplomatic conservatism springs from a new anxiety, which has been increasingly perceptible since 1985 (and in particular the first anti-Japanese demonstrations in China): everything is happening as if Beijing's

7. Jean-Louis Margolin has analysed in detail the reactions of the 'Chinese world' to the massacre of 4 June 1989 in 'La Chine et les petits dragons: un bloc paradoxal?', *M. Mensuel, marxisme, mouvement*, 31 September 1989, pp. 4–28 (special issue, 'Chine notre douleur').

partners were increasingly afraid of the effects of China's internal crisis on her foreign policy.

Such fears are understandable. Although China had never entirely abolished all her *zones d'ombre* (in particular in Indochina), her foreign policy became normalised during the 1980s. A clear direction was identified: to work for the modernisation of the country. To this end she maintained active links with the West and with Japan, balancing their political disadvantages by her rapprochement with the fading Soviet world, and appeased relations with her main neighbours, Taiwan, South Korea and even Vietnam. Since 1989, while keeping up appearances, China has to some extent become disconnected. The various mechanisms of foreign policy often operate with surprising autonomy. The special services have redoubled their activities, at the risk of embarrassing the efforts of the diplomatic services, and the armaments industry has redoubled its exports (including those to the most 'sensitive' areas of the Middle East), disregarding Western alarms and the commitments agreed on by Chinese diplomats.[8] Certain sectors of the army and conservative milieux appear to hold a sizeable proportion of the various internal and external 'ideological' dossiers. On the other hand, commercial logic is being given free rein in other areas. Furthermore, the cellularisation of the nation (which we will return to later) makes Chinese foreign policy more disjointed. Certain provinces see their exports in a way which affects Beijing's precautions, to say the least. Fujian is opening up to Taiwan, and Guangdong to Hong Kong; through the investments they receive, the goods they purchase and the travellers they welcome, these two provinces are virtually 'economic protectorates'. It is significant that Guangdong is taking an active part in the construction of a 'Chinatown' in the Paris area.[9] The export activities of units of forced labour can be seen in the same way – there is nothing new about this, for it dates back to the 1950s. The crisis in Sino-American relations after June 1989 should have made the Chinese authorities more careful, but the need for currency and the keen awareness of money among the cadres of the 'system' of forced labour were stronger. By using the staging-post of the coastal provinces they have skilfully increased their exports, leaving Beijing diplomats with the impossible task of responding to protestations from financially interested American lobbies.[10]

8. On the exports of Chinese arms and the military lobby which organised them, see the excellent article by John W. Lewis, Hua Di and Xue Litai, 'Beijing's Defense Establishment. Solving the Arms Export Enigma', *International Security*, 15 (4.1), Spring 1991.

9. *Libération*, 2 July 1991.

10. See in particular the dossier in the *Courrier international*, 24 April 1991 and the *Far Eastern Economic Review*, 2 May 1991.

The disarticulation of the weapons of foreign policy is beginning to threaten its implementation, particularly near at hand. The contrast with the past is certainly far from complete; as before, Beijing is engaged primarily in evicting the Great Powers from Asia, in preventing any regional power from imposing itself and in maintaining its traditional pressure on China's immediate neighbours. The continuity of this policy can be seen most clearly in the necessarily ambiguous relationships with Japan. China seeks to puncture the immense Japanese financial power and to set up Tokyo against the Soviet Union and the United States; but she is also concerned that Japan's possible 'move into politics' would make her the regent of eastern Asia. On the other hand, Chinese policy in the rest of the region is increasingly fragmented. In relations with the former Soviet Union the classic decoupling of the economic, territorial and political levels has been strengthened by that country's disintegration. Chinese policy over the Korean peninsula has long been muddled and hypocritical, and probably governed by opposing groups: the conservatives sought to sustain reasonable relations with Kim Il Sung while the reforming lobbies, which won in the summer of 1992, want extended trade links and recognition for Seoul. In Indochina Beijing has normalised its relations with Hanoi (but without giving up its ambitions to regain its influence) and is pushing the Khmer Rouge towards a compromise (but without withdrawing her support completely); such ambiguities cover more than simple nuances in the Chinese leadership.

This evolution is probably the result of growing fragmentation, of circumstances and of the stakes to be played for in the region, but it also reveals the changes on the Chinese politico-administrative scene. In effect, the nation finds itself engaged in a waiting game for the succession, a game intensified by rivalries between individuals and groups. The previous similar era, Mao Tse-tung's final years (1974–6) provides an interesting comparison. Internal conflicts were evident at that time, in matters of foreign policy, in increased verbal obduracy, dissent and contradictions in various affairs, and above all in actual paralysis; now, fragmentation appears to be winning. The orchestra of Chinese diplomacy is playing with as much virtuosity as before, but the programmes have changed little and its playing sometimes sounds discordant. In foreign policy, post-communism is engaged in a disorder which is the result not of gentle variations but of fierce contradictions.

Internal Loosening

These contradictions relate above all to internal changes. Twenty years ago society was awakening (with difficulty, and fearfully), while in the last decade it has largely reoccupied the space left open to it by those in power. And yet (and herein lies the full ambiguity of the Chinese situation, distinguishing it from that of the Poles or the Czechs) the diffuse emergence of society, however effective it may be in the economic domain, is not creating any political positivity. Quite the reverse: it is confirming, extending and deepening the loosening out of which it has grown. The internal crisis is much more serious than the one affecting foreign policy.

Firstly, it is more radical, for to some extent foreign policy can enjoy a dispensation from rigorous official recognition: the first consideration is a community to be defended or to promote. Internally, however, the crisis now challenges the very idea that politics can still carry purpose and achieve it. In China as elsewhere, this concept formed the foundation of contemporary history; today it is affected by the failure – unequal, it is true – of the two ideologies which fought between themselves over the burden of modernising the nation: communism (which is collapsing but is taking a long time to die) and democracy (which is winning but is proving incapable of taking over effectively). The modernisation of the country remains an objective necessity; but its human planning, like its language, remains to be invented.

History is now indeed at work. As so often, it is beginning with the revival of traditional or external models. In the past few years, the Chinese ideological scene has been accepting political formulae which communism and democracy claimed to have rendered unfashionable, some of them inspired by the memory of the traditional imperial system. Many leaders now see themselves as mandarins and operate in the order/disorder and centre/periphery structure which has taken over as the legacy of imperial politics. It was through concentrating their criticisms on the mandarins' corruption and opposing it with the traditional ideal of a clean government that the students were able to mobilise the people of Beijing in the spring of 1989.[11] More generally, the concept of a restoration of the old virtues and social rituals is spreading, feeding on the examples of Taiwan, Singapore and South Korea (and even that of Japan) which prove that social traditionalism need not necessarily clash with economic modernisation and political détente. Fundamentally, it is assumed ever more widely that there must be a return to those healthy traditions which alone can legitimise governmental authority. These ideas reach right into some of the leading circles and are often combined with the ideal of 'enlightened despotism'.[12] Some consider

11. Jane Macartney, 'The Students: Heroes, Pawns or Power-Brokers?' in George Hicks, *The Broken Mirror. China after Tiananmen*, Harlow, Longman, 1990, pp. 4–23.

12. On this point, it is useful to read the interview with Ruan Ming, a former counsellor of Hu Yaobang, the hero of communist reformism, who describes the development among the Chinese leaders of a 'neo-authoritarian' current, in 'Les rêves scandinaves de Ruan Ming', *Cosmopolitiques*, 17 September 1990, pp. 123–136.

that if democracy has any chance of finally taking root in China it will be on condition that it first combines with authoritarian formulae based on a social traditionalism. Meanwhile, however, the progress of these concepts is deepening the political crisis in China. Traditional formulae heighten the importance of ritual conformity in respect of the law, and of legitimate authority in respect of negotiated compromises. Authoritarian formulae remove the universal dimension from politics.

In these circumstances it is hardly surprising that the Chinese state is going through a severe crisis, although this is neither new nor definitive. Contrary to accepted stereotypes, the state does not run itself in China: traditional culture retains a primordial role in the ritual bowing of individuals and the interlocking of organisations. The state is a twentieth-century entity which has proved its effectiveness under the nationalists and even more under the communists. Today the general disturbance of order and the civic spirit in China should not be allowed to hide the solidity of public services in basic areas: defence, security, education, even the economy. The trains are dirty but they run. Up to a certain point it is the survival of this framework which makes the general easing of the social fabric possible: the Chinese disorder is partly, as in the past, a sort of temporary by-product of a greater order.

In the immediate present, however, the state is undergoing the effects of a decisive process, the breaking-up of the social fabric into cells, which is derived from the specific history of communism in China. The very factor that gave the Maoist enterprise its strength – its capacity to rake through society and to build relay-networks within it – turned against it as it lost its totalitarian dynamism. The heart of communist history in China is the change from continuous mobilisation into cells of solidarity, following the two central failures of the Great Leap Forward and the Cultural Revolution. The ambiguity of this phenomenon (which partly explains the political weakness of civil society) is derived from the fact that such social fragmentation was not only acknowledged but very often directed by the communist cadres themselves. The Chinese administration has increasingly turned into an untidy interlocking of concurrent cells, sometimes linked between themselves by clannish networks or interest groups.

For political legitimacy has been transformed. What once legitimised the exercise of power was its ideological purpose; today, in contrast, it is the satisfaction of a particular community, that of the cadres of the communist apparatus. Corruption among civil servants is certainly rarer than in many other countries, but it is spreading steadily, is visible to all, and scandalises a society imbued with Confucianism. The servants of the state are engaged in feathering their own nests and its subjects are engaged in escaping from the state: the sickness itself is commonplace but it seriously weakens a vast and diverse nation like China, which considers itself (and is considered by others) as forced into unity.

The second result of this cellularisation is the disintegration of vertical hierarchies. Central power is losing its cohesion and its authority. At its highest level it is now divided into factions and bureaucratic 'systems' which squabble over sinecures. Its chain of command is falling apart as each unit tends to free itself from the one which formerly dominated it, with results varying according to geography, economy and politics. The administrative level which has profited most from this evolution is that of the province or the municipality. This is the level of revenue raising, which constitutes the chief power relationship with the central authority. It is also the most powerful level within the administrative structure. Maoist totalitarianism was based on provincial bureaucracies which today are turning against the central power. Moreover, the provinces often constitute veritable economic entities which are encouraged by Beijing to develop their exports. Since the early 1980s Guangdong, Fujian and Sichuan have become considerable powers which negotiate ferociously over the transfer of taxes to Beijing. The cities of Shanghai and Canton pose a particular problem because of their size and status in the régime's history. Their leaders are seen in the corridors of central power, either because they have great influence there or because Beijing is trying hard to separate them from their base. Thus it is that the two 'strong men' of Canton and Shanghai were summoned to important posts in the spring of 1991: the first, Ye Xuanping, as Vice-Chairman of the National Assembly; the second, Zhu Rongji, as Vice-Prime Minister (and in fact master of economic policy).[13]

It is therefore likely that the provinces (and, in the country's most remote areas, the military districts) will play an important part in the reconstruction of post-communist political power, although they cannot impose a complete fragmentation. There remains in effect a very strong 'state demand' nourished by bad memories of the Kuomintang period and above all by the claim to unity engraved on the heart of Chinese political culture. The internal disorders are perceived by many intellectuals as a shameful illness requiring treatment, with violence if necessary. The leaders manipulate this perception successfully by skilfully concealing the fact that they are adapting very well to the provincial fragmentation of the nation.

The compromise between central power and provincial bureaucracies has in effect been one of the most substantial bases of Deng Xiaoping's régime since 1978. Deng converted Mao Tse-tung's bureaucracy to the

13. *Far Eastern Economic Review*, 15 August 1991, pp. 18–19.

reforms by promising fresh prerogatives and supplementary advantages drawn from broader local powers. His delay in organising the military strike of 4 June 1989 against democratic protest can be explained largely by the need to rally provincial leaders and commandants of military regions beforehand.

But in doing so, Deng has opened Pandora's box. China has always been attracted by a dual organisation of powers: at the centre, power symbolically strong but practically weak; at its base, a multitude of cells, subordinate in theory but independent in practice. As in the Soviet Union (but for reasons among which ethnic circumstances and national identity reflexes rank lower), the unity of the nation today appears compromised by the excesses of communist power – at the same time, moreover, as by economic differences. The case of the minorities in Tibet, Xinjiang or Mongolia is secondary to the enormous phenomenon exercising China herself. Units that are in principle subordinated to the provinces are raising their heads. The movement stirring in society is the exact inverse of that which the new communist power introduced after 1949: it is tendentially weakening all the bonds of subordination. ·

In this collapse the provinces are profiting from the fact that they can offer the smallest units a certain degree of protection against central government. Their cities, like Beijing, benefit from the prestige of power and above all from an economic force of attraction accentuated by rural underemployment. They draw in hundreds of thousands, sometimes millions, of temporary and migrant workers.[14] But the lower echelons are all seeking to emancipate themselves, using every means at their disposal. In coastal regions, for example, the call to overseas Chinese for capital funds is a significant element. More or less everywhere, local powers and notably the districts, are trying to impose internal customs charges, often in order to protect their own businesses from neighbouring competition. In most cases security bodies operate first and foremost for local interests. This confused movement contains two self-contradictory tendencies. The authority of the leaders is strongest at the lowest levels: the village in the country, the working unit in the towns. Conversely, local managers have limited administrative means at their disposal and reduced political weight. The levels of compromise between the two vary with place and time, often favouring the 3,400 districts which constitute the basic level of administration. Overall, the map of the whole of China is cracking on a vast scale. After forty years of a power which took its purpose of metamorphosis to incandescent levels, the setback (which is ordinary enough) is stinging.

14. Jean-Louis Rocca, 'A Pékin, ruraux et citadins', *Le Monde diplomatique*, September 1991.

The question is therefore not one of knowing whether communism will last, nor even whether there may be other forms of compromise for survival: it is condemned in all its forms and its disappearance is no more than a matter of time. Nor is the question one of economic development, for the diagnosis varies enormously with the region. The problem of China's unity is henceforward posed in the most difficult terms of all: if it is not possible to see how the nation might preserve its unity, it is no longer possible to discern the lines on which it might carve up its space. The China that was once unified and self-confident appears to be stuck in an uncertain state of partial disunity and experimentation.

Spaces and Flux

This enigmatic policy drift provokes more general comments, some concerning the question of spaces appropriate for analysis, which are less clearly defined than formerly. The permeability of frontiers, a phenomenon often mentioned in analyses of international relations, has particular relevance in the case of China. The question of frontiers has remained central for this country both because it is the only empire which has survived more than twenty centuries of history and because it still retains its old claims to difference. The solidity of its barriers has always been a measure of the health of successive Chinese dynasties. This has engendered a particular sensitivity to the effects of the recent openness. The current situation in China inevitably recalls that of the empire or of the 1930s, when a weakened central power failed to control either local feudalisms or openness to the exterior.

The comparison between these different periods leads to some central questions, and firstly to this: is the globalisation of phenomena more powerful today, in central Asia at least? It seems to me that important and possibly decisive steps have been taken towards the globalisation of a significant part of the internal Chinese space during the 1980s, for three reasons: the currents of influence are more powerful because they are emitted, or rather re-emitted, by poles of prosperity that are very close and on a world scale: Japan and the NICs; they are sustained and enriched by the flow of images which illustrate the great currents of world time; and finally, forms of resistance to globalisation have been weakened in China by the crisis in the state and by the disintegration of the social fabric. True, this does not mean that the Chinese space is becoming uniform; on the contrary it means that, following the original dividing lines, it is undergoing deconstructions and reconstructions that are induced by the changes in international relations.

The second point concerns the modification of the relationship between world space and regional space. Although eastern Asia was thrust into world history in the middle of the nineteenth century, some of its countries (Burma, Vietnam, and even more so North Korea) retain the means to filter external influences and to delay their effects. Overall, however, its integration into the great world currents was successively reinforced by the Second World War, the wars of decolonisation, the Cold War, and more recently by two linked phenomena: the retreat of the great powers which operated the networks of regional alliances and the expansion of Asian economies into the major currents of world trade. This evolution did not reduce the importance of proximity – we have already seen how recent Chinese history was influenced by phenomena that were all the more powerful as examples because they were close. But the regional space has changed. At ground level it is still a strategic space marked out by East–West dividing lines, noticeably by conflicts which are more or less isolated and unchanging (Korea, Cambodia); yet this space is extended and further fragmented by economic, social and cultural exchanges. Economic currents dismantle the region and connect it to the world's great cities, the great migrations are aimed at capitalist nations outside their zone. The triumph of the Western mass culture in its Japanese version is total. In the cinema, on the radio or television, in magazines for the young, fashions from the West are established, a few years late, but their vectors (radio and television sets, newspapers, drawings, fashion products) are generally of Japanese manufacture. The truly regional stakes have thus diminished in importance. Every country watches its own security and frontiers (and China watches them more closely than others), but the question of regional leadership does not arise, partly because none of the great nations in the region can put forward serious claims to it: China and Japan are hindered by the extent of their world aspirations, political in one case and economic in the other; and India is hampered by its subregional status, limited to southern Asia. In eastern Asia the era of strategic spheres of influence appears to be giving way temporarily to an era of economic fluxes and ideological influences.

The third point concerns the role and content of the ideological mutations in Chinese history. Historians are largely agreed in thinking that their seizure of nationalism broadly explains the Chinese communists' accession to power.[15] The mandate which the latter gave themselves was twofold: they had to both apply their ideological programme and restore China to the rank from which Western aggression had deposed her. They therefore systematically associated the pursuit of meaning with that of power: it was through socialism that China would recover her greatness.

15. We should remember here the great classic work of Lucien Bianco on *Les origines de la révolution chinoise*, Paris, Gallimard, 1967.

This synthesis failed politically at first, as China's modernisation was delayed by the régime's transformations. Next it was devitalised by the invasion of foreign goods and models, in other words by China's entry into the world climate of market democracy. Having failed, communism was submerged beneath hostile models. But this setback also represented a change in status for ideology in China. For thirty years she had borne strong indicators – 'socialism', 'paths of national development', etc. – which promoted murderous projects. These strong pressures have been replaced by indecisive and confused lesser ones. China still preserves a degree of power that is notable given the hitherto unfavourable environment but, as in the aftermath of the empire, she no longer has a strong and original message. Increasingly loosened and penetrated by the world's goods, sounds and images, she finds herself once more forced to create her own history.

THE FAR EAST: THE MEANING OF PROSPERITY

JEAN-LOUIS MARGOLIN

The principal theatre of the bipolar confrontation known as the 'Cold War' consisted of Europe together with eastern Asia. The latter area suffered violent confrontations, in Korea, Indochina, Quemoy and Matsu, the 'revolutionary wars' in the Philippines, Malaysia, Thailand and Burma, and the massacre of Indonesian communists in 1965. No other region represents so many concentrated vital interests of the non-Western European powers (Japan, China, the Soviet Union, the United States through Alaska and 'their' Pacific), and the concentration of weapons here, particularly nuclear ones, has momentarily resisted the détente between the great powers. Could this mean that the *loosening of the world order*, so clearly perceptible elsewhere, has not made itself felt here and that the post-Cold War period has failed to reach the western shores of the Pacific?

To accept this assumption would mean falling into the reductive illusion of over-estimating the single geostrategic dimension as well as the universally regulating power of the great powers. Yet everything in the Far East indicates the weight of economic logic and the growth in capacity of the middle-ranking States. But the 'Cold' War itself, which was at least tepid in the Far East, was nevertheless not as clearly bipolar here as in Europe. In essence it died during the 1970s – more than a decade before its death at the other end of Eurasia – and in fact eastern Asia was surely something of a global laboratory in the relaxation of the post-war order. By 1960 the Sino-Soviet schism had embarked on an irreversible and increasingly complex pattern of the confrontation between capitalism and communism. In 1978–9 the first war (on two fronts) between communist states indicated the possible turning of the 'domino theory' against its supposed beneficiaries and the resurgence of tenacious national hatreds beneath the cracked gloss of 'Marxism-Leninism'. During the 1980s the poorly controlled headlong rush of communist China towards the market revealed the inability of 'real socialism' to develop without renouncing its fundamental economic foundations; and the surprising capacity of the 'four dragons' to overcome internal and international crises promptly indicated the flexibility of the

North/South barrier, the resources of capitalist development for the periphery and finally the superiority of economic logic. Without success on this economic front surely none of the four would have survived. Finally, Japan was for everyone, if not a model, at least the proof that autonomy and power could still be achieved without rejecting the strategic order dominated by the United States.

Of all the world's regions the Far East undoubtedly shows most clearly the great hegemonies' tendency to dislocation, and this has long been so. Surely this is a link combining a tradition of openness (often poorly recognised) with the effects of complex influences? Contrary to accepted Western wisdom, the Middle Kingdom always remained aware of the world outside, even if only through the redoubtable nomads of the steppes. Today we can distinguish at least *six Far Easts*, largely overlapping, four of which overflow onto other parts of the world. China, Korea, Japan and Vietnam make up *sinicized* Asia. An independent *nipponised* space has developed on this cultural foundation, so durable was Japan's imprint on its former colonies (Korea, Taiwan) and also, to some extent, on its less permanent possessions in northern China and South-East Asia. The latter area (excluding Vietnam) was for centuries almost wholly part of the *indianised* area of influence. This is apparent in religious and/or political systems, and it is from India that the Buddhist element of Chinese civilisation was derived. The *Islamic* world extended substantially into the Far East, particularly through Indonesia and Malaysia; but from the eighth century onwards the Arabs also played a significant part in the commercial and outward-looking spirit of south-eastern China. The Philippines symbolise the more recent grafting of the region on to the *Pacific* world, consolidated by a myriad economic, strategic and cultural bonds. Finally *communist* Asia, now entirely Far Eastern, may for some time still to come constitute the final bastion of Marxist-Leninist orthodoxy.

Can a universe endowed with so many fracture lines and so great an inherited capacity for synthesis, accustomed to foreigners but only marginally to their lasting domination, and inhabited by a good third of the human race, remain content with front-line status under the command of Washington or Moscow? The Far East has loosened the bonds without breaking the links, apparently effortlessly (certainly without bitterness or a wish for revenge) and has thrown itself, new order or no, into the new world.

But is there a total equivalence between the Asian *regional time* and that *world time* defined by Zaki Laïdi? In strong contrast to the situation of a few years ago, the response depends less on geographical orientation than on the societal aspect under consideration. In fact, however great the apparent gradual economic rallying everywhere to the same norms (a more or less enthusiastic harmonisation with the great globalising current), when it comes to culture and politics the particularities of local times still show a capacity for survival which few would have foreseen at the end of the 1980s.

Finally, the question of the final years of the millennium – the purpose of Japan – is inescapable, urgent for the whole planet and, *a fortiori*, for the former Japanese 'zone of co-prosperity'. The mysterious and confusing archipelago cultivates ambiguity, when ambiguity is not imposed on it. In which direction is Japan's power unfolding? Does she see the construction of a solid East Asian bastion as her priority? Is her position there one of hegemony or simply one of primacy? In short, does the loosening described earlier represent a genuine shift to a new system of international relations or a simple transitional stage between domination by America and domination by Japan? Finally, to what extent is the latter's economic *imperium* accompanied by penetration of political, cultural or social values, as was earlier the case with the United States?

The Age of Bipolarity

The first quarter-century after the Second World War may seem to have followed the line of an ever-increasing bipolarisation. Yet the years 1945–50 showed other possibilities: the Vietnamese declaration of independence, signed by Ho Chi Minh, was drawn up with the help of an American, Major Patti;[1] in 1949 Washington played a decisive role in the emancipation of India, operating against its European ally the Netherlands; the Malayan and Philippine communists seriously attempted to join in the constitutional political game, at the cost of relinquishing most of their weapons; the United States, whose help for Chiang Kai Shek in the Chinese civil war was too little and too late, almost had to abandon the bastion of Taiwan and at one moment saw Mao more as a second Tito than as Stalin's ally; the State Department's Korean policy was chiefly characterised by doubts and vacillation. The Soviet side appeared to be characterised by both almost exclusive concentration on European affairs and the maintenance, evident until at least the end of 1947, of several irons in the fire; the revolutionary seizure of power and the constitution of an entrenched socialist camp was probably only one option among several. Furthermore, if only for reasons of communication, it was difficult to see the Asian communist parties as simple operators of Moscow's wishes. In short, with so many autonomous operators, with so many indefinable 'grey areas', the Far Eastern order appeared somewhat 'loosened'.

1. Daniel Hémery, *Ho Chi Minh. De l'Indochine au Vietnam*, Paris, Gallimard, 1990, p. 89.

But the area in which this loosening took place was to fade like the Cheshire cat during the following decade. The onset of the Korean War in June 1950, followed by the United States' increasingly significant involvement in the anti-communist struggle in Indochina and the conclusion of the Manilla Pact at the end of 1954 (giving birth to SEATO, the South-East Asia Treaty Organisation), were to precipitate alignments. A continental mass dominated by communist régimes (except in South-East Asia), which showed its expansionist intent in China's aggressive frontier behaviour and the encouragement given to the guerrillas of South-East Asia, was opposed by peninsular and island fringes, violently anti-communist and closely controlled, militarily and also economically (in particular in South Korea and Taiwan) by the United States.[2] It was difficult to escape enrolment in one or other of these two camps, as was proved by the sad fate of the neutralist attempt in South-East Asia, whose spirit animated the Bandung Conference in April 1955. U Nu, Sukarno and Sihanouk were to fall one after the other and the Indonesian massacres of 1965, followed by Cambodia's 1970 entry into the tumult of war, were to ensure the death (temporarily?) of a grand idea. Only militaristic Burma remained neutral, and degenerated into a dictatorial autarchy which was characterised by economic failure.

China, as is better understood today, aligned herself with the Soviet Union more through fear of an American intervention in the wake of the Korean War than through genuine enthusiasm; and less than a decade later disagreements with Stalin's successors were already flourishing. However, from the point of view of Asia's geopolitical configuration, Beijing's firm intention to build on Soviet positions at first appeared to harden still more, making major frontal opposition more dangerous. Although it was somewhat simplistic to see Japan's foreign policy as no more than that of a 'transistor salesman' (as De Gaulle said of Prime Minister Sato),[3] the San Francisco Agreement of bilateral security of September 1951, extended with slight modifications in 1960, confirmed her place in the American orbit; and even if their low-price textile exports provoked commercial friction with the United States from 1957–8 onwards,[4] Washington's primary concern was rather to ensure sufficient prosperity in Japan to prevent any possible leanings towards 'treason'.

2. Cf. François Joyaux, *Géopolitique de l'Extrême-Orient*, vol. 1, Brussels, Complexe, 1991, pp. 27–49.

3. Cf. Warren I. Cohen, Akira Iriye, *The Great Powers in East Asia 1953–1960*, New York, Columbia University Press, 1990.

4. Ibid., pp. 115–16.

The Birth of Complexity

The succeeding period (1970–86), which may be seen retrospectively as a transitional phase, was marked by a growing disarray in the earlier bipolar structure. The sequel was a quadripolar format in which the (relative) decline of the United States was balanced more by China's seizure of autonomy and growing power in political terms, and by Japan in economic terms, than by the advance of the Soviet Union. But this first complexification to some extent conceals another: the six ASEAN nations (Brunei, Indonesia, Malaysia, the Philippines, Singapore, Thailand) and the two North-East Asian NICs, South Korea and Taiwan, are using their economic successes to participate more extensively and more independently in the region's future. This increase in the power of Japan and the 'little dragons', building on the foundations of their material success, was less obvious in the military expansion of the 1970s than the twistings of American policy; yet it constituted the least cyclical evolution of that period and therefore the most irresistible in the long term.

The point of departure for the upset in the Cold War system appears to have been President Richard Nixon's speech in Guam in July 1969. Not content with announcing the gradual retreat of American forces from Indochina as well as the new policy of 'Vietnamisation', he promised a sort of 'Asia for the Asians' and reorganised the US strategy on the island fringes of the continent itself as well as in the Pacific island groups. This indicated to America's anti-communist protégés that they could no longer count on a last-resort military intervention. In view of the Asian geopolitical configuration, they should therefore now regroup to protect each other and above all attempt to reach direct understanding with the two communist continent-states. The United States went on to prove the seriousness of their intentions by the following actions: the total withdrawal of their combat land forces in 1973; the simultaneous mothballing of SEATO, which died quietly in 1977; the denial in 1975 of any substantial aid to a South Vietnam at bay, despite Hanoi's flagrant violation of the Paris Agreements; the retreat from Thailand in 1975; and President Carter's announcement (eventually without after-effects) of the American contingent's departure from Korea, despite the evidence that Kim Il Sung still clung to the notion of reuniting the peninsula by force.

The dynamic issuing from this American semi-retreat became overwhelming with the turnaround of China's foreign policy in 1971–2. After more than a decade of delay this finally showed the logical consequences of the Sino-Soviet rupture: the move to politico-strategic tripolarity; the greatly increased possibility of balancing manoeuvres, and therefore the inclination towards autonomy, for the nations in general; and the reintroduction of Beijing into normal multiple relations. Briefly, the unexpected rapprochement between Washington and Beijing was interpreted as a powerful reinforcement of the US strategy towards the Soviet Union. At a time when the latter no longer exists, the true winners appear to be China herself (discovering in this way how to emerge without major political upset from the tragic Maoist impasse) and Asia, which, no longer a pawn in the confrontation between the great powers, was able to resume autonomous progress. Finally, the capacity of the People's Republic of China (concerning Taiwan) and of North Vietnam to extract significant concessions from the colossal American power without giving away anything fundamental continues to encourage the smaller nations of the region. The step towards loosening was, in fact, decisive.

This loosening was, however, to remain disguised for some fifteen years by the phenomenon, easily resistible in itself, of the growth of Soviet power. The Soviet Union's massive support for the Vietnamese communists automatically established her among the victors of the Indochina conflict. But, more profoundly, eastern Asia occupied an advantageous strategic position in Brezhnev's attempt to get round the unassailable European status quo by the south and the east and thus, in contrast to his predecessors, to comprehend the Soviet Union genuinely as a world power. This was proved by the Soviet proposal of a 'collective security pact', put to the Asiatic nations in 1969, although in the aftermath of Nixon's visit to Beijing they preferred – with the remarkable exception of India – to reach agreement with China (the nearer and more traditional partner as well as the natural patron of the restless Chinese communities and the quasi-totality of communist parties, then still often a threat to the governments in power). This is why Moscow, deriving political advantage from the communist victory in Indochina and then from Vietnam's total financial dependence, adopted a strategy of confrontation based on a reinforced military presence in the Far East and the use of Indochina as a stepping-stone. In 1979 Hanoi and Vientiane, then Phnom Penh, became locked into the economic-strategic network ruled by the Kremlin, and the constant reinforcement of aeronaval forces based in Vladivostock underwent a (limited) extension as far as Cam Ranh Bay, in Vietnam.[5] However, the Vietnamese inability to eliminate the resistance fighters on the Khmer-Thai frontier, and the unsustainable economic burden of an endless war for a nation almost without resources, would soon make the Soviet Union to some extent the prison-

5. Cf. François Joyaux, *La nouvelle question d'Extrême Orient*, vol. 2, *L'ère du conflit sinosoviétique, 1959–1978*, Paris, Payot, 1988, chap. 14.

er of her conquest as she waited for the domino theory (which was finally proven but in reverse) to bring her past gains into question once more. Thus from the 1970s onwards the communicating vessels of hegemony no longer functioned: what the United States lost the other superpower did not manage to win.

Still more surprisingly, neither Tokyo nor Beijing really managed to reap the dividends of the American decline and the absence of any Soviet breakthrough. Quadripartite polarity was indeed achieved, but this was no simple subdivision of the former bipolarity. The very phenomenon of hegemony was apparently becoming increasingly blurred and the lines of power, the networks of influence (which still exist and will continue to do so) operate less and less as one-way channels; increasingly they overlap and are less and less clearly hierarchical.

It is true that Japan is gradually assuming control of the security of shipping lines within a radius of one thousand nautical miles; but her offensive capacity remains virtually non-existent and she could only be an onlooker through the 1980s, observing the growing tension surrounding the Spratly Archipelago in the South China Sea, i.e. right on the Gulf route. Despite many efforts, and the sending of a limited unarmed contingent under the UN banner (an operation without precedent since the Second World War), Japan remains a secondary partner in the grand regional diplomatic saga of Cambodia. For many years the provocative attitude of her history books concerning colonisation and the Second World War (tending to deny imperial responsibility and minimise the atrocities committed by her forces) clouded her relations (which were already less than confident) with China, Taiwan and the two Koreas. Even at the economic level the powerful growth of her investments brought less profit to eastern Asia – they dropped by two-thirds in relative value from 1970 to the middle of the following decade – than to any other part of the world. Her market share was relatively stagnant, the United States remaining the leading partner in many cases.

As for China, she made virtually no appreciable gains, apart from receiving diplomatic recognition almost everywhere (although not from Jakarta until 1990 and from Seoul until 1992) and obtaining from London in 1983 a promise to return Hong Kong to Chinese control in 1997. But the 'punishment' which she expected to inflict on Vietnam in 1979 turned into a stinging military setback; she was unable to make progress towards the recovery of Taiwan or to gain genuine acceptance of her (highly questionable) rights over the island groups of the South China Sea. She had even less success with the vagaries of establishing a zone of influence, however small. It is true that she armed North Korea, Thailand and the Khmer Rouge forces; but can it be said of ferocious nationalists such as Kim Il

Sung (who managed to be supplied with weapons by the Soviet Union until 1990) or Pol Pot, or those dizzyingly flexible and opportunist Thai generals, that they became client subjects? China, with less trade than Taiwan but with fifty times her population, is an essential trading partner only for Hong Hong and, in percentage terms, her trade with some nations in the region remains less than before the Cultural Revolution.

These two cases of weakness in Japan and China may appear contrasting: here a lack of will, there a lack of means; here internal contradictions, sometimes paralysing, as is shown in this book by Jean-Marie Bouissou, there the inability to conduct economic modernisation at the same time as constructing an effective army, and the presence on several essential frontiers of somewhat 'unsympathetic' neighbours (Vietnam, Russia, India). Beijing's international credit also suffered greatly from conflicting impulses (here less simultaneous than successive) and above all perhaps from a deep lack of realism (rooted in the imperial past), as was seen in the perpetual hesitation between a myopic frontier policy, and a hypermetropic world vision, as discussed by Jean-Luc Domenach. The particularist and fundamentally insular past of the two nations, and the absence of any genuine tradition of international relations based on the recognition of others as simultaneously different and endowed with equal rights, are responsible for the tendency to hide in isolationism when the construction of an empire appears inconceivable.

From the 1970s onwards the world time was less than propitious for the establishment of new hegemonic systems. Decolonisation had all too rarely paved the way for the establishment of stable economies; much more often, it had encouraged the emergence of nation-states which were disinclined to be submissive and which generally managed to acquire substantial means to achieve this end – army, police, media, educational and administrative systems, the elements of a welfare state. The economic boom in eastern Asia (and also the fairly general presence of strong traditions of statehood) here, more than anywhere else except for Western Europe, turned the smallest territory into a hard nut to crack, even for the greatest of powers. The history of Vietnam is proof of this, but so too is the improbable survival of Taiwan, of South Korea or of Singapore, where economic success was a necessary prerequisite for existence. The virtual disappearance of foreign aid (whether American or British) during the 1970s was counterbalanced here by major works programmes, there by the accelerated launch of heavy industry, elsewhere by offers of maximal facilities to multinational companies.

Despite what the World Bank may have said, the political and economic systems were liberal,[6] but the national administrations soon took over from the Western counsellors who had trained them; frequent incidents of corruption and arbitrariness did not hinder the fundamental preoccupation with effectiveness. Economies that were generally seen as open and fragile (like that of Japan ten years earlier) were spared in their essentials during the world shift to lower rates of growth after 1973. The serious crises suffered by the NICs (1973–4 in Taiwan, 1979–80 in Korea, 1985–6 in Singapore), which were the result of internal factors as much as of international ones, were swiftly overcome and, above all, provided the opportunity to move into a higher economic gear through financial and administrative reforms and the launching of new and more advanced branches of activity (see below). The birth of a powerful non-Japanese East Asian brand of capitalism confirmed the pertinence of Japan's fundamental societal choices at the same time as it indicated the existence of formidable competitors.

The other great and unexpected success of these years was ASEAN, established in 1967 but principally active from 1975–6 onwards (although it did not preside over any economic integration of its member states or create a potential supranationalism). Formalised dialogues have been established with nations (or groups of nations such as the European Community) important to South-East Asia, but the gains have been modest and Japan, a leading participant, has generated at least as much disappointment as satisfaction. Gradually, however, under the aegis of ASEAN, rapprochement developed between political leaderships and managing groups of all kinds as they adjusted to reciprocal concessions and then to speaking with a single voice; this may also be seen as the great success of the EC.

For nearly a quarter of a century the six nations have formed a zone of peace – at the cost, admittedly, of the persistence until 1991 of the running sore of Cambodia, the fundamental factor of unity and the occasion in

6. Cf. for example M. Shahid Alam, *Governments and Markets in Economic Development Strategies. Lessons from Korea, Taiwan and Japan*, New York, Praeger, 1989; Alice Amsden, *Asia's Next Giant. South Korea and Late Industrialisation*, Oxford, Oxford University Press, 1989; Cal Clark, *Taiwan's Development. Implications for Contending Political Economy Paradigms*, New York, Greenwood Press, 1989; Thomas B. Gold, *State and Society in the Taiwan Miracle*, Armonk NY, Sharpe, 1986; Stephan Haggard, *Pathways from the Periphery. The Politics of Growth in the Newly Industrializing Countries*, Ithaca, Cornell University Press, 1990; Zaki Laïdi, *Enquête sur la Banque mondiale*, Paris, Fayard, 1989; Jean-Louis Margolin, *Singapour 1959–1987. Genèse d'un nouveau pays industriel*, Paris, L'Harmattan, 1989; Garry Rodan, *The Political Economy of Singapore's Industrialisation. National State and International Capital*, London, Macmillan, 1989; Robert Wade, *Governing the Market. Economic Theory and the Role of Government in East Asian Industrialization*, Princeton, Princeton University Press, 1990.

1979 for ASEAN to achieve the rank of international pressure-group. But the causes of friction between the nations (frontiers, minorities, migrations, religious traditions and differing colonial backgrounds) were so evident that their settlement or regulation by peaceful means without intervention from the great powers has been a tremendous success. The great powers frequently had to come to terms with the ASEAN stance in international dealings, particularly over Cambodia. One indirect result of the *pax aseanica* was the Six's enviable reputation for political, social and economic stability, a climate favouring foreign investments and rapid expansion. Even in the Philippines, the weak link in the group, Cory Aquino's hold on power and the survival of modest growth – against and despite most expectations – owed much to the support of the other ASEAN leaders. This success, at least in relative terms, achieved the elimination of the earlier rigid configuration and in contrast also underlines the failures of the new beggar-nations (Indochina and, to an even greater extent, Myanmar/Burma). The road to independence surely began with integration.

Loosening and Reorganisation

In a speech at Vladivostok in July 1986, seventeen years after Richard Nixon's speech in Guam, Mikhail Gorbachev demonstrated the Soviet Union's awareness of these new realities with proposals aimed at integrating the Soviet Union into Asia in its current form, without any longer seeking to take over leadership or even to create a Soviet fiefdom there.[7] The speech marked the end of the Brezhnev venture; it also hinted at substantial leanings towards looser relationships of hegemony. Following the erratic movements and violent confrontations which came to a head during the second half of the 1970s, the Gorbachev move now seemed to veer towards a certain degree of restabilisation, although on foundations profoundly different from those of the 1950s and 1960s: no more lines of major confrontation, a general will to resolve conflicts pragmatically by 'de- demonising' the 'other', a quest for economic synergy.

In the end the US Seventh Fleet retained its primacy and even re-established a form of strategic monopoly. Has the Pacific once more become the 'American lake' which some writers described with reference to the post-war period? Yes, but by default: the Soviets have to some extent thrown in the sponge and withdrawn to defences nearer their coasts. The old com-

7. Nayan Chanda, 'The External Environment for Southeast Asia Foreign Policy', in David Wurfel, Bruce Burton (eds), *The Political Economy of Foreign Policy in Southeast Asia*, London, Macmillan, 1990, pp. 54–73.

municating vessels of hegemony have been called into play; but it should not be forgotten that although the United States have largely taken over from the Soviet Union, the two protagonists already exercised no more than a limited *imperium* over the region. The indications of power nonetheless appear highly favourable for Washington. The Chinese navy is virtually incapable of threatening any nation larger than Vietnam and still appears entirely incapable of ensuring effective control of the island groups in the South China Sea, however noisily she has laid claim to them. Australia has given up maintaining bases in Asia and despite the survival of the Five-Power Defence Agreement (FPDA), which has linked her with Malaysia, Singapore, the United Kingdom and New Zealand since 1971, the Commonwealth's military engagement in the Asia-Pacific area is now wholly symbolic. But what about Japan? Apart from the United States she is the only Pacific basin nation with both the means and the interest to sustain a substantial naval presence. But both the greater part of Japanese opinion and the nations which experienced her colonial or wartime yoke regard her offensive rearmament as unacceptable; and the Tokyo authorities have never done anything to provoke fundamental suspicions of their hidden intentions. The collapse of the Soviet empire is the best proof of the futility of military force without economic, political and cultural support.

Faced with ever-increasing nationalism and global change, the United States seem certain to abandon their bases in the Philippines, and popular anti-American feeling is growing in South Korea. But they have been offered new facilities by Singapore (and probably by Brunei) and no one except Pyongyang still genuinely disputes the advantages of their presence in the Pacific region. Even if it meant their reappearance and local re-establishment, Vietnam herself would welcome US involvement in her recovery. The combination of the Soviet collapse, the uncertainties of China's foreign policy and the distrust with which Japanese initiatives are perceived may place the United States (here again chiefly by default) in the role of an arbiter who is acceptable to the numerous contenders in regional conflicts; but the species of global triumph which the United States enjoy today may turn out to be a Pyrrhic victory, in view of the gap between their reduced resources and the scale of their commitments.

Although the Vladivostok speech simply hinted that Soviet expansion would change to self-limitation, it changed first to a controlled retreat and then to implosion. In the wake of the Soviet retreat from Afghanistan (1988), Moscow forced Hanoi, by reducing aid, to do the same in Cambodia. The departure of Soviet forces from Mongolia removed the final obstacle to a Deng-Gorbachev summit in Beijing in May 1989, which, but for Tiananmen Square, would have appeared as a triumph for the Chinese.

In 1990 the Soviet Union decided to recognise South Korea, which meant relinquishing the unwelcome ally in Pyongyang. It must, no doubt, be particularly hard for Russia to be forced to go begging in Seoul for capital and technology, from a country where, in the early 1960s, peasants were still occasionally reduced to eating the bark from trees to avoid starvation; but it is in fact in relation to the Soviet Union and Eastern Europe that the growth in East Asia (including coastal China) is most dazzling.[8]

In 1991 Soviet aid and the Soviet presence virtually ceased in Indochina. The many Vietnamese teachers of Russian sought to retrain in French and above all in English. Financially on its knees, the government sought sympathy and help from the IMF, Thailand and Japan, and adopted some ultra-liberal measures. Laos is counting on the revival of Chinese penetration to avoid falling wholly into Bangkok's orbit. The next stage on the Russian way of the cross in Asia will probably be to give up part or all of the southern Kurile Islands to Japan, an inevitable precondition for any active economic agreement with Tokyo. The loosening of Russian hegemony may now spread internally and lead to growing independence, in some form still to be determined, for a new *Republic of the Far East*. Free-trade zones (the first have already passed the planning stage) and a massive opening to Japanese and South Korean businesses should lead to the formation of a credible 'bridge' between Asia and Europe, with an almost inexhaustible reserve of raw materials and energy for hungry neighbouring economies.[9] Even more acutely than in Australia, which is at the other end of the dynamic East Asian axis, the very low number of inhabitants would present difficulties (there are some six million people, fewer than the population of Seoul, in an area nearly twenty times as large as Japan). In any case, Russia (in one form or another) can now scarcely think of being anything except a medium-size power in the region in the short or medium term, and it will be with patience and via the very long route of Siberian development that she may one day benefit genuinely from the unique advantage of a territory spreading from one Eurasian coast to the other.

With the fundamental handicaps of China and Japan still far from resolution, their situation has changed little. As Jean-Luc Domenach shows in this book, the incoherence and myopia of Beijing's foreign policy are even more clearly apparent in the after-effects of Tiananmen Square and the end-of-reign atmosphere. China may, however, take advantage of the Soviet withdrawal to establish the semblance of a bastion of Asian commu-

8. 'Shampoo for Caviar', *Far Eastern Economic Review*, 27 June 1991, pp. 32–3 (concerning 'wealthy' tourists from neighbouring China in the poor Primorje region of the former Soviet Union).

9. 'Soviets Make Pacific Plans', *The Australian*, 9 January 1991.

nism with Vietnam and North Korea; the first major effect, as from autumn 1991, would appear to be the suddenly more conciliatory attitudes of both Beijing and Hanoi's Cambodian protégés, even if that moderation, one year later, looks increasingly fragile. A significant trump card for communist China – and here the contrast with Russia is radical – is the relative success of her modernisation and economic openness, undertaken from 1978 onwards. This baroque mixture, which is always under revision, of administrative management and encouragement to private enrichment, reflects with almost total accuracy the 'model' presented by the Asian NICs, the main fact being that its economy has grown at the rate of 8 per cent for more than a decade, although at the cost of growing disparities between social groupings and between provinces. Beijing is strengthened still more by the myriad bonds created or renewed with the 60-odd million Chinese living outside the People's Republic. They constitute a discreet but effective support for modernisation despite their political reluctance to support the hierarchy of CCP structures.

Under the influence of *endaka* (the rise of the yen, particularly apparent in the mid-1980s) and of the natural consequences of her own growth, Japan is at last truly launched on the internationalisation of her economy, some fifteen years after the United States or the European Community (in 1987, still only 4 per cent of Japanese industrial production was based abroad, against 20 per cent for West German firms)[10]. But little of this external growth took place in the region, where investments from the NICs were often locally more substantial; and her internal lack of decisiveness was shown up harshly on the occasion of the breathless international situation at the turn of the decade. The Malaysian proposal in late 1990 for an East Asia Economic Grouping (EAEG), closed to 'white' powers and with Tokyo as its leader, revealed that Japan still aroused great distrust in East Asia (although during the Japanese occupation the Malay élite, traditionally hostile to the Chinese, collaborated extensively). In the local GATT negotiations, Tokyo can use the threat of a Far Eastern block as a form of pressure. Conversely, the resistance provoked by this vague project from a small country, both among those excluded and among many of the nations approached,[11] proved the impracticability of any such association and the considerable caution still felt about Japan. No nation declared itself in full agreement with Prime Minister Mahathir, not even Tokyo.

Nothing is lost, nothing is new, everything is transformed. If this dictum can be applied to social phenomena, it is right to enquire where the 'hege-

10. Gerald Segal, *Rethinking the Pacific*, Oxford, Clarendon Press, 1990, p. 304.

11. Lee Kuan Yew, in a conference in Paris in May 1991, declared his opposition to any attempt to divide the world into 'racial blocs', for the sake of Singapore's status as a 'global city'.

monic material' lost by the United States–Soviet Union pair, and which neither China or Japan has managed to pick up, has gone. The answer is simple, even if the phenomenon is complex: it has gone more or less everywhere, but more particularly to the NICs, followed by the ASEAN nations. Long-distance dealings between Asia and America have certainly not ceased. A sort of triangle can be perceived within the Pacific interchanges: ASEAN sells its raw materials to Japan and the NICs, which transform them and sell consumer goods to the United States; the latter re-exports durable goods and certain agricultural products; the NICs act further as Japan's subcontractors.[12] But the picture becomes increasingly blurred, for increasingly important independent networks proliferate on the fringe of this triangle, straddling the dividing line between 'centre' and 'periphery' and cutting across over-simple specialisations: what we are seeing is well and truly a logic of loosening. This turbulence affects more than the economy alone. Ideas, ways of life, political power, all are equally involved. The governments in Seoul, Taipei and Bangkok, submissive clients of Washington yesterday, now have their own *Nordpolitik*,[13] reunification strategy or policy for hegemony on the scale of the Indochina peninsula. Coaches in the Chinese province of Guangdong follow Hong Kong time and show videos in Cantonese, not Mandarin. Brochures in the 'How South Korea has achieved success' style are very popular in Vietnamese markets.

Economic logic, however, predominates. The governments of Burma and Vietnam (not to mention Pol Pot's autarchy in Cambodia), thinking it possible to make political advances at the cost of the economy, have simply achieved disaster in both respects. It is therefore necessary to consider how a series of secondary poles and bi- or trilateral synergies, which lie essentially outside the sphere of influence of Tokyo and the other great powers, are being consolidated.

The vast reserve of drive and dynamism which is today's East Asia represents the fundamental source of a reorganisation which is as massive as it is swift. The cake is growing to such an extent that everyone can expect a slice of it. The key word in this process is 'complexification'; it indicates primarily that everyone is seeking to escape from his role, accepted since colonial times, in the regional division of labour. In a particularly significant manner, paradise areas of mineral and agricultural resources like Malaysia, Indonesia and, to a lesser extent, Thailand, have more than made

12. Cf., among others, Michel Fouquin *et al.*, *Pacifique. Le recentrage asiatique*, Paris, CEPII-Economica, 1991.

13. An expression which, adapted from the West German *Ostpolitik*, designates for South Korea its policy relating to North Korea and, by extension, to all communist countries (or former communist countries).

up for the unfavourable shift in the markets for their main raw materials, by encouraging industrialisation on a massive scale since the mid-1980s. In countries where rubber, rice, tin and crude oil made up the bulk of exports, light industrial goods have taken the lead within the space of only a few years. Electronic components and materials head the Malaysian sales graph. Indonesia now has a considerable aeronautical industry and is the only OPEC nation to have at least sustained its penetration of the world markets. The virtuous circle of increasing revenue has pushed forward other impressive forms of diversification: the automobile industry in Malaysia (although not technologically independent), the tourism boom in Thailand, and more generally the explosion of services of all kinds.

As for the existing NICs, the growth in power of this 'second generation' of industrialising nations will surely not hinder their advance. Although their industrial expansion only began in earnest around 1960, these pioneers are already experiencing the painful effects of closing factories or, more often, their delocalisation. But, faced with the triple shock of the rise in wage costs, growing popular intervention in economic decision-making (particularly through the claims of the ecological movement) and the surge of new regional competitors, they have responded with unprecedented efforts to acquire technological mastery in record time. Adapting to international specialisation, training or retraining most of the labour force in appropriate skills, introducing science parks[14] and international exhibitions, establishing financial centres of global importance, disseminating information technology: it is no less than a move to excellence, to the international 'state of the art', which is the aim and sometimes already the achievement. In this sense the harmonious simplicity and strict hierarchical order of the famous 'flight of the wild geese' directed by Tokyo has now surely been interrupted: everyone wishes to do a little of everything, at the same time, and everything which works well is quickly copied. It is no longer a case of following a leader but of gaining a good place within the system.

This strong tendency towards complexification also affects interstate relationships and, overall, the very geo-economic configuration of East Asia. A sure sign of this is the more or less universal burgeoning of what are described, with some disregard for geometric rigour, as 'growth triangles'; and the new bilateral synergies also deserve attention. Most remarkable of all is the sight of yesterday's political or economic adversaries harmonising their economies, opening frontiers that were formerly hermetically sealed, and the sensation that major readjustments are on the way which will affect

14. Cf. the dossier on 'Science and Society', *Free China Review*, (Taipei), 40 (12), December 1990, pp. 1–27.

everything, not excluding the configuration of nations with which we are familiar.

The only 'growth triangle' formalised by governmental declarations and international agreements is the one linking the Indonesian archipelago of Riau and the Malaysian state of Johore to Singapore, the major southern pole of South-East Asia. The city-state feels uncomfortably restricted, particularly over developing its leisure facilities, and would like to relocate its labour-intensive industries in a controlled manner. The unformalised, but already very real, continental triangle further north, which Bangkok is currently establishing for its own benefit with the largely unco-ordinated economies of its Burmese and Indochinese neighbours, is a counterweight to this peninsular and insular triangle. The advantages for Burma and Indochina are not obvious, but the autarchical dreams of the generals in Rangoon and the hegemonic ambitions of the commissars in Hanoi are now thereby eliminated. As for the third triangle, which reunites the Chinese economic area by stepping up daily the rate of human, financial and commercial interchange between Taiwan, Hong Kong and the coastal provinces of communist China, Jean-Luc Domenach reveals elsewhere in this book that this too may end in a decoupling of the 'greater South-East' from the subcontinent of China.

The other synergetic phenomena are more bilateral. The rapprochement between South Korea and the former Soviet Union, with the apparently complementary nature of the two economies, is rich in possibilities: Moscow needs manpower, technology and markets near at hand for its Siberian products; Seoul lacks raw materials and space, and confidently expects to 'get round' the North Korean obstacle by the northern route.[15] The substantial NIC relocations to Malaysia, Thailand and Indonesia offer these nations new major partners, with investments sometimes greater than those of Japan (such as Taiwan's in Malaysia). We may go further: the purposeful drive of the NICs in leaping from one staging post to another in order to gain a better launching pad for their onslaught on world markets by creating their national *sogo shoshas* (general trading companies), their interest in the opening of Eastern Europe, prove that Asian tendencies are more global than internal.

In Time to the World Rhythm?

The Far East has long been recognised as an area heavily affected by external influences which it manages to absorb in an original way and over-

15. Scott Atkinson, 'The USSR and the Pacific Century', *Asian Survey*, 30(8), July 1990, pp. 639–45.

come. If we recall that for centuries China was ahead in many domains (particularly the technical and administrative ones), that colonisation – here more often than elsewhere – turned towards productive activity and the establishment of infrastructures, and that Japan was the first non-European nation to achieve developed capitalism, it is clear that the *world time* was never far from the western shores of the Pacific. According to Marco Polo it was Venice which was provincial in the thirteenth century, not the vast Hangzhou.

But what about today? The region yearns to be in the fast stream of the outside world, and does not fear it. Its earlier reluctance to accept that it was no longer the centre of the world died before the end of the nineteenth century with the break-up imposed by the West and also by internal transformations. And during the second half of the twentieth century the traditional modes of thought (specifically Confucianism), of which Max Weber, like many others, recognised only the conservative aspects, were to reveal their flexibility and their paradoxical ability to serve modernity.[16]

Indeed, the Far East is slightly in advance of certain world tendencies. From having been the setting for the hottest phases of the Cold War it became the setting for the first great departure from the reality and language of bipolar confrontation, perhaps precisely because it had suffered terrible ordeals and was undergoing a catharsis. As early as 1975 ASEAN, formed eight years earlier round an explicitly anti-communist plan and hitherto seen as a form of 'civilian' extension of SEATO, invited the new Indochinese régimes to join it. Hanoi refused, no doubt believing at the time that it knew how to play the domino game; but the offer was never explicitly withdrawn and has been accepted in principle by all the nations since 1978 (and formally by Vietnam and Laos in 1992). Moreover, Khmer Rouge-dominated 'Democratic Cambodia' has forged a strange alliance with ASEAN from its remote frontier exile, more particularly with Thailand and Singapore. Beijing has long been running Hong Kong jointly with the ultra-liberal administrators sent from London, the colony's Chinese magnates and the gangs. Since the mid-1980s Seoul has sought to apply pressure on Pyongyang by weaving numerous bonds with Communist China (including diplomatic recognition in 1992), while Kim Il Sung's régime tries to nestle up, against the South, with certain sections of the Japanese conservatives. Singapore did not open diplomatic relations with Beijing until 1991 but her Prime Minister, Lee Kuan Yew, was officially received by Mao Tse-tung as early as 1976 and it has become impossible to keep a count of investments

---

16. Cf. Kim Kyong-dong, 'Confucianisme introuvable, confucianisme retrouvé', in 'Sortir du tiers-monde – espace-monde, nouveaux maillages', *EspacesTemps*, 45–6, 1991, p. 62 –72.

and contracts in both directions: eastern Asians know how to go for what is essential. And on the Chinese mainland the village of Xikou, Chiang Kai-Shek's birthplace, is now a tourist stopping place, suitable for extracting Taiwan dollars and symbolising the intended dialogue with the Kuomintang. The 'bamboo curtain' was never so hermetically sealed as the Iron Curtain, even though the armistice line between the two Koreas remains the most strictly sealed frontier in the world.

The Far East was also extremely advanced in its attempts at reforming communism, both in China and to a lesser degree in Vietnam and Laos. Private enterprise flourished in these nations, and the autonomy conferred on the Chinese provinces, even on the municipalities, has already virtually put an end to the concept of a plan. Foreign investments are increasing and enjoying the same advantages and guarantees as in officially liberal nations: 90 per cent of Hong Kong industrial firms are said to carry out part of their manufacturing in China. It is possible to see in all this the absolute triumph of market logic, of private enterprise and of international competition, which the success of the NICs foreshadowed. The region is probably therefore on the point of accepting this globalisation of capitalist norms of management and structure as the legitimate standard, as what 'goes without saying'.[17]

Ahead of the world time in economic matters and in the de-ideologisation of international relationships, the region appears, by contrast, to be 'behind' on matters of internal policy: market democracy is imposed without becoming positively established. Yet democracy was thought to be virtually taken for granted in the second part of the 1980s, as the following events suggested: democratic revolution in the Philippines (1986); the imposition of a free presidential election with universal suffrage in South Korea (1987); the withdrawal of martial law (1987), and the acceptance of plurality and the first free elections (1989) in Taiwan; the rise of opposition to authoritarian power in Malaysia; the end-of-reign atmosphere for the immovable Japanese Liberal Democratic party (LDP); and finally the Chinese democratic movement in 1989, which quickly spread to Hong Kong, the first time the colony had seen such widespread demonstrations.

But the drama of Tiananmen Square coincided with a change in circumstances. Contrary to most expectations, the Beijing régime regained its authority and stability without even having to introduce massive repression. The good old methods of police suppression, imprisonment of trade-union militants, and of gratuitous violence in the students' camp, tended to slow down the advance of democracy in South Korea. Opposition to Taiwan's Kuomintang revealed only demagogic ineptitude and

17. *Le Monde,* 8 October 1991.

internecine struggles, and the previously unique party had no great difficulty in becoming the dominant party in the free and fair 1991 election. It won three-quarters of the vote: Mahathir crushed the opposition in the 1990 election. And in the same year the People's Action Party (PAP), even without Lee Kuan Yew as its leader, was confirmed in power in Singapore. Despite recurrent scandals, the LDP in Japan regained its briefly shaken stability; while in the Philippines, 'people's power' is no more than a beautiful memory – domination by the traditional clan oligarchy has taken over smoothly from the self-made cronies of Ferdinand Marcos.

Less than the actual setbacks to certain democratisation processes, the most upsetting element is surely the ease of such setbacks. Do the people and even the middle classes want democratic liberties as much as was claimed? Are they not moved much more by nationalistic, ethnic or religious passions, or simply by the desire to live better in material terms, without too much concern for the political context? The acquisition of better living standards for most people constitutes the Chinese communist leaders' best, and apparently most persuasive, argument. From this point of view the 60 per cent abstention rate in the 1991 Hungarian elections and the rapid rise in nationalism and racism in Eastern Europe should help to incriminate less the backwardness of obscurantist peoples than the actual falsity of the notion which makes market democracy an essential and irresistible element of world time. What works well, what wins over the Asian masses in 1992, are rather the particularisms of all kinds – Islam or Buddhism, Japanese clientèlism, Korean regionalism; and even where communism rules it is not (yet?) seriously threatened, as was shown by the Mongolian communists' triumph in the 1992 elections. Economic prosperity itself helps to discredit opposition and to establish the existing régimes permanently: 'It's us or chaos.' So, is world time (economic) out of rhythm with world time (political)?

Japan: Relative Power, Limited Purpose

The bonds wrought by Tokyo with surrounding nations are strengthening. Yet they should not be overestimated, and the modifications which they involve should also be noted. They do not entirely (far from it) lead towards a progressive reconstitution of the Japanese *imperium*.

None of the great domains of international economic relations is entirely free from ambiguity. True, Japan on her own supplies one third of the exports of Pacific basin nations to other Pacific countries, against one quarter from the other great power, the United States. True, her hegemony on the more restricted level of the Far East is even more impressive: by reason of the very high level of income per head (23,000 dollars in 1989,

against 400 dollars, for example, in communist China), Japan supplies
nearly three quarters of the region's GNP (2,830 million dollars in 1989,
and 1,020 million dollars for the other nations combined). And all her
bonds with eastern Asia have been greatly strengthened since she
embarked on the serious internationalisation of her economy in the mid-
1980s. Boom in direct investments: half her capital invested in Asia
between 1951 and 1989 was placed after 1985.[18] Boom in trade: it more
than doubled between 1985 and 1989. Boom in public development aid:
nearly two-thirds was devoted to continental Asia in 1989, against one-sev-
enth in the case of the United States;[19] and, in parallel, Japanese aid has
now become quantitatively the world leader.

But although the empire would like to strengthen its Asian influence,
although it aims to benefit to the utmost from the dynamics emerging
almost everywhere in the region, it is not interested in exclusive domination; even supposing it were possible, this would be politically ruinous
for its relations both with the nations of the area and with the United
States. Japan's priority is the Pacific, and beyond that, the world.
Exchanges with the United States, traditionally important ever since the
Meiji era (when it was the Americans who 'opened up' Japan, a remarkable exception in that period of European supremacy), have been confirmed in their primacy: 30 per cent of Japanese trade in 1985–9 was
with the United States.[20]

The great development of the last thirty years has been the explosion of
trade with the European Community, moving from 5 per cent to 16 per
cent of the total, while trade with the rest of eastern Asia is stagnant at
around 25 per cent – a comparatively low value compared with the
approximately 58 per cent of their external trade achieved on average
between them by the EC nations in 1989. The ASEAN nations have even
lost much of their importance for Japan because of the poor reputation of
most of their raw materials. Japan is certainly the primary supplier for
most of the region's nations, but it is only (and this is nothing new) the
leading customer for those nations producing raw materials such as
Indonesia, Brunei and the slightly more distant Australia. The American
market remains in the lead for both the ASEAN nations and, to an even
greater extent, the NICs. Furthermore, any new growth in Japan's market
share in the region now appears conditional on the reduction of the colos-

18. 'Empire of the Sun', *Far Eastern Economic Review*, 3 May 1990, p. 46–8, and 'Drop in
the Bucket', *Far Eastern Economic Review*, 20 December 1990, pp. 48–9.
   19. Fouquin, *Pacifique*, pp. 173–5.
   20. *Far Eastern Economic Review*, 3 May 1990, p. 46.

sal commercial deficit accumulated over a few years by region's nations in Japan's favour: Taiwan and South Korea are in a particularly difficult situation, with a total deficit of 18 billion dollars in 1990[21] – greater, relatively speaking, than that of the United States.

The position is even clearer in the case of direct foreign investments. They have certainly leapt upwards from 11 billion dollars in 1981 to 282 billion dollars in September 1990;[22] this shows their rapid growth in absolute terms, in Asia as almost everywhere else in the world. In her own region, however, Japan placed only 12.4 per cent of her capital overseas in 1986–91, against 33 per cent in 1975! True, 1990 saw a substantial rise once more, with 16.5 per cent, but it is still not clear whether this marks a permanent reversal of the trend. Within the same period it is in North America and Europe that Japanese investments have truly exploded, rising from 27 per cent of the Japanese total to 48 per cent in the first case and from 10 per cent to 21 per cent in the second.[23] Obviously we are still a long way from the new 'yen bloc' so feared by Tokyo's Western partners, and of which the mere mention sends shivers running throughout virtually the whole of East Asia. Japan pays for only 14 per cent of her imports in her own currency against, for example, 50 per cent in the case of Germany.[24] And yet there is no 'mark bloc' on the horizon.

The reason for the Asiatic nations' firm rejection (with the possible exception of Malaysia) of anything which might resemble an institutionalisation of Japanese leadership is their long list of complaints, explicit or implicit. Their growing deficit *vis-à-vis* the Japanese empire has been evoked; but they have not managed to obtain even a timid opening of the domestic market or self-limitations of Japanese exports achieved by the United States and the European Community; the ASEAN nations are entirely lacking in any Lomé-style system of price stabilisation for their raw materials. Branches of Japanese multinationals are bitterly reproached for their harmful protectionism concerning transfers of technology and the internal promotion of native-born managers. Japan is denounced for her massive destruction of the South-East Asian environment, particularly the forests, to protect her own; not content with exporting goods and capital, the Japanese are relocating their pollution. Aid itself has often appeared unacceptably tied to imports from Japan, as if Japan was incapable of not

21. *L'état du monde 1993*, Paris, La Découverte, 1992, pp. 190, 363.

22. *Far Eastern Economic Review*, 20 December 1990, p. 48.

23. According to Segal, *Rethinking the Pacific*, p. 304; *Far Eastern Economic Review*, 18 June 1992, p. 44.

24. Cf. Andras Hernadi, 'Japan's Role in the Asia-Pacific Region', *Japan Forum*, 2 (2), October 1990, pp. 185–92; 'Model of Paradox', *Far Eastern Economic Review*, 31 January 1991, p. 40 and 'Unequal Partners', *Far Eastern Economic Review*, 21 January 1991, p. 43.

taking with one hand what it had just given with the other. And yet the Japanese and other Asians are getting used to living together once again (before 1941 several Far Eastern nations had substantial Japanese communities) through scholarships offered by Japanese universities, through the very numerous overseas placements of Japanese managers (20,000 in Singapore, against 200 in 1960), and of course through tourism. And the Tokyo-style department stores, among many fashions adopted from Japan, are sometimes tremendously successful even while they irritate the most nationalistically minded.

The power of Japan in eastern Asia is thus both genuine and limited, and will no doubt remain so for a long time to come. More or less the same is true of her purpose. As is appropriate for any major power, her influence takes very diverse forms – a lighthearted example being the fashion for *karaoke*. More serious are the quality-control circles which were quickly established within business structures, the 'just-in-time' style of management, or the custom of company trade unions which developed in Singapore during the 1980s in place of the British-style industrial federations. Although the introduction in Taiwan, South Korea and Singapore of a heavily government-directed form of mass teaching can be attributed to Confucian tradition, the Japanese meritocratic diploma-hungry system has been a role model since late Meiji days: it is very much more difficult for someone without a doctorate to become a minister in Singapore than in the old British metropolis; the strict hierarchy between universities, the links between public and private establishments and the very substantial financial sacrifices required in all cases from families are characteristic of advanced education in Seoul and Taipei as much as in Tokyo; the 'mafias' of graduation classes from the most sought-after universities hold a controlling place in political and economic life. Although the higher civil servants and business managing directors in the NICs have in most cases completed their education in the United States, trading houses of the *sogo shosha* type are being established on all sides as well as economic management boards similar to the MITI (the Singapore Economic Development Board, the Taiwan Council for Economic Planning and Development, and the Korean Economic Planning Board, whose chairman automatically holds the rank of vice Prime Minister); as in Japan, a major factor of economic success is the symbiosis between the public and private sectors, without the pecking order between the two always being apparent.

At the political level, mention should be made of the implicit model of catch-all party of patronage (epitomised by the LDP) that has been adopted, for example, by the Kuomintang or, even more clearly, by the new Democratic Liberal Party in power in Seoul. The enduring power of Japanese conservatives enables their Korean or Taiwanese counterparts to look with confidence on the current process of democratisation – as in Japan, the interplay between the factions of a dominant party may take the place of the alternation in power between the majority and the opposition. Some other features should be mentioned: the neighbourhood system of policing (the Japanese koban system) established by the Singapore authorities as part of their determination to keep a close watch, with the collaboration of the populace, over the slightest form of deviation; or even that business-combined-with-politics symbiosis which seems to be inseparable from democratisation in Taiwan, Korea and Thailand (the scandals linked to the corruption of the political leadership are as recurrent there as they are harmless to the overall stability of the system, and might almost be assimilated into a system for renewing the élite, or even for rotating its members in power). Is it not the Japanese rather than the Chinese version of Confucianism that provides the model of unconditional loyalty to the State and of sacrifice for the community (through work as well as through sharing in the island's 'Total Defence') which the PAP seeks to make Singapore's national ideology? Chinese tradition insists much more on family duty and harmony between rulers and ruled, based on the rulers' goodwill, while the Japanese version prefers the absolute obedience due to the hierarchical superior in whatever he may ordain.[25]

Administrative regulation, corporatism, the combination of fluidity and respect for the hierarchy in social relationships, universal communication – this is what the most advanced East Asian nations envy in Japan and attempt to reproduce. In some cases it is explicit: the Singapore *Learn from Japan* campaign in 1978; Malaysia's *Look East* policy launched in 1982. Both were concerned to break with the over-exclusive hold of the British tradition and to proceed simultaneously towards better training for the labour force, general mobilisation for economic progress and greater authoritarianism in labour relations. In the Philippines the minister of Trade and Industry, José Concepción, stated that his country must 'become something like Japan Incorporated'. Yet, although the Japanese model may be more seductive than the American one, inasmuch as a certain harmony of life-styles and effective regulation of social relations are concerned, the Western cultural influence still remains the determining factor (even inside Japan itself) and makes new advances through the universalisation of the American televisual model, as is seen in the rapid growth of Christianity within the élites of the NICs.

25. Michio Morishima, *Why has Japan 'succeeded'?,* Cambridge, Cambridge University Press, 1982.

The Far East: A Model of Original Development?

The question is inescapable: although the region shows convincing evidence (more than Europe itself) of a tempting diversity in virtually all areas, there is (as in Europe) the hint of one or more common elements, barely perceptible and virtually imponderable. This is the place to assess them.

It is a delicate task, if one prefers to avoid reductionist caricatures. In effect, the nations of the Far East do not appear to be homogeneous either at the micro-economic level of the company (the great anonymous Japanese conglomerate, the giant Korean family firm, the modest Chinese company),[26] or at the macro-economic level of public/private relationships or industrial strategy. Although the power of attraction of the Japanese political model is increasingly obvious, although communism has entered on its regressive stage in Asia as elsewhere, the differences between styles of government and of protest will probably remain fundamental. When it comes to explaining the success of Japan and the NICs, the range of explanations and the irreconcilable differences between them leave an impression of doubt and uncertainty. This applies regardless of whether they concern economic factors (the 'benefits of liberalism', the 'advantages of state intervention', the 'mechanisms of interdependent development'), political ones (superiority of authoritarian and/or anti-communist régimes), or cultural matters (Confucianism, Buddhism, the 'Sinicized' ethos of development).[27] Surely it is unsatisfactory to rely on analyses, however precise, of the institutional frameworks of business or of the state, in their interaction with social systems,[28] at the cost of ignoring the intriguing similarity of success in nations with widely differing institutions? It is as difficult to determine the common mechanisms of success as it is to understand the reasons for failure in other nations in the region, which are similar in many aspects to its 'wunderkinder'.

Should we therefore give up the search for the East Asian master plan, of which Japan would present only the most highly developed variation and historically the first in the field, but which would in the end be as little Asiatic, and as fundamentally global, as the system whose praises were sung by the Britons Smith and Ricardo two centuries ago? This would

26. Cf. Simon Tam, 'Centrifugal Versus Centripetal Growth Processes. Contrasting Ideal Types for Conceptualizing the Developmental Patterns of Chinese and Japanese Firms' in Stewart R. Clegg and S. Gordon Redding, *Capitalism in Contrasting Cultures*, Berlin and New York, De Gruyter, 1990, pp. 153–83.

27. Cf. Léon Vandermeersch, *Le nouveau monde sinisé*, Paris, Presses Universitaires de France, 1986, and Kim Kyong-dong, *Confucianisme* (see note 16 above).

28. This is the approach in particular of Benjamin Coriat in *'Penser à l'envers'. Travail et organisation dans l'entreprise japonaise*, Paris, Christian Bourgois, 1991, and of Clegg and Redding, *Capitalism* (see note 26 above).

mean a failure to answer what is undoubtedly the most significant question raised by late twentieth-century East Asia.

The most disconcerting element for us, and one that is almost invisible because it is so obvious, may be the rehabilitation of values which are traditional but which have never been forgotten in the Far East: effort, rigour, discipline, frugality, saving, dedication. These values, which in the West tend to be integrated into an overall conservative vision – frequently in a religious framework (the famous 'Protestant work ethic', for example) – have no abstract meaning in Asia. They are set to the service of purely material aims and above all of enrichment. Furthermore they have very few political associations, the difference between various régimes and cultures lying less in principles than in how they are implemented.

Much closer to the 'post-modern' sensibility is the dialectical counterpart of this rigidity of principle that is often associated with Confucianism: the insistence (which is itself strongly Taoist) on flexibility, malleability, the rejection of oppositions and forceful contradictions. Is it really necessary to choose between public and private, between small independent firms and giant companies, between robots and the standards of quality represented by craft workmanship? Why not seek to develop reserves of productivity and prosperity wherever they occur? Exporting is aggressive, but its profits help to develop the internal market. The rigours of the laws of the market are accepted; it is reasonable to increase one's wealth and to manage others without sharing the decision-making with them. But this is counterbalanced by the continual rise in income and standards of living for the most disadvantaged: the cultures of the NICs are on the whole relatively egalitarian. This economy of the new 'information age' has been described in Japan as 'softonomics':[29] the term seems appropriate for the whole of the Far Eastern system where, as in Heraclitean philosophy, 'everything flows', without any intangible vested interest, without a fixed point in profession or social status (in Hong Kong four bosses out of five began as wage-earners),[30] but yet with a group solidarity softening the sharp edges of cultures which tend to function, as in Japan, on 'tightrope' lines. Christian Sautter's definition of the East Asian success is based on the reconciliation of opposites: Government/Business, Savings/Education.[31] If 'true socialism' is dying from excessive concentration on government, the great mid-century model – the United States – is increasingly paralysed by having sacrificed everything to business.

29. Lee Poh Ping, 'ASEAN and the Asia-Pacific in the 1990s', *Contemporary Southeast Asia*, 9 (2), September 1987, p. 159.

30. Simon Tam, 'Centrifugal versus centipetal', p.161.

31. Christian Sautter, 'Préface' in Fouquin *et al.*, *Pacifique*, (see note 12 above), pp. iii–vi.

The least tangible element, which is established in the everyday nature of individual behaviour as much as in the interplay of political forces and the life of states, is a profound pragmatism which is an- or even anti-ideological; material success, and primarily the enrichment *hic et nunc,* to which even Deng Xiaoping invited the Chinese peasants, replaces transcendent values which have collapsed here more completely than elsewhere because they undoubtedly never entirely won over the masses. Religious and ethnic hatreds appear to be in retreat: fundamentalist Islam is less popular than in the early 1980s. Communism has lost its dynamism virtually everywhere; but where it does hold power, there is less inclination to overthrow it, or simply to challenge it, than to win the freedom to pursue one's private business as one wishes. This détente, which is undeniably only relative, is favoured by the current prosperity, but the example of Europe or of North America reveals overwhelmingly that wealth and education are not enough to eliminate the foundations of hatred and outbreaks of fanaticism.

It is true that these characteristic elements are not universal, and in any case do not apply in the same proportions to the Far East as a whole. They concern much more the 'Group of Five' (Japan and the NICs) than countries such as Vietnam or Indonesia at the other end of the scale. Yet national systems are not isolated entities, as is proved, particularly in South-East Asia, by the turbulent interplay dating from the remotest past of Chinese, Indian, Middle Eastern, Japanese or colonial influences. Consequently these five advanced nations are the birthplaces of an exceptional dynamism which is extremely attractive to the surrounding countries. More or less everywhere the economic and cultural structures conceived in Japan are taken as models, as are also, sometimes, Korea's industrial policy, Singapore's urban planning (in Indonesia or Malaysia), or Hong Kong's financial structures. The strong tendency today is that the nations of ASEAN, then Indochina, Burma (and even North Korea) will gradually be won over by the 'Japan-NICs model'. A certain uniformity is doubtless on the way, but the nations can find in it the means of achieving their own autonomy. The world order is loosening, undoubtedly, and the Far East is part of this relaxation. Yet East Asia is deriving from it a stronger coherence at the same time as it is raising itself to the rank of major operator in world affairs; this is surely the fundamental shift of balance of the final third of the twentieth century.

8

THE INTER-AMERICAN SYSTEM AFTER THE COLD WAR

GEORGES COUFFIGNAL

One of the first foreign policy moves of the newly created United States of America was to express support for the emancipation movements in the Spanish and Portuguese colonies between 1810 and 1823. Independence had barely been achieved when James Monroe laid the foundations of the doctrine which later bore his name, concerning inter-American relationships. Initially the United States disregarded or scorned the republics whose birth they had applauded but were unable to stabilise.[1] As the United States grew more powerful, economically and militarily, in the middle of the nineteenth century, relations between the two halves of the continent deteriorated into conflict and passion, and were generally marked by mutual incomprehension. Their paths diverged from the first, in fact, with Anglo-Saxon Protestant America resolutely engaged in building a prosperous nation while the ruling élites in Roman Catholic Latin America retained close intellectual and cultural ties with Europe, which continued to supply a steady stream of immigrants. The Mexican War and the first military interventions, which were almost always motivated by defence of North American interests, added lack of balance to the original lack of comprehension – a tendency that was heightened in the twentieth century, particularly by the Cold War, which added an East-West dimension to the North-South polarisation, which was at the same time geographic and economic.

The character and operation of these relations may change radically as a result of the new world order which has been developing since the fall of the Berlin Wall. Substantial modifications are appearing in the regulation of this loosened world order, in which purpose and power no longer necessarily go hand in hand. It can be said today of inter-American relations that they are noticeably more contradictory and ambiguous, more conciliatory and more conflicting, more interdependent and more autonomous.

---

1. See the remarkable study by John J. Johnson, *A Hemisphere Apart. The Foundation of United States Policy Toward Latin America*, The Johns Hopkins symposia in Comparative History, Baltimore and London, The Johns Hopkins University Press, 1990.

More contradictory, because the renewal of Latin American interest in the United States is associated with greater displays of political autonomy among the states to the south of the Rio Grande *vis-à-vis* their powerful neighbour and protector. More ambiguous and more interdependent because in many areas (economic and labour policies, the struggle against drugs, etc.) each depends on the goodwill of the other. Simultaneously more conciliatory and more conflicting, because politico-military submission has faded with the disappearance of the 'red peril'. The Latin American states are effectively gaining a political autonomy which was unattainable in the struggle to resist subversion.

How will these relationships evolve? Will the economic crisis affecting the whole region mean greater dependence on the North? Yet surely the North's crisis of productivity must mean a measure of dependence on the South, for both its market and its labour force. And surely the battle against drugs, by forcing ever-greater constraints on North American policy, must mean a possible reduction in autonomy for nations which won greater independence in the 1980s? What are the relationships between the centre and the new élites which have emerged and quickly taken over in most countries? Firstly, what is the centre? Latin America's new élites have always seen themselves in relation to a centre located somewhere else – in Europe or the United States. This is also the origin of the interaction, so strong in this region, between internal and external factors, between national political practices and international pressures. Does the United States now have a free rein in the enormous void created by the Soviet Union's disappearance from the ideological field, so leaving relationships more one-sided than ever in the absence of a counter-balance? Or should we agree with Albert Hirschman that this ideological vacuum and its accompanying social changes are creating a new breathing space for societies in sore need of it?

It is impossible to answer such questions without first looking at the traditional facts underlying relationships between the United States and Latin America as they have developed over nearly two centuries. As will be apparent, the 1980s brought major changes even before the Gorbachev era and the fall of the Berlin Wall, with the emergence of ethics and of rights in the thinking and exercise of inter-American relations on the one hand, and a Latin American diplomacy, associating several nations of this region in its common aims, on the other. The loosened world order emerging since then has radically modified relationships throughout the Americas, both between the two Americas and between distinct units within each grouping. We are seeing a decoupling in operation, between the economic and the political, which is shaping an entirely new American order.

Traditionally Unequivocal and Asymmetric Relationships

James Monroe's message to Congress on 2 December 1823 established the principle which has formed the basis for inter-American relationships ever since: the United States felt their security threatened by any European attack on the independence of any one of the nations in the region.[2] This was clearly a message with two parts. The first, often put forward subsequently, is the US emphasis on the overriding importance of security. The many local North American military interventions, including the latest to date (Panama in December 1989) have always invoked this principle of security. The second had been forgotten in the course of these interventions: faced with a colonising Europe, the United States, which had long since won their independence, greeted the young and newly established nations with assurances of protection against any attempt at European interference. In the nineteenth century the promise was not always kept, but the myth of 'America for the Americans' became deeply rooted in the collective imagination and continued (as we shall see) right up to the Falklands War. Furthermore, this notion of the duty (or right) of protection expanded to match the growing military and economic inequality between the two halves of the continent.

The war which deprived Mexico of nearly half her territory in 1848 (Texas, New Mexico, Arizona, California, Utah, part of Colorado and Wyoming) moved the United States southward. General Grant (1869–77) asserted the 'common destiny' of the two Americas and claimed the right of intervention throughout the whole continent, a right transformed at the beginning of the century into one of international policing with Theodore Roosevelt's 'Big Stick' corollary to the Monroe Doctrine. The growth in military power accompanied an increasingly visible economic hegemony. The big American agro-exporting and mining companies established in Central American and in certain South American nations intervened directly in governmental policy to promote their own interests. This phenomenon was particularly noticeable among the small Central American nations, devoid of any clear identity, which together constitute what has since been described as the 'backyard' of the United States. Governments in South America, with its much larger and strategically less important nations, often enjoyed greater autonomy but knew that their powers were limited

2. There is a sound presentation of the history of United States-Latin America relationships in Harold Molineu, *US Policy Toward Latin America from Regionalism to Globalism*, Boulder, Westview Press, 1986. It is also worth referring to the very full work (which is strongly convinced of the justice of the foundations of US Latin American policy) of Lester D. Langley, *America and the Americas. The United States in the Western Hemisphere*, Athens GA, University of Georgia Press, 1989.

whenever the interests of locally established North American companies were at stake: the affirmations of hegemony were evidently relative in their effect. The 'good neighbourhood policy' of Franklin D. Roosevelt (1932–45) did not last: the 1930s crisis, with the establishment of the German-Italian axis in Europe and the rise of populisms tainted with fascism in Latin America, encouraged the South American communist parties to seek conciliation with the United States. The end of the Second World War and the Cold War restored the relationship of domination. The 'Alliance for Progress' of John F. Kennedy (1961–3) was a great utopian pact for the modernisation of Latin-American societies, initiating a number of vast engineering projects; but it did not survive, nor did it fundamentally challenge either the North American right to oversee the Latin American economy or its complementary right to intervene militarily.

The Cold War strengthened this traditional status quo, supplying the will for hegemony founded primarily on a well-understood national interest with a geopolitical justification,[3] and here as elsewhere helping the politico-strategic factor to dominate over economics. At the same time, however, it made the region's politics infinitely more complex than their strategic position, particularly in Central America and the Caribbean. Fidel Castro's victory in Cuba in 1959 supported the Latin American belief in the possibility of changing régimes through military force despite US hostility. The Castroists' successful defeat of attempted landings or destabilisation created an alternative which thoroughly upset internal policies. Cuba began to crop up everywhere across the continent, either because governments were forced to deal with Cuban-inspired guerrillas or because Cuba was useful as a negotiating weapon with which to scare the United States. It is interesting to note here that these remained largely American phenomena, with the competition from the East often purely speculative, relating more to collective imaginings than to reality. Various recent works have indeed shown that the Soviet Union, after being reminded at the time of the Cuban missile crisis of the rules which must not be transgressed, was much more concerned to develop its trade with the large South American nations than to support the continent's revolutionary movements.[4] This priority accorded by the Soviet Union to the economic over the political was genuine; it covered the Brezhnev era, for whom Latin America ranked behind Asia and Africa in importance. Cuba was used as an

3. Cf. Margaret D. Hayes, *Latin America and the US National Interest*, Boulder, Westview Press, 1984.
4. See the works brought together by Eusebio Mujal-Leon (ed.), *The USSR and Latin America. A Developing Relationship*, Boston, Unwin Hyman, 1989, and in particular David Albright's study, 'Latin America in the Soviet Third World Strategy. The Political Dimension', pp. 3–65.

outpost for the Soviet network (which included Nicaragua and El Salvador) only when she could act as a form of exchange currency for Afghanistan in possible negotiations with the United States over world-wide spheres of influence. But the Soviet Union nonetheless observed the growth of nationalism in the region attentively, seeing it as likely to favour greater national autonomy despite growing economic dependence.

More perhaps than in other regions, *purpose* and *power* were thus linked in Latin America. The universalist messages of the two great powers were asserted by internal political operators, with that of the Soviet Union appealing the more strongly to intellectuals because the only power perceived as militarily threatening was the United States. The Cold War also supplied forms of expression for the anti-Americanism created by a century-and-a-half of military interventions and economic imperialism. This anti-American feeling was sustained throughout virtually the whole subcontinent, in the form of either nationalism or guerrillas. In the case of the United States the Cold War formed the basis for their support for the installation or maintenance during the 1970s of the military dictatorships from which few nations escaped. The leaders of these dictatorships were trained in the 'School of the Americas' in Panama, the North American military school where the doctrine of 'national security' was elaborated; its aim was to combat the 'enemy within' as represented by movements which could at any level be described as 'communist'. Here as elsewhere the thinking behind East-West competition entailed the imposition of force as the *ultima ratio* within the United States' oldest zone of influence.

The Emergence of Ethics and Rights

The end of the 1970s and the beginning of the 1980s mark a major turning point in US relations with Latin America, even if they do not appear to have changed much. This was the introduction, probably enduring, by the United States' references to respect for universal rights and democratic legality in their relations with their southern neighbours. Jimmy Carter (1977–81) was not content with vigorous condemnation of dictatorships. He linked American economic aid with respect for human rights in nations receiving aid, even (notably in El Salvador) suspending credits that had already been approved, in cases of repeated violations of human rights. Elsewhere he showed an entirely new understanding of political claims from the subcontinent, whether they concerned problems of sovereignty (the signature in 1977 of treaties returning sovereignty over the canal to Panama at the end of 1999) or social justice (aid granted in 1979 to the Sandinista government which had just gained power through the naked use of force).

Carter has too easily been contrasted with his successor, Ronald Reagan. Careful observation reveals that behind their very different styles of rhetoric their policies were not dissimilar.[5] It is true that Ronald Reagan wished to reduce all regional conflicts to the East–West dimension alone, which his predecessor had ignored. Literally obsessed by Nicaragua, he wished to *contain* and then *roll back* communism in Central America at all costs.[6] However, he operated by constantly invoking universal principles (reintroducing the creation of purpose), making it impossible to interpret these conflicts according to traditional categories of imperalism or of the United States' domination over their own backyard.[7] International opinion thus held pride of place, together with the image that the United States wished to promote of themselves. Thus Grenada was invaded in 1983 in order to 'overthrow a communist dictator' and to restore free elections. It was to help the 'freedom fighters' that Washington armed and financed the anti-Sandinista rebellion (the Contras). It was to prevent the installation of a 'communist dictatorship' that they did the same for the army in El Salvador.

This philosophy has had a paradoxical and significant effect. The swift return of freely elected régimes throughout most of the continent is partly due to the Reagan crusade. In order to isolate the Nicaraguan Sandinistas on the international stage, Ronald Reagan had to prove the validity of the 'theorem' formulated by his UN ambassador, Jane Kirkpatrick. This held that it was possible to escape from dictatorship in the Western sphere of influence (the 'free world') but impossible in the communist zone. Thus, El Salvador, Honduras and Guatemala are seeing their military rulers ejected by the United States in favour of civilians. That human rights are recognised scarcely more in these new 'democracies' than in the former dictatorships is of little importance: electoral reality is what matters. North American ambassadors *en poste* in Latin America are tireless in their efforts to promote civilian alternatives which would be sympathetic to the United States. When it becomes apparent that only the forces of the Left can immediately step into the places left vacant by the military, or when the risk of chaos appears too great, there is a preference for temporising and

5. Cf. Michèle Soulignac, *La politique de Jimmy Carter et Ronald Reagan en Amérique central*, DEA memoir of international relations, University of Paris I-Sorbonne, unpublished, 1987.

6. American production (in the North or the South) is very significant in this question. A good presentation of the most recent works can be found in Cheryl L. Eschback, 'Explaining US Policy Toward Central America and the Caribbean', *Latin American Research Review*, 25 (2), 1990, p. 204–16, and in Thomas P. Anderson, 'Recent Studies on Intervention and Politics in Central America', *Latin American Research Review*, 25 (3) 1990, pp. 214–21.

7. The Gulf crisis was to confirm what Marie-Claude Smouts calls 'the alliance of *universal* rights and *American* force' (in 'L'ordre neuf du président Bush', *Esprit*, 6 June 1991, p. 185).

allowing a moderate opposition to emerge. Argentina, Brazil and Uruguay gained their elected civilian régimes rapidly in this way, while Bolivia, Chile and Paraguay had to wait a little longer. In the first three cases, internal political dynamics were undoubtedly prominent: the Argentinian army lost all legitimacy with its rout in the Falklands, the Brazilian army tried to pass the buck, and the Uruguayan army never achieved popular acceptance (the people rejected the proposed constitution submitted to referendum in 1980). But this return to democracy would not have been easy without US support. The case of Chile is a perfect illustration of this situation. In 1980 the constitution proposed by General Pinochet was largely approved by referendum, giving it an undeniable whiff of legitimacy. In 1988 he lost the referendum provided for in this same constitution and was therefore obliged to hold a presidential election in 1989. The US embassy then exercised its influence to the full to dissuade officers who were tempted not to recognise the results of the election. Meanwhile, it helped to reconstruct an opposition which was deeply fragmented – the classic situation in authoritarian régimes.

The latest North American military intervention on the continent, the invasion of Panama in December 1989, designed to get rid of a comic-opera dictator who was irritating the United States, was blessed with this double seal of ethics and of right. In many respects the military operation, baptised 'Just Cause' by George Bush, anticipated the 'Desert Storm' type of intervention in the Middle East:[8] constant concern for international public opinion before (presenting a very negative image of the enemy) and during the intervention (giving the illusion of a 'clean' operation without significant harm to civilians), requests for the support or understanding of partners (Soviet Union, the Organization of American States – OAS) and allies, speed of execution, limitation of objectives (ousting a dictator, regaining territory), etc.

Here again, comparisons setting George Bush the pragmatist against Ronald Reagan the ideologue may have been over-hasty. Like his predecessor, Bush set about bringing down Noriega, chasing the Sandinistas out of power in Nicaragua, and preventing an FMLN victory in El Salvador. He succeeded where his predecessor had failed, using the same methods but applying them in different countries. Military pressure was declared to be pointless in Nicaragua or El Salvador, so he substituted diplomatic pressure and the reconstruction of alternative political powers. Diplomatic and economic pressure and internal opposition had misfired in Panama, so he used

8. This type of operation had already been tried by Great Britain during the Falklands War. Cf. Virginia Gamba-Stonehouse, *The Falklands/Malvina War. A Model for North-South Crisis Prevention*, London, Pinter Publishers, 1987.

armed intervention instead. Following this success some wondered, in view of the appreciable reduction in credits granted to the zone, whether Central America was not 'on the point of returning to her traditional place in the list of priorities of US foreign policy: virtually at the bottom'.[9] The case of Panama included some factors which would also be present in the war against Iraq and which meant that that operation could in no way be compared to past interventions (contrary to the assertions of many Latin American commentators). These factors also appear in the developing new world order:[10] the reference to ethics, the call to respect human rights, particular consideration for the Soviet Union, concern for international public opinion.

The appeal to ethics, so prominent in the Gulf intervention, was a constant feature from the beginning of the Panama operation. In his televised addresses George Bush sought to 'demonise' Noriega, stressing his amorality and his involvement in drug trafficking, i.e. playing on two of the most sensitive registers of American public opinion. Certainly his adversary helped him, as in the case of Iraq, by piling up provocations ahead of the invasion and then disregarding the slow-burning international or Latin American reaction. The call for respect for rights and democratic legality appeared in the four objectives assigned to the US Marines. They had to: (1) overturn Noriega; (2) re-establish democracy (allowing the president elected in 1988 to assume his functions); (3) protect American citizens; (4) defend treaties concerning the canal.[11] Protection of US citizens is a traditional basis for American military interventions and one always emphasised in variations on the Monroe Doctrine; but the other three objectives established by George Bush are all related to rights. Noriega had to be overthrown because he did not respect his nation's legality and, furthermore, was under indictment by American justice. Democracy must be re-established: the American troops enthroned the legitimately elected president, taking his oath (at a US military base) within the first few hours of the invasion. Finally, the call to respect treaties referred to Noriega's recent nomination of a Canal administrator who was unwelcome to the United States

9. William M. Leogrande, 'From Reagan to Bush. The Transition in US Policy Toward Central America', *Journal of Latin American Studies*, 22 (3), October 1990, p. 621.

10. It is now customary to talk of the 'new international disorder' (the title, for example, shown in the review *Politique étrangère* on its publication in autumn 1991, no.3). One may wonder if this is a happy phrase at a time when, following the disappearance of many East-West confrontations in peripheral areas, it is the turn of infinitely more complicated conflicts to die down: Lebanon, Cambodia, the Israeli-Arab conflict. The Kurd drama, the Serbo-Croat war, the probable dissolution of many artificial multinational entities, cannot efface the knowledge that the old 'order' was in its day infinitely more murderous and oppressive for the people concerned than the current 'disorder'.

11. Cf. Georges Couffignal, 'L'intervention de décembre 1989 à Panama. 'Big stick', 'bulletin de vote' et 'mare nostrum'', *Hérodote*, April-June 1990, pp. 76–87.

(on 1 January 1990, according to the terms of the Carter-Torrijos agreement, the post was to be filled by an administrator who was initially to be nominated by Panama but who had to be approved by the United States).

The particular consideration granted to the USSR was necessary in order to prevent the conflict becoming international. The intervention began on 20 December 1989, just as Ceaucescu was hanging on to power in Romania, where the worst was feared. The United States let it be known officially that they would understand if Moscow intervened to force the Romanian dictator out of office. At the same time the French foreign minister, Roland Dumas, claimed a 'right to intervene' and a 'duty to help an endangered nation' – claims which would surface again later, on the liberation of Kuwait, the Kurd exodus and the EC attempts to prevent violence breaking out in Yugoslavia. Concern for international public opinion was in fact something of a novelty. From the beginning of the intervention George Bush and the Pentagon paid particular attention to the use of information aimed at American and foreign media. Possible reactions of allied governments must be anticipated (they were informed immediately, as were the principal chancelleries in Latin America), as were those of their peoples. The four objectives were achieved in satisfactory style, including (as later in the Gulf War) passing over in silence the realities of material damage and human losses among the enemy. A new conflict-management style had been tried successfully.

It can therefore be stated that the United States' relations with Latin America changed appreciably during the 1980s, probably permanently. Whereas previously in Washington's eyes American interests had long taken precedence over all other considerations, the primacy henceforward granted to matters of legal rights and democracy (which might have been no more than coincidental and likely to fade with the Sandinista defeat) was strengthened by the collapse of the Soviet bloc. Today – and this is a notable change for America – it is reasonable to suggest that there will be no more North American armed interventions against Latin-American nations led by democratically chosen governments, except in the very improbable case of a military threat against the United States (all Latin American nations have now ratified the Tlatelolco nuclear non-proliferation treaty of 1974).

With the fading of the military threat, political bonds are now tending to loosen just as, in contrast, those of the economy are tending to tighten under the effect of the economic crisis and the management of debt-related problems. (At the end of 1990 the debts for Latin America and the Caribbean together amounted to 423 billion dollars.)[12] Will economics no

12. UNECLA, 'Balance preliminar de la economia de América latina y el Caribe 1990', *Notas sobre la economia y el desarrollo,* 500–501, December 1990, p. 17.

longer lead politics? This is one of the many uncertainties of the present situation. Others are apparent within inter-American relationships, no longer from the United States point of view but from that of Latin America. There too the 1980s were decisive, engendering developments which may become part of the new world order in the long term. What yesterday was unequivocal is now complex, fluctuating, contradictory. The first characteristic of the new inter-American relationships, like the world order in which they occur, is to construct new ground rules which must include the emergence of a Latin American diplomacy.

The Birth of a Self-governing Latin American Diplomacy

Henry Kissinger once remarked that Latin America was an abstraction. His words emphasised the very great national diversity within the region, in all respects. Bolivarian dreams of unity may have sustained many fantasies but have never begun to be realised. The Pan American Union created in 1910 was no more than the buttress of US economic expansionism. The Organisation of American States created in 1948 was long notable chiefly for submitting to North American wishes. Fidel Castro's comment is well-known: when the majority of its members voted to expel Cuba in 1962 he observed that the organisation was the 'United States' colonial ministry'. Actual regional cooperation is minimal, despite a proliferation of organisations: FTALA, LAIA, ECLAC, UNECLA, PCLAPP, CACM, the Andean Pact, LAES, TIAA, etc.[13] On the other hand, most large South American countries had foreign policies which could on occasion be distinguished from that of the United States. Among them, only Mexico showed a steady wish for independence. She was the only nation, for example, never to break off relations with Fidel Castro despite American pressure. How else, in such conditions, can the coincidence of three apparently contradictory processes be explained: greater economic dependence on the North, greater political autonomy and the proliferation of genuine interstate agreements?

In 1983, faced with a regional conflagration fanned by Ronald Reagan's Central America policy, Mexico, Colombia, Venezuela and Panama set up the 'Contadora group' which for four years stubbornly sought for negotiated solutions to the Nicaraguan conflict. From the beginning the European

13. Free Trade Association of Latin America (1960), Latin American Integration Association (1980, sequel to the preceding body), Economic Commission for Latin America and the Caribbean, United Nations Economic Commission for Latin America, Permanent Conference of Latin American Political Parties, Central American Common Market (1960), Andean Pact (1969), Latin American Economic System (1975), Treaty for Inter-American Aid (1947). The list could be extended considerably by including all the specialised inter-regional bodies. None of them ever played an important role in achieving common action.

Community supported this undertaking, despite outspoken US hostility. In 1985 Contadora received the support of a four-nation pressure group (Argentina, Brazil, Peru, Uruguay), three of which had just returned to democracy. The significance of Contadora has never been sufficiently recognised. The first objective was to 'de-internationalise' a conflict which Ronald Reagan saw purely in terms of East-West confrontation, even though the Soviet Union showed no desire to become engaged in any depth.[14] 'De-internationalisation' of this conflict meant that it must first be 'regionalised' – in other words reduced to a regional scale. The group saw this as the only possible way to resolve the problem satisfactorily.

In this search to 'regionalise' the conflict, Contadora systematically exploited the international dimensions of its initiatives. Following the European Community, the OAS and UN Secretaries General gave their support. The European Community continued to show an interest in the region by signing aid and economic cooperation agreements in 1985 (the San José Agreements) which have been regularly renegotiated and renewed every year since then. As soon as so many institutions became concerned with its future, Central America ceased to be the backyard of the United States,[15] a new state of affairs illustrated by the Central American presidents' adoption in August 1987 of the plan proposed by Oscar Arias (the Esquipulas Plan). On the eve of the meeting of the heads of state, Ronald Reagan, who was hostile to the plan, sent a counter-proposal which was not even examined at their meeting. True, the Esquipulas Plan's objective (as has often been stressed) was essentially the same as that of the United States, to chase the Sandinistas out of power. The essential point in this argument is not what is left unspoken but the worldwide echo aroused by the Esquipulas Plan, an echo that was amplified by the Nobel Peace Prize awarded to its progenitor. The Esquipulas Plan's essential importance was also reflected in the provision made for the realisation of its various stages, which were to be verified by *ad hoc* international

14. Various works have shown that the Soviet Union always adopted a low profile in Central American conflicts. These observers include Nicola Miller, who in a heavily documented study of relations between the Soviet Union and Latin America stresses, with reference to Central America, that in contrast with Cuba, the Soviet Union had little interest in the region and from the beginning of the Reagan administration refused to be drawn into confrontation with the United States in this area. Although Soviet aid grew considerably between 1984 and 1986, it was above all to create a counter-balance to Afghanistan, in the possibility of a negotiation on spheres of influence. After 1987, and particularly from the beginning of the withdrawal of their troops from Afghanistan (15 May 1988), she indicated several times to Managua that the days of her aid were now numbered (cf. Nichola Miller, *Soviet Relations with Latin America*, Cambridge, Cambridge University Press, 1989, pp. 188–216).

15. Cf. Georges Couffignal, 'Amérique centrale, démocratie et relations internationales', in *Quel avenir pour la démocratie en Amérique latine?*, Paris, Editions du CNRS, 1989, pp. 73–83.

investigations. The 'backyard' was no longer the 'private hunting ground': on the one hand, the five Central American states followed eight Latin American states in confirming an impressive wish for autonomy; on the other, many nations in the outside world took an interest in an area which they had traditionally ignored. These leanings towards autonomy may appear to have genuinely faded since the electoral defeat of the Sandinistas and the election of new presidents in the five nations. Although the scale of the crisis reduced such overtures, no return to the status quo ante is now possible because the order in which it arose no longer exists. What we are seeing here is further proof of the ambivalence of the new inter-American relationships.

Even though the politico-strategic element has given way to the economic factor the developments of the past decade cannot vanish so easily, particularly because they have been reinforced by parallel economic and ideological developments further south. In economic matters the diversification within Latin America is modest but genuine and the widespread opening of frontiers should speed up the process. For the last ten years Japan, and to a lesser degree Germany, have had a sustained volume of investment in the area. In Africa, Brazil is now competing seriously with France, particularly in building infrastructures. During the whole period of the United States-decreed embargo on the Soviet Union following the invasion of Afghanistan, Argentina developed its former relationships with the Soviet Union and was for a time its premier supplier of cereals. As has been seen, the European Community has been cooperating with Central America and the Caribbean since 1985, and is now seeking to extend the scope of its relations.[16] Spain is investing heavily in the region and hopes, increasingly openly, to become the link between Europe and Latin America. But alongside this diversification of partners there have been some profound ideological mutations.

One of the greatest of these changes probably arises from Great Britain's victory in 1982 in the Falkland Islands, unexpectedly invaded and annexed by Argentina, who had always claimed sovereignty over them. The United States and most European nations supported Great Britain in this operation, while overall the Latin American states, the press and most political parties of the Left or the Right on the continent were wholeheartedly behind Argentina and her generals, even though in other respects the latter were undesirable company. This war has probably had a considerable effect on how Latin Americans see their relationship with the United

---

16. Instituto de Relaciones Europa-América latina, '¿Hacia una nueva relación con América Latina? Nuevos enfoques y desafíos', unpublished, and 'Relaciones Europa-América latina. Una agenda para los 90', Madrid, IRELA, 1989, unpublished.

States. The myth of the Monroe Doctrine, of 'America for the Americans', has been destroyed. In breaking with continental solidarity (which was in fact more imaginary than real) the United States released the Latin American states from an exclusively bilateral perception of their relations with Washington. Contadora, the 'pressure group' and the Esquipulas Plan bear witness to the end of this exclusive bilateralism; and confirmation that these regroupings were more than purely coincidental is to be found in their permanent establishment and proliferation since the disappearance of their original objective.

In Acapulco in December 1987 these eight nations, henceforward known as the 'Rio Group', implemented the Esquipulas Plan and adopted an 'Engagement for peace, development and democracy' to establish a permanent organisation for cooperation at the highest level. Significantly, this cooperation was designed to operate without the presence of the United States. The group has met periodically (Panama was not invited after 1988), and has enjoyed such success that many nations have demanded to be 'admitted' to a group which has no legal existence and which now consists of thirteen members. Its gatherings may be the occasion for official meetings with the representatives of other regional groups.[17] Elsewhere Mexico, Colombia and Venezuela, ex-members of Contadora, have formed a 'Group of Three' and as such have signed agreements of cooperation.[18] Demonstrating independence when North America was increasing the pressure on Cuba, the group invited Fidel Castro to participate in one of its meetings at Caracas in November 1991, to consider possible solutions to the Cuban energy problem. In the same order of ideas the Esquipulas Plan introduced regular summits of Central American heads of state or vice-presidents, meetings which continued after peace had been achieved in Nicaragua and new presidents had been elected in each of these nations.

All this took place as if the existing structures (OAS, LAIA, CACM, etc.) were considered inappropriate for the current needs for cooperation, so that legally informal and unbureaucratic structures were created to encourage direct contacts rather than the elaboration of texts. Far from producing chaos, the loosening of the world order here appears to have created more widely based procedures for encounters, cooperation and regrouping between partners who, if not equal, are at least concerned to

17. On 12 April 1990, for example, the Rio Group met the chancellors of Central and Eastern European nations in order to match experiences and problems.

18. At the time of the Central American nations' meeting with the European Community and the Contadora Group in July 1989 (San José V), during which the creation of the 'Group of Three' was made official, the Group signed an accord of positive cooperation with the five nations of Central America (see the text in *Revista Mexicana de Politica Exterior*, 7 (28), Autumn 1990, pp. 77–8).

avoid creating other forms of political dependence or becoming trapped in constricting judicial frameworks, thereby retaining the freedom to diversify relationships inside or outside the American continent. It is thus truly a new inter-American order that is being constructed in this new world order.

Towards a New Inter-American Order

One cannot but be amazed at this proliferation of groups and gatherings, as every possible opportunity for informal meeting is promptly seized. Investiture ceremonies for a newly elected president are used as meeting points for heads of state.[19] In July 1991, at the invitation of Mexico, all were present at the first summit meeting of the Latin American heads of state with those of Spain and Portugal, to prepare the ceremonies marking the fifth centenary of the discovery of America. It was an occasion of many intense bilateral exchanges, particularly with Fidel Castro; it showed that Latin America is now seeking a peaceful solution to the inevitable fall of his régime. The principle of annual meetings was adopted here: there were to be meetings in 1992 in Spain and in 1993 in Brazil. This passion for regional or subregional meetings, outside any formal structure, is entirely new. It marks the end of the traditional dual relationship with the United States, which persisted within OAS-type organisations. The new pattern is one of groupings which also aim to avoid isolated approaches to future negotiations with the United States.

They were all thinking of George Bush's 'Enterprise for the Americas' initiative, launched in June 1990, which planned for the creation of a 'common market from Alaska to Tierra del Fuego'.[20] The proposition was threefold, aimed at a global free-trade agreement for Latin America, the creation of a multilateral investment fund supported by the IBRD (International Bank for Reconstruction and Development) and the World Bank to finance privatisation and development, and finally the use of money due to the North American government (a public debt of only 12 billion dollars) to finance environmental protection. In associating debt, investments and trade in a new way, the proposal seeks, through this immense potential

19. Thus they allowed Fidel Castro to make his first visits to the continent for a long time, notably for the investiture of Carlos Salinas de Gortari in Mexico and Rodrigo Borja in Ecuador.

20. This 'Enterprise' corresponded to the interest shown by George Bush in Latin America from the moment he took office. Cf. David C. Jordan, 'The Emerging of Latin American Policy of the Bush Administration', *Strategic Review*, Summer 1989, p. 21–31. See also Thomas Carothers, *The United States and Latin America after the Cold War*, Washington, Wilson Center, Working Paper no. 184, 1990.

market, a return to economic health from the present weakness in the face of European and Japanese competition. To achieve it, Latin American economies must escape from the present crisis. All have committed themselves to the route towards 'structural adjustments', with greater (Mexico) or lesser (Brazil) determination. Among the great nations of the region several have regained health and dynamism, although at enormous social cost (Chile, Venezuela, Colombia, Argentina, Mexico). Others remain less certain (Brazil, Bolivia), while clearer skies are beginning to appear for some (Peru, Nicaragua). Concerning debts, the application of the 'Brady Plan' has made it possible to relieve the repayments burden and in 1990, during a visit to the southern latitudes of the subcontinent, George Bush announced the cancellation of certain debts for the most heavily indebted nations.[21] Will this great market come into being? The thinking behind the proposition must survive the president who formulated it. One way or another, Latin America (or certain Latin American countries) constitutes a trump-card for the United States in the contest of economic blocs.

The announcement of this 'Enterprise for the Americas' has not to date been followed up by any dramatic propositions, the United States having been absorbed with preparations for the great North American market with Mexico and Canada. In 1991 the Americas Investment Fund was still in limbo but the project appears in all commentaries and the Latin-American states know that it is one of the possible routes to their future development. Furthermore, it was clearly in order to approach the negotiations in the most advantageous way that regroupings speeded up in 1991. In March of that year Argentina, Brazil, Uruguay and Paraguay signed the Asunción Treaty which created a free exchange zone to be called 'Mercosur' with effect from 1 January 1995, for more than 200 million consumers and a GNP greater than that of China. In the light of the history of these nations, which has been marked by frontier disputes or constant political tension, the change is remarkable; the ground had been prepared for it by the signature in 1986 of a 'programme of integration' of the Brazilian and Argentinian economies. The president of Brazil, José Sarney spoke without dissembling in his comments on the Treaty: 'Brazil, Argentina and Uruguay are opening up a vision for all the other countries of Latin America: implementing active integration means not having integration imposed. On their own, our nations change nothing in the world order, but together we shall gradually be able to affect international decisions.' Alongside this major regrouping, decisions for the progressive cre-

21. It should be noted here that, as far as we know, no president of the United States had travelled to this southern part of Latin America since John F. Kennedy. George Bush also undertook two other visits to the region. He clearly showed much interest in the continent.

ation of free-trade zones (taking between one and six years) have gone well: in January 1991 between Mexico and the five nations of Central America, in April between the member nations of the 'Group of Three', in May between the members of the Andean Pact (Venezuela, Colombia, Ecuador, Peru, Bolivia). As the economies of these countries appeared to be too different from each other, Colombia and Venezuela decided at the beginning of 1992 to go ahead alone; they drew up a bilateral programme for the integration of their economies. Finally, in December, the thirteen nations of the 'Rio Group' decided to create between them a total free-trade zone by the end of the decade at the latest.

The proliferation of these agreements and the speed of their introduction may raise doubts as to their actual implementation on the dates proposed; nevertheless, they show that the continent is on the move, is redefining itself, is discovering areas of cooperation. The only nation that remains outside these collective rearrangements, Chile, prefers for the moment to go on emphasising its bilateral relationships (in September 1991 it signed a free-trade agreement with Mexico) and above all concentrating on the delicate reconstruction of consensual democracy.[22] In the case of Mexico analysis is far more ambiguous and complex, with multilateral factors operating to serve bilateral relations.

Before being elected both George Bush and Carlos Salinas de Gortari announced their intention to bring Mexico into the proposed common market with Canada. This meant overcoming serious obstacles relating to trade unions in the United States (because of low Mexican wage-rates) and ideology in Mexico (where anti-Americanism, even hatred of the *gringo*, has long formed part of the national identity). Furthermore, Canada was hostile to the plan. The United States interest was threefold: to ensure secure access to Mexican oil, to integrate the already largely complementary economies (Mexico is their third largest trading partner) and to relocate labour-intensive companies south of the Rio Grande, where hourly wage rates are twelve times lower. The stake is to win back their lost competitiveness through this potential market of 360 million consumers (the European Common Market has only 326 million). Mexico in turn hopes above all for an influx of investors attracted by the vision of this vast market, who will stimulate growth and resolve problems of unemployment.[23] Negotiations began in 1991 and the North American Free Trade Agreement (NAFTA) was signed in August 1992, before the accomplishment of the great European market.

22. Cf. the studies analysed by Paulo J. Krischke, 'Chile Reinvents the Democracy', *Latin American Research Review*, 25 (3), 1990, pp. 221–37.

23. Cf. the studies assembled by Gustav Vega Cánovas (ed.), *México ante el libre comercio con América del Norte*, Mexico, El Colegio de México, 1991.

This budding market completely upsets analytical data for the continent. Mexico traditionally took care to preserve an equal distance between the United States and Latin America. She played on her cultural links with Spanish America to avoid being absorbed by the all-powerful Anglo-Saxon America, her principal trading partner and work-place for millions of her people, whether as legal seasonal workers or as clandestine immigrants. Alliance with the South, whether geographic or economic, was always resisted, being of little interest and not to be trusted. Mexico's absence from membership of the Latin Union is proof of this, although all the other nations of the subcontinent belong to it. Further evidence of Mexico's reluctance to ally herself with the South lies in her refusal to join OPEC (in contrast to Venezuela), or again in the very low number of centres for research into Latin America in Mexican universities, despite their proliferation in the United States and elsewhere in the world. Standing upon the dignity of her independence, Mexico was the only nation which always showed off her difference within the OAS, refusing to accede to North American pressure or injunctions at times of great crisis in the continent (Guatemala in 1954, Cuba in 1962, Nicaragua in 1982). She flirted briefly with Third World ideologies during the 1970s (under the presidencies of Luis Echeverria and José Luis Portillo), but this did not survive the economic crisis. As we have seen with the Contadora Group, Mexico quickly returned to the traditional foundations of her diplomacy, with the addition of greater multilateralism and greater purpose.[24]

How then should we judge the current situation, which sees Mexico resolutely plunging into the economic and ideological adventure of the great North American market but also multiplying Latin American initiatives and involvement? It is clear that Mexico's future lies with the United States, her major trading partner and the home of between 8 and 10 million of her citizens. The Mexican people understand this well, having in less than four years (1988–92) not only grown used to the notion of the great market but also for the most part having learned to approve of it. The Mexican government had two trump-cards in the negotiations: the first was Mexico's spectacular economic recovery and her recovered confidence in investment. The second was the Latin American card, which was successfully exploited by Salinas. Here too we can see the ambivalence of this new inter-American order, an ambivalence that is also visible in other Latin

24. A great deal has been written on Mexican foreign policy and United States–Mexico relations. Three classic works should be mentioned, which display well the complexity of these relations: Mario Ojeda, *Alcances y limites de la politica exterior de México*, Mexico City, El Colegio de México, 1976 and *El surgimiento de una politica exterior activa*, Mexico City, SEP, 1986; Jorge G. Castañeda and Robert A. Pastor, *Limits to Friendship: The United States and Mexico*, New York, Knopf, 1988.

American nations and which is a direct consequence of the loosening created by the disappearance of East-West competition.

Ideological Void and Ambivalent Relationships

The explanation for the ideological void which characterises the current period lies at least as much in the economic crisis as in the scale and speed of the changes affecting most of Latin America. Internally, representative democracy is clearly here to stay; but it is accompanied by extremely high rates of electoral abstention almost everywhere, not excluding those countries where voting is obligatory. The path to democracy is probably still very long.[25] Perhaps, as Albert Hirschman suggested,[26] it may take root in the social reforms which the upper middle classes can no longer defer locally under the pretext of the communist threat? For the moment, political democracy has not brought about social democracy. In fact there appears to be a complete lack of connection between the logics of politics and economics which are customarily perceived as being linked. The world time which establishes a direct relationship between the market, development and democracy is appearing here according to very different rhythms. Representative democracy has taken over everywhere with an enthusiasm which soon lapsed, without apparently following the path to which Alexis de Tocqueville linked it indissolubly – that of equality. The market has taken root very quickly, destroying existing state or corporatist structures without allowing time for other structures to emerge. Social differences are more marked than ever before and the economic hierarchy of the various nations has been completely overturned during the last ten years. What we are witnessing, in fact, is the growth of what the Latin Americans call 'ungovernability': the impossibility for governments (or states) to manage society or even the economy.[27] The dizzy growth of alternative economies, the dynamism, in many nations, of associative movements which regulate society outside traditional structures, the growing importance of new powers (including those linked to drugs), demonstrate an increasing breakdown of the links between political power and civil society.

One of the many current paradoxes is thus that social divisions which in

25. Cf. my study 'A quoi sert le vote en Amérique latine?' in Georges Couffignal (ed.), *Réinventer la démocratie. Le défi latino-américain*, Paris, Presses de la Fondation nationale des sciences politiques, 1992.

26. Albert O. Hirschman, 'Un sage et salutaire abandon. Les événements de l'Est et les pays du Sud', *Esprit*, 11, November 1990, pp. 63–9.

27. On the concept of 'governability', see the chapter on this topic by Jean Leca in Jean Leca, Roberto Papini (ed.), *Les démocraties sont-elles gouvernables?*, Paris, Economica, 1985, p. 15–29.

the past led to political tensions are tending to increase under the effect of 'structural adjustments', while political divisions are concurrently fading. Guerrilla forces have laid down their arms in Nicaragua, Colombia, El Salvador and Chile, or negotiated a place for themselves in the legal political game, as in Guatemala and Colombia. The single exception is Peru. Armies or governments here and there (Venezuela, Peru) may still be tempted to launch *putschs* to combat corruption or in response to popular disenchantment, but in the absence of any exterior support, either from within South America or from elsewhere, these are only peripheral events. By eliminating such points of outside reference, either as inspiration or for rejection, the end of the Cold War has restored purpose to natural geopolitical bonds. Central America, the southern portion of South America and the Andean region are attempting to construct homogeneous entities ready for dialogue with the forthcoming North American ensemble. Mexico is establishing herself in a North America to which she belongs geographically. Ties between the North and the South of the continent have largely lost the passion which characterised them for so long. Anti-Americanism, contrary to many expectations, did not spread after the Falklands War. Furthermore, indeed, the Peronist president of Argentina (Peron had been one of the great bullies of 'Yankee imperialism') does not know how to anticipate American aims. On all sides the United States hegemony now appears to be acknowledged and accepted.

Yet it remains difficult to eliminate decades of distrust and incomprehension. Do the United States loom too large? There are negative popular reactions. It is certainly significant that the massive support given by the United States to certain candidates or groups in electoral contests does not necessarily ensure their victory, as was seen in the 1990 and 1991 elections in Central America and Peru. This new variation on the Monroe Doctrine, which could well be called 'ballot-paper diplomacy' is, in the final analysis, less reliable than its predecessors. One may also wonder whether anti-American movements may not in the end resurface in the internal politics of many nations in the face of the omnipresent United States, when they are incapable of even maintaining their economies at a satisfactory level of prosperity. In such conditions hegemony is perceived only as a sanction, with all the potential ensuing frustrations. The case of Central America is the most obvious, but in Argentina also the American ambassador is known in the press as the 'viceroy', referring to the colonial period. Yet, apart from sporadic outbreaks of revolt, American ideological victory and economic domination currently produce only political passivity among peoples who have a greater tendency to turn inwards to the micro-society. On the other hand their rulers, who realise that there is now an alternative to 'America for the Americans' (for Europe is concentrating too heavily on its centre and its East) are stirring themselves into cooperation, as we have already seen, and are establishing new groups, with Mexico seeking to become the link between the two Americas.

The present period is characterised at the same time by a strengthening of economic links and a loosening of political ties. This complex blend of greater dependence and greater autonomy is perfectly illustrated by the struggle against the manufacture and distribution of cocaine. Washington has not stinted in its efforts to persuade the producing nations, where traffickers have sometimes won excessive power and openly defy the state, to aim at eradicating the drugs trade. The year 1990 was an unprecedented one for the Colombian and American authorities in their war against the 'Medellin Cartel', with several of its leaders being killed or arrested and extradited to the United States. Public opinion was stirred by the growing militarisation of Colombian society, with the dependence on American military counsellors. In June 1991 the Colombian constituent assembly decided to make non-extradition a constitutional principle, in open defiance of the United States. In Peru president Alberto Fujimori, engaged in the struggle against the Shining Path, had no wish to accept American aid, despite the guerrilla movement's links with the drugs trade. Yet the Peruvian economy has been bled white and, having initially refused, Fujimori has had to agree to cooperate in the struggle against drugs in return for being granted new credits.

Will this hinder the expansion of the coca crop and trade? It seems doubtful. The Drug Enforcement Administration estimated that cocaine production in South America was 361 tonnes in 1988, 685 tonnes in 1989 and 900 tonnes in 1990. It is difficult to see how this increase in production can be halted, since, like any product, cocaine is subject to market forces (and demand is growing), its growth is difficult to observe and most of the producing nations have weak governments. The struggle against drugs may acquire a different meaning, which appeared in the second 'Drug Summit' in Houston in 1992: it may make possible the tightening of political bonds which have been visibly relaxed. This has probably been noted by Colombia and Peru, perhaps ahead of similar developments in the other producing countries and those which operate as staging posts for the distribution or laundering of drug funds. (In 1991 growers demonstrated in Bolivia.) All the Latin American nations have, sometimes reluctantly, agreed to 'structural adjustments' in their economy; they have observed that such adjustments, in view of the loosening of the world order, did not prevent them from acquiring formerly non-existent areas of autonomy and it is doubtful whether they would accept the loss of such areas for the sake of the struggle against a harvest which injects attractive sums of money into their economies. Growers and traffickers must however recognise the limits beyond which they must not pass, those where the state authority is openly flouted. No one can doubt that the example of Medellin will be pondered on. In Colombia the Cali cartel has avoided the errors of its rival: it has not been disturbed and is developing unhindered.

An unchallenged North American hegemony, but with a relaxation of political ties; the wish to define a new continental order, but increasing 'ungovernability' in many countries; massive electoral commitment, but the election of undesirable candidates; proposals for continental economic cooperation, but the creation of regional subgroups and attempts at diversification of trading partners; imposition of the struggle against drugs, but demonstrations of autonomy relating to the struggle; the highly ambiguous linchpin position of Mexico in the current patterns of rearrangement – the inter-American system is indeed, like the world order, loosened. Its entities are both more autonomous and more interdependent. The American continent certainly has a centre, but there is no automatic implication that the peripheral areas surrounding this centre are always dependent on it.[28] In other words, now and for the future inter-American relationships are no longer what they used to be.

28. Here I have adopted the image used by Jean Leca in the presentation text of the World Congress of Political Science which was held in 1991 in Buenos Aires.

9 AFRICA: ADJUSTMENT AND CONDITIONALITY

FRANÇOIS CONSTANTIN

A common theme runs through virtually all the projections made in the last two years concerning the post-communist world order where they deal with Africa south of the Sahara. The area appears to be evoked in order to stress its transience or even decrepitude, as if some curse of dubious scientific basis had been laid on political analysis of the whole continent. Ignored by theoreticians of power politics until, like Kissinger, they were forced to pay attention to it on becoming advisers to heads of state,[1] discredited by the militant attackers of imperialism whose dialectical reasoning proved Africa's impotence in international society,[2] an anachronism in the era of nuclear deterrence and computer-assisted war, Africa has always appeared to exist only as a reminder, always the subject, the stake, the victim, and never a genuine actor.

The circumstances of the late 1980s are irrefutable. The generalised decline in standards of living among African peoples, and therefore in the material and symbolic capacity of African actors, both internationally and internally, is an established fact of daily life as well as of statistics. The leading analyses and attitudes, however, often fall into the trap of generalisation and theoretical projections, which transform intolerable hard facts (famine, violence) spread unevenly across the continent, into stern structural data. The scholarly report of a death foretold regards the significance of the terrain, the substratum or African humanity as negligible or even aggravating factors.

1. They had to plunge into the whole mass of problems relating to southern Africa: Portuguese decolonisation, the fight for liberation in Rhodesia, the place of South Africa in the American diplomatic system. See Zaki Laïdi, *The Superpowers and Africa. The Constraints of a Rivalry, 1960–1990*, Chicago, University of Chicago Press, 1990.

2. The endurance of this tradition is confirmed in the collection of essays edited by Bade Onimode, *The IMF, the World Bank and the African Debt*, 2 vols, London, Zed Books, 1989. See Douglas Rimmer's critique, 'External Debt and Structural Adjustment in Tropical Africa', *African Affairs*, 89 (355), 1990, pp.283–91.

There is a certain Manicheism in many analyses of North-South relations. The rigour of economic reasoning has taken over from the stereotypes of the Cold War. However essential, this dominant neo-materialism which concentrates on quantitative variables should always be seen as only one approach among others; it is also necessary to reason in qualitative terms in order to avoid reducing to an immediate problem of inadequate resources (in a specific area such as finance) something which may partly be a problem of political mismanagement.[3]

Internationalist political analysis is traditionally handicapped by the urge towards globalisation. To speak of 'Africa' (even limiting discussion to Africa south of the Sahara) is a bold but inevitable simplification, whether Africa is regarded as an actor or a single indivisible subject. Whatever common traits may be identified – including international ones – Africa is a plural entity and all generalisations are open to refutation on well-founded particularistic grounds: Nigeria is not the Niger and widespread poverty does not exclude poles of relative wealth (Botswana). Similarly, to make the 'state' the chief actor is convenient but expresses only part of the truth and something of a fiction when sovereignty is breaking down throughout the world and transnationality in all its forms is prospering.[4] To concentrate only on Africa, the state actor – in principle of course the government – is only one of the protagonists in the international relations being created every day by various public and private actors (businessmen, traders, individuals, etc.), not all of whom respect state or international norms.[5]

Another problem is the loss of a sense of relativity beneath the apparent rigour of the quantitative: the wealth of (approximate) statistical data may create a mirage effect.[6] The accumulation of figures gives a promise of truth and is a temptation to engage in futurist scientific projections which announce either growth or decline; yet over the years it can be seen that the scientifically produced plans of groups of national or international experts can be contradicted by the same experts. Past fluctuations in eternal truths concerning development prospects encourage prudence in the

3. An analysis of this approach can be seen in UNDP, *Human Development Report*, Oxford, Oxford University Press, 1990.

4. See for example David P. Rapkin (ed.), *World Leadership and Hegemony*, Boulder, Lynne Rienner Publ., 1990; R. B. J. Walker, Saul H. Mendlovitz (eds), *Contending Sovereignties. Redefining Political Community*, Boulder, Lynne Rienner Publ., 1990; Robert H. Jackson, *Quasi States. Sovereignty, International Relations and the Third World*, Cambridge, Cambridge University Press, 1991.

5. See 'L'Afrique sans frontière', *Politique africaine*, 9, March 1983; Daniel C. Bach and Olivier Vallée, 'L'intégration régionale. Espaces politiques et marchés parallèles', *Politique africaine*, 39, September 1990, pp. 68–78.

6. Is it better to live in the Zambian copper belt (GNP per head: 390 US dollars in 1989) or rural Burundi (GNP per head: 220 US dollars in 1989)?

face of current certainties, even when they are supported by figures.[7] And although catastrophe theory may be a political method for mobilising energy, it may equally be a motive for discouragement and distrust.

Certainly, the dilapidated infrastructures and social conditions in much of Africa require the internationalist to pay more serious attention to actual national living conditions. The futility of some diplomatic-ideological arguments (who is supporting whom in the struggles between armed gangs in Liberia?) justifies this reassessment, provided it does not simply become the latest fashion. Knowledge of business strategies is one element in an understanding of local, regional, continental and intercontinental dynamics; yet this should not mean emptying the world of emotions, representations and beliefs and returning to the backward thinking of the 1960s, which confused the crisis of Marxism with the end of ideology. On its own terms, Africa is a place for business, but also for imagination, international sympathies, the creation and diffusion of purpose (religious networks, Western-style élitist socialisation, etc.), the effects of which may otherwise prove more durable than the eye-catching activities of some successful and high-profile personalities.

The criteria for appreciating Africa's place in the international dynamic cannot be reduced to stock-exchange fluctuations – analysts of international financial markets may resemble the 1960s nuclear strategy experts who saw Africa, which was virtually without nuclear weapons, as unworthy of consideration. In theory the changes in the East will bring the continent even lower because money hitherto destined for Africa will now be redirected to Eastern Europe.[8] According to the methodological propositions of, for example, Achille Mbembe or Jean Coussy,[9] any research into Africa's place in the world order should question the relevance of such perspectives produced by the centres of the international system. Behind their genuine expertise they may be suspected of creating a new ideology which does not meet the demands of scientific advance and, in the worst cases, of reviving ancient racist demons.

7. See, for a self-critique, the World Bank, *World Development Report, 1991. The Challenge of Development*, Oxford, Oxford University Press, 1991. Cf. also Christian Coméliau, 'Les impasses de l'économisme', in *La paix des grands, l'espoir des pauvres*, Paris, La Découverte/Le Monde, 1989, pp. 185–91; *Le Monde*, 29 May 1991; Zaki Laïdi, 'Berlin-Koweit. Les rapports Nord-Sud après la double secousse', *Politique étrangère*, 2, 1991

8. The point was made by Zaki Laïdi in 'La crainte d'une éviction au Sud par l'Est est-elle fondée?', *Marchés tropicaux*, 14 September 1990, pp. 2569–72.

9. Achille Mbembe, 'Pouvoir, violence et accumulation', *Politique africaine*, 39, September 1990, pp. 5–6; Jean Coussy, 'L'impact des ressources extérieures sur les Etats en voie de développement' in Daniel Pécaud and Bernard Sorj (eds), *Métamorphoses de la représentation politique au Brésil et en Europe*, Paris, Editions du CNRS, 1991, pp. 173–4.

With the dismantling of the Eastern bloc the African governments are caught in a paradox. The loosening of the world order may mean their increased marginalisation in the international system as the great powers turn their attention towards Eastern Europe; but this demotion will not necessarily mean being ignored and gaining greater freedom of action. In fact, in view of deteriorating economic conditions and the continued existence of foreign interests at stake in the continent, the African governments are exposed to a more closely supervised structural adjustment combined with political conditions imposed on them by the World Bank and the Western powers without any credible or reliable alternative being available. In this respect the world order is for them less relaxed than ever. Thus, while the possibilities of manoeuvre opened up by bipolarity have led to a world crisis, the new order is manifested as a reshaping of African dependence. Yet, theoretically, new initiatives may emerge from today's (possibly intensified) marginalisation which could form the basis of an effective regrouping.

The Faded Flowers of Bipolarity

The world in which the African peoples achieved international sovereignty contained two opposing visions of the ideal society, under the protection of two creators of purpose and power supported by unrivalled means of intervention: the United States and the Soviet Union. Competing anticolonialist demagogues, they set themselves up as models of political, economic and social development struggling in the global ideological market-place.

This emphasis on ideological action in building international hierarchies strengthened African leaders in their determination to assert, beyond formal independence, African autonomy and the contribution of African nations to world affairs. Although they lacked the material reserves necessary for genuine power, it seemed possible for them to compete on the intellectual terrain of creating purpose. The new nations' fresh view of the old world which made colonialism possible might achieve a profound reform of this excessively inegalitarian world order. Even after they had called on the extended resources of the Third World network, the attempt was a slow business. Pragmatists determined to create local power in the shadow of international hierarchies took over from the visionaries: but the guarantees of clientelism[10] could only operate inside a closed system (such as Franco-African cooperation), and in the long run the globalisation of strategies and economic variations which was a characteristic of the post-war period destroyed this strategy.

10. On international clientelism, see François Constantin and Christian Coulon, 'La difficile décolonisation de la diplomatie africaine', in *L'évolution récente du pouvoir en Afrique noire*, Bordeaux, CEAN-IEP, 1977, pp. 219–36; S. N. Eisenstadt and René Lemarchand (eds), *Political Clientelism, Patronage and Development*, London, Sage, 1981.

The African Creation of Purpose

In the nationalist pressure for independence, many African leaders expected to take an active part in the debates shaping the world. Unable to act with material strength against major powers armed with weapons of a different kind, they developed local initiatives to create purpose and to define a new world time. There were even secret hopes that this would mean a relative increase in power, for individuals or for Africa, if only as a result of the expected downgrading of the traditional great powers, which had already begun with the defeat of colonialism. This policy was apparent in Nkrumah's speeches on African unity and the liberation of oppressed peoples; it was also articulated, less actively but equally significantly, in Senghor's references to black culture or Nyerere's teaching on African socialism.

Approval of anticolonialism and indictment of the South African racist system were effective: between 1960 and 1990 the political map of Africa changed profoundly and apartheid finally melted away. Lacking her own power, Africa used the institutional resources of the international order (the United Nations in this case) to impose purpose and action. Politically and diplomatically, success was never in doubt, but it must be remembered that it was achieved not only with the support of the Third World as a whole but also with the cooperation of the United States and the Soviet Union.

In the absence of such cooperation, other attempts at world revolution through the creation of new purpose came to a halt. The radical critique of the international order stated in Latin American theories of dependence showed that political independence left the fundamental structure of hierarchies and world domination unaltered. Similarly, the subtle tactics of Nasser and Nehru, the masters of neutralism who manipulated the ambitions of the great powers to strengthen their own material resources on the most advantageous terms and conserve their enlarged internal and international autonomy, ended in their accepting the bipolar and imperial nature of the international system and not breaking it.

Certainly no one seriously foresaw a reversal of the military order simply because of the efforts of the united non-aligned governments. Illusions were more serious during the 1970s when these nations attacked the New International Economic Order (NIEO). Certain African governments promptly tried to revise their cooperation agreements with France, notably in monetary matters;[11] but the anticipated radical changes did not materialise despite mobilisation of the Group of 77 in the UNCTAD (United Nations Conference on Trade and Development) or the UN

---

11. Renegotiation of the agreements had to be undertaken in 1973–4, particularly with Niger, Mauritania and Madagascar, when the two last-named left the franc zone.

General Assembly. Insofar as it is possible to identify Africa's contribution to this failed debate, it may be that the setback arose primarily – in contrast to anticolonial action – because the values and principles of interventionism and egalitarianism underlying the African claims were rejected by the holders of the world order, who represented hierarchy and market freedom. It also arose from the weak mobilisation of the less poor African states, such as Nigeria, Zaire and the Ivory Coast, which acted in accordance with other logics and other, more effective alignments: OPEC for Nigeria, or forms of clientelism linked to the strength of the United States or France.[12] Finally, it arose from the fact that time is short and that while the debate continues the conditions to be faced in the field are deteriorating.

Virtually nothing survives from this attempt at innovation except do-it-yourself efforts and baroque constructions such as the scientific socialism of Siad Barre, the political liberalism of Daniel Arap Moi or Benin's Marxism-Leninism. The borrowing of schemes from East and West (the centralism of the Democratic Party of the Ivory Coast, parastatals developing in 'liberal' economic systems, etc.) indicated attempts to respond to local problems of order or employment rather than subjugation to Washington or Moscow. The increased range of accessible frames of reference also made it possible to distort a dominant traditionalism, notably among first generation leaders who are more at ease in the familiarity of the renewed dependence of clientelism (the French Community, the British Commonwealth) than in fresh ventures.

It was possible to be devious on the East-West ideological front (an attitude of moderation for Paris, militancy for Moscow), but mobility was much more difficult to achieve on the North-South axis, which creates roles within an international framework and is a source of power in the statist system.

The Clientelist Option

The internationalist may question the practice of 'voluntary servitude'. Temptations to subvert the clientelist system have proved futile not only because of the great powers' capacity for survival but also because few of the holders of power are inclined to disturb the order that forms the basis of their status. The legitimacy of government in new state-systems – if not of the state-systems themselves – is based as much on the acknowledgement and support of the international community as on domestic support;

---

12. In the case of Nigeria, substantial internal constraints also come into play. On this weakness of the American presence, cf. Marie-Claude Smouts, 'L'Afrique dans la diplomatie multi-latérale', *Etudes internationales*, 22 (2), June 1991, pp. 267–78.

the former is capable, at least temporarily, of mitigating the failures of the latter, as in Uganda between 1979 and 1985. In cases of internal contradictions or incapacity in former colonial capitals, one or other of the guardians of the world order managed to use their power and reputation to maintain the respectability or, at least, the effectiveness of more or less authoritarian African governments (e.g. that of Mobutu in Zaire).

The policy of cooperation was one of redistribution, the transfer of public and private funds, military and other materials, communications and other technologies to make the government better known and better respected, if not better admired by its subjects. This internal function of foreign policy explains the widespread preference for a clientelist strategy, renewing old colonial North-South vertical networks within a normative context of sovereign and equal states. The powerful personalisation of power in both North and South, and the élites' shared experiences of socialisation, helped to sustain an approach to external relations which combined the purpose of public (or even private) affairs and attitudes to the greatest advantage of the protagonists. Despite certain vicissitudes (the abandonment of embarrassing allies, such as F. Youlou or M. Yameogo, by France, the treatment of apartheid in the Commonwealth), clientelism responded to the expectations of African clients. It appeared to guarantee them privileged political, military, financial or monetary protection in return for sustaining structures of exchange and economic dependence which would bring public and private operators together to achieve a surplus. The stakes at issue consisted fundamentally of negotiating the share-out most likely to satisfy everyone concerned.

Governments that had been left without an effective and/or legitimising patron by the historical circumstances of colonisation (Ethiopia, Zaire, the Portuguese colonies, etc.) adopted a coded political language and ritualised measures enabling them to attract or retain the benign attention of Washington or Moscow. This provided the superpowers with an opportunity to bring Africa into the Cold War, in total contradiction to their repeated declarations of neutralism concerning Africa, and brought about something that was not self-evident initially, the subordination of African conflicts to the vicissitudes of East-West confrontation.

The perverse effects and risks of the clientelist relationship were substantially underestimated, as if the leaders' political horizon were restricted to the imperatives of holding on to power.

A Time for Regrets

The over-politicisation of purely African concerns appears to have been one of these perverse effects. On the eve of the great upheavals of the late

1980s it seemed that the African leaders had achieved only limited success. They had thought that the major rules of the international order were decided within the universal international organisations where decisions are taken on a majority basis. The law of the greatest number carried the day for Africa and the Third World; but the democracy of the UN system is a mere delusion. The repeated triumphs in the full sessions produce only 'recommendations', with the true decisions being taken either in the Security Council, under the influence of the great powers (which wield the power of veto) or within financial institutions such as the IMF or the World Bank. These are still hierarchical organisations, with votes weighted according to the financial strength of the member nations. Popular political sovereignty was therefore not enough to achieve independence of action in international society. In drawing up the fundamental principles of the world order after 1945, the great powers (with the United States and the Soviet Union at their head) had no wish to see it either genuinely democratic or genuinely egalitarian. The participation of African delegations in the great international organisations created an illusion; the essence of power remained elsewhere.

Voluntarist declarations to the effect that, once independence was gained, Africa would be for the Africans and no longer the theatre of imperialist confrontation, were equally illusory, a political ambition asserted firmly against a background of generalised dependence which immediately proved misguided. The emblems of sovereignty, such as state ceremonial, banners, armies, ambassadors, did little to disguise the clientelist choice or the increasingly urgent and increasingly obvious recourse to humiliating external support. Such assistance might be needed to make ends meet financially (contributions towards balancing the budget) or simply to feed the populace (emergency food aid). Africa was still not genuinely for the Africans.

The illusion lay in believing the assertions that the way out of these difficulties was partly political: authoritarian rule for development. This philosophy was astonishingly widespread and was expounded, listened to and accepted throughout the world. Priority was therefore given to the objective of reinforcing power, i.e. to politico-military aid. But, with the strong personalisation of politics, policies of development aid were led astray into logics of patronage, thus sustaining power among leading families whose loyalty could be bartered among the major operators in the world market and the international order.

In due course, therefore, ambitions were reduced to the immediate political imperative (to remain in power), under various guises taken either from African cultures (Zairean or Togolese 'authenticity') or from the world ideological market and international monetary and financial flexibility. Nervousness among the élites over the outward appearance of immediate power accentuated a catastrophic dialectic, because it combined a growing identification with the norms proclaimed by the North in its poles of liberal capitalism and Marxism-Leninism with a growing tendency towards decoupling from African cultures whose styles of thinking, acting and operating have been pushed to the periphery of the 'historical post-colonial bloc'.[13]

The broken bipolarity of the world order, the result of the Eastern pole's 'implosion', had the immediate effect of clarifying facts concealed by summary ideological discourse: the stakes in Africa were not, as incompetent political actors and commentators insisted on stating, a struggle between 'liberal' and 'socialist' régimes,[14] but between tyrannies and forms of authoritarianism and patronage on the one hand, and the acknowledgement of pluralism, human rights and development policy on the other.

Ambivalence in the World Time

Whatever its causes, the implosion of the Eastern bloc was followed by spectacular changes on the African political scene. The South African army withdrew from Namibia once independence had successfully been negotiated; Angola's rival factions celebrated the end of the civil war on 1 May 1991, leading the way for the Frelimo and Renamo negotiators in Mozambique; single parties of all kinds (of both the Right and the Left) were questioned publicly and sometimes forced to accept competition (Zambia, Gabon, Ivory Coast, etc.); Zambia's judges condemned their government for its ban on press discussion of opposition activities, while the bureaucracy and shifts (not to mention the extravagances) in the management of the economy were acknowledged and tackled. Apartheid itself collapsed.

Order was to reign, diffusing throughout the African continent the themes of an international culture hitherto dominated by a unique frame of reference, of pluralist and competitive liberal order: market democracy. This product of westernised Northern hegemony has its supreme guardian, the United States (or the World Bank group), its occasionally turbulent supporters (Europe) and its obedient pupils, excessively well-behaved except perhaps in political matters (Japan, South Korea, etc.). The westernised cultures' historical experience was even supposed to enable them to establish the criteria of the sound new international culture: economic norms (mar-

13. I use the terms adopted by Jean-François Bayart, *L'Etat en Afrique*, Paris, Fayard, 1989, p. 249.

14. These caricaturising images can still be found, for example in Claude Collin-Delavaud, *Territoires à prendre. Le marché face aux idéologies*, Paris, Presses Universitaires de France, 1988, particularly pp. 75–8.

ket, competition, privatisation), political norms (organised pluralism, 'human rights'), even cultural norms (valorisation of the 'managerial' culture).

But for Africa, the most vulnerable element of the South, the end of bipolarity does not mean the end of interference, still less the end of delays and uncertainties. Relations with the international system waver between the risks of more intensive guardianship (access to international aid being conditional on economic and political liberalisation, dangerous for any leader of dubious legitimacy in need of resources) and of a supreme indifference, confirming the downgrading of Africa (and depriving the present power-holders of possible access to the resources of the international system).

Siad Barre has gone, closely followed by Hailé Mariam Mengistu, a symbolic association recalling that yesterday's subtle game of pro-American and pro-Soviet alliances and appearances could not prevent economic decline, famine, civil war and the final fall from power. But the reformed international order does not mean immediate total control over the images, concerns or changes that may be necessary or desirable. The question of survival, for social cultures themselves as well as for political régimes, remains uncertain, although the current hierarchy is not based entirely on an expertise which will flourish in the market economy; it is also the line of defence for a morality of human rights and is thus responsible for legitimate internal political power. Conditionality is a reminder that, from this point of view, the world order has not relaxed at all. For Africa the world time means an adjusted democracy.

Euro-optimism and Afro-pessimism

The prevailing economism, dramatised by deteriorating statistics, is not purely arbitrary. The crisis in African society which was apparent throughout the 1980s may grow worse if the last known form of emergency support – international aid and particularly financial aid – runs out.[15] Subject to its own financial, energy or social constraints, the westernised North has been engaged for more than a decade on a re-evaluation of the clientelist relationship, where business takes the lead over emotion. In this respect, the collapse of the Eastern bloc created a set of images which have apparently immediately taken over the business world: the opening of the

---

15. This drop effectively adds to the slowing down of production (the rate of annual industrial growth has gone from 7.5 per cent (1965–80) to 0.7 per cent (1980–9) and of trading activity (exports: from 6.1 per cent to -0.6 per cent; imports: from 5.7 per cent to -5.9 per cent). Public aid payments for development have gone from 14,079 million US dollars (1988) to 13,145m US dollars (1989). See World Bank *Report*, 1991.

European East, where everything has to be reconstructed, offers an extraordinary opportunity for fruitful investments, combining efficiency (even in Eastern Europe, some infrastructures and *savoir-faire* exist), emotion (the brotherhood of European culture) and even redemption (expiation for the cowardly abandonment of these brothers between 1945 and 1948).

The impending rush to the East, no matter how much the reality is mythologised, is indicative of the new order and its implications for Africa. The long papers on interdependence, the duty to assist the weakest nations, the North's historic responsibilities, the mutual advantages of policies of cooperation, were no more than diversions masking highly realistic objectives: the sustaining or relaunching of economic activity and international trade so as to maximise Northern operating profits, public as well as private.[16] Cooperation for development meant that Africa's prosperity depended on the North's prosperity, with Northern expansion taking priority. Whatever the sound technical reasons, the South is financing the North.

This logic of international cooperation becomes even more strict as soon as the West takes on responsibility for regulating development everywhere in the world. With means failing to match needs, we are back with the racist tendencies of colonial exploitation. The insignificance of African governmental economic and cultural achievements would seem to reveal a fundamental inability to think in rational economic terms. Although there is room for charity towards Africans, partnership seems more attractive, serious business with those who are culturally closest and better prepared to respect if not understand the demands of technological modernisation: Romania before Zambia. The argument in favour of the rush eastward is strengthened by references to North-North dynamics: the European West must fight hard to resist the expansionism of the westernised Far East, which represents a serious threat to the commercial power and financial bases of the dominant United States.[17] One possibility, a form of acknowledgement of despair, is to abandon the exhausting labours of Sisyphus on the dark continent in order to concentrate on resisting the new yellow peril where it does not yet exist: in Eastern Europe.

International practice impedes the creation of purpose just when everything appears to be straightforward. The liberal humanism of the discourse on universal values is accompanied by reactions and attitudes, if not practices, stemming from the old *realpolitik*. This unspoken return to

16. Establishing the primacy of the profit motive has nothing disreputable about it when seen from a capitalist logic. See F. Akwireng-Obeng, 'Some Influences in African Entrepreneurship', *Journal of Contemporary African Studies*, 5 (1–2), August-October 1986, pp. 41–65.

17. Cf. Zaki Laïdi, 'De l'hégémonie à la prédation? Hypothèses sur la transformation de la puissance américaine', *Cahiers du CERI*, 1, October 1991.

the mystique of the illusory 'national interest' entails not only an élitist and nationalist, possibly racist, approach to international society; it is manifested in the strengthening of measures wholly contrary to the principles of economic liberalism which the African nations are firmly invited to put into effect. Protectionist regulations (import quotas, rules, subsidies) protect American and European economies, or those of the Far Eastern 'models', affecting the supposed openings for African exports (of cotton or meat products, for example), and when there are no such barriers, the subtle game of monetary fluctuations, interest rates or the cost of raw materials consistently restricts the most vulnerable economies.[18]

Intensifying a fairly generalised breakdown of African economies, and particularly of production systems, the spectre of international aid being redirected from the South to the East together with the generalised spread of predatory practices (the search for profit without reciprocation) has led African leaders and chroniclers to question the conditions or even of the possibilities of Africa's survival. This amounts to questioning the effectiveness of the policies of structural adjustment which integrate Africa ever more closely into a world order with strictly defined principles.

The Time for Adjustment

The generalised application of plans of structural adjustment, in response to the generalised failure of African economic performance, has finally put the Africans under the ultimate authority of the IMF and the World Bank. Forced to acknowledge in broad terms that they have mistakenly led their people into an impasse (shortages, famine, civil war, armed struggles to seize power), no matter which models were adopted from the world market (unrestrained capitalism, state capitalism, cynical patronage, dogmatic *dirigisme*), no matter what their effective resources (oil, copper, etc.) and, forced to disregard the impressive personal successes of certain leaders and entrepreneurs, those in power can only acknowledge the collapse of all possible bases for improvement, either political (legitimacy) or material (financial resources). A certain equalisation of status between African states is emerging as potential regional powers find themselves forced to concentrate their energies on the management of internal political and/or economic difficulties, the sporadic use of the military argument simply adding to past and/or future claims (Nigerian leadership of the intervention force in Liberia, Zairean intervention in Rwanda).

18. One illustration of the combination of these variables and its catastrophic effects is the collapse of the Zambian copper market between 1974 (£1,400 per tonne) and 1977 (£612 per tonne). Werner Biermann, 'The Decline of the Zambian Copper Industry', *ZAST*, 5, 1989, pp. 11–29. See also World Bank, *Report*, 1991.

The world time has set all the clocks to the same hour in what is known as the market economy. In a world where security and the maintenance of peace is no longer relevant (or so it was supposed until August 1990), the protection of international order now rests less with the Security Council than with the monetary-financial system of the United Nations. Since the early 1980s the United Nations have played the part of enlightened guide in the reforms required to unblock the jammed economic systems of the Third World and limit the risks of credit transfers to nations with diminishing solvency. Most African states are now obsessed with plans for structural adjustment and other formulae proposed by the IMF and the World Bank, each one approaching negotiations in its own way.[19] Difficulties here arise less from the scale of the problems to be resolved than from certain concerns for dignity and the political will to go on creating purpose in the face of the prosperous world, and from the disquiet of populist leaders faced with the social risks incurred. But delaying tactics (Tanzania) or noisy ruptures (Zambia), which are overwhelmingly symbolic, have never done more than delay matters. Taking all ideological tendencies as a whole, the African states have been led to implement a panoply of measures, with variations, to liberalise their economies: devaluation, reduction of the budgetary deficit, dismantling of the public sector, abolition of interventionist measures (notably on prices), the search for international competitiveness, etc. All these measures are intended to disengage the state, challenging practices (such as state enterprises) which might have genuine social ends (training or health-related expenditure, employment, social security) rather than patronage alone.

It is, therefore, impossible now for African leaders to define a distinct social and economic policy.[20] The economic sovereignty solemnly voted through in 1974 by the United Nations has been suspended in favour of an international regulation imposing, in the name of expertise and economic rationality, plans to 'depoliticise' economic management in order to bring to an end the 'chaos' to which national 'political' management had led.[21] In this sense, Africa as a whole has fallen back into *de facto* trusteeship (which has been accepted, even if it was not wished for), in response to the deployment of a new form of hegemony based on methods of action

19. See the examples discussed in 'Stabilisation. For Growth or Decay?', IDS Bulletin, 19 (1), January 1988, as well as Kjell J. Havnevik (ed.), *The IMF and the World Bank in Africa. Conditionality, Impact and Alternatives*, Uppsala, Scandinavian Institute of African Studies, 1987.

20. See, for example, Judith Marshall, 'Structural Adjustment and Social Policy in Mozambique', *Review of African Political Economy*, 47, 1990.

21. Jean Coussy, 'Etat minimum, contrainte de compétivité et ajustements structurels', Paris, unpublished, 1988.

recommended by international experts and managerial technocratic ideology. For these experts, the 'adjustment' of the African economies begins with an ideological move towards liberal capitalism. Although this shift is exemplified by the United States (the resemblance to the ideology of the Reagan era is unavoidable) it is also fostered by the scale of the achievements of the Far Eastern dragons and the simultaneous collapse of the theoreticians of *dirigisme*. The question of political legitimacy arouses even less concern because, in the second half of the 1980s, the current (world) climate favoured a well-mannered liberalism setting the pace for all the political managers dependent on the international mechanisms of redistribution in return for extra persuasiveness and for pushing a bit of optimism into intermediary balance-sheets, just as the UNDP and the World Bank itself thought it reasonable to do in 1989.[22]

World ideological orthodoxy, however, brings with it a worrying contradiction for African governments. Budgetary, financial and monetary rigour and the managerial culture are deferring the operation of social policies to some indeterminate future date; economic rigour can only achieve the expected objectives if the government can control public-sector strikes. The simplistic judgement that sustained the credo of earlier decades required a strong government, but today conditionality is expressed more delicately: to remain master in its own house a government must be legitimate – which in the new dominant liberal tradition means that it must be based on the principle of pluralist liberal democracy. This is adjusted democracy.

Back to Democracy?

For the African states as a whole, the political field thus comes under close international scrutiny. This scrutiny extends beyond the terms of reference of the world financial organisations (although, while ostensibly devoting its 1990 report to 'poverty', the World Bank sent out a clear signal which was reinforced by the quiet suggestions of its president at the OAU in 1991).[23] Programmes for structural reforms are backed up with strong pressure for institutional reform, thereby turning the democratisation of political systems into a requirement for a trusting (and thus effective?) form of assistance between Northern and Southern nations.

22. World Bank-UNDP, *Africa's Adjustment and Growth in the 1980s*, Washington, World Bank, 1989. See also *IDS Bulletin*, 19 (1), January 1988, dealing in particular with Ghana.

23. 'He said that the World Bank had no intention of introducing political conditionalities in its relations with African countries, but would intensify scrutiny of those aspects of governance that directly affect development, especially accountability, transparency and adherence to the rule of law ...' *Weekly Review*, 7 June 1991.

The theme of the rule of law and pluralist democracy had already been advanced by the Europeans both collectively (notably in the renegotiation of the Lomé agreement, in 1984–5 and 1989–90), and separately (by the French government, for example). At the La Baule conference in June 1990 President Mitterrand spoke up very clearly for the concept, if not the proposals, held (prematurely) by his former aid minister at the beginning of the decade.[24] Less than a year later the UN Security Council debated very seriously whether they should recognise a 'duty' to interfere in a set of circumstances which was undoubtedly specific and non-African, but which created an interesting precedent. In this respect the new world order appears to be anything but loosened.

And yet practical experience is misleading. France's military intervention in Gabon undoubtedly hindered the opposition's active development, although her passive presence in Chad supported it. But do opposition groups necessarily represent democracy? The extended non-intervention of the international community was not the best way to promote democracy in Liberia. Throughout the whole of Africa the upheavals in Eastern Europe created doubt among rulers and relieved the anxieties of various opposition forces which had already sporadically expressed their unease at the rise in prices required by systematic structural adjustment plans (SAPs).[25] Actual riots are not simply associated with food supplies; and subsequent political claims are serious enough to make single parties and authoritarian régimes submit to public challenge and even to accept competition. Comparable conditions are occurring everywhere across the continent, from Abidjan to Maputo via Brazzaville, Dar-es-Salaam and Cotonou. Depending on the context, attempts at negotiated settlement of crises may be attributed to rulers' awareness of the delicacy of their situation once the international community (and not only state bodies) has warned them firmly against over-zealous methods of dealing with disputes. The world order has encouraged a loosening of the internal political climate. This process, known as 'strengthened conditionality', leaves few unaffected (Malawi) but may be managed very skilfully, as is demonstrated by the stability of governments in Abidjan and Libreville. This, too, is adjusted democracy.

Generalised concessions made to elementary forms of pluralist democracy do not indicate an enthusiastic ideological conversion. To some extent the overcoming of successive outbreaks of protest is a supporting argument for African rulers in economic and financial negotiations. A dete-

24. 'France will contribute in any way she can to the efforts needed for progress towards greater liberty' (statement reported in *Le Monde*, 22 June 1990).

25. Since the beginning of the 1980s, 'hunger riots' had been worrying African governments. They were even behind the fall of President Tolbert in Liberia (1979–80).

riorating internal political situation may be shown as favouring radical (or Islamist) elements whose initiatives can usefully be dramatised to persuade Northern powers to write off or reschedule debts, relax the conditions imposed by the SAP, or simply to provide active political support for the government in power – which would appear to be the current tactic of the Kenyan government in response to rising protests. The disadvantage may be that it confirms an irresistible rising tide of new dangers and inescapable irrationality in African political systems.[26]

By imposing political conditionality the North is paradoxically obliged to amend the SAP conditions and to recognise the (socio-political) qualitative element, thus departing from the technical logic of the expert, who is deprived of political responsibility. Yet the African leaders are unable to regain the initiative. By engaging in a ritual of non-cooperation with the IMF before finally applying its remedies, Kenneth Kaunda has allowed Zambia's economic and financial situation, and his own political position, to deteriorate even further.[27] A potential breakdown in negotiations is no great threat to the IMF, the World Bank or the great powers; the global homogenisation of conditions leaves the excessively rigid African client with little chance of finding an ally capable of helping him out of any impasse he may get into. Such a hypothesis would represent the most serious risk of marginalisation for Africa (or certain parts of the continent). But such dogmatism is hardly part of the political culture of the African ruling classes.

Unimaginable Marginalisation

We must return to our introductory methodological caveat. Taken as a whole, the globalising imperative which stresses the spectacular (growing negative GNPs, outstanding billion-dollar debts), the national institutional actors (states, governments, central banks) and international ones (large business, international organisations), simplifies realities, artificially ironing out the diversity of practices and social logics. The search for effective publicity, which has consequences that are as ambiguous as its motivations, adds to an Afro-pessimism which is based on an approach which may be incomplete or distorted.[28]

26. Cf. the warnings in Mbembe, 'Pouvoir, violence et accumulation'.

27. Apart from *IDS Bulletin*, 19 (1), January 1988, see Kenneth Good, 'Debt and the One-Party State in Zambia', *Journal of Modern African Studies*, 27 (2), 1989, pp. 297–313; John Loxley, 'Structural Adjustment in Africa: Reflections on Ghana and Zambia', *Review of African Political Economy*, 47, 1990, pp. 8–27.

28. This links up with the criticism of the 'Kennedy scenario' developed by Georges Modelski in 'Global Leadership: End Game Scenarios' in Rapkin, *World Leadership*, pp. 241–56. For Africa one may compare the contributions brought together in 'L'Afrique autrement', *Politique africaine*, 39, September 1990, and, somewhat more forceful, Eric Fottorino, 'Le Sud pour mémoire', *Le Monde*, 17 September 1991.

The constraints imposed by the new world order on African governments and public and private entrepreneurs play a part in reclassifying Africa within international society. Their universality, from the SAP to political conditionality, does not however entail the immediate involvement of all elements of society. There are individual and collective actors (and the latter are not necessarily the least important) who invent strategies for evasion, exit options, or at least their own methods of international action, in order to pursue what they see as their proper objectives.[29] Africa's international policy is not only decided in Wall Street, Washington, or the Elysée Palace. The unfolding of violent episodes in Somalia (1989–91) or Liberia (1990) was not planned from the North because there was no longer a Cold War to serve as a primary cause. Perhaps that is why they were deliberately seen as irrational and outdated; yet they were nonetheless decisive, so much so that the North had to respond and try to impose its own solution (Ethiopia in 1991). The thesis of African marginality or insignificance becomes even less credible as the financial retreat of the westernised North reveals the intervention of other elements seeking international opportunities and influence, or the dynamism of populations whose micro-achievements ensure their survival and sometimes even individual prosperity (including that of the élites in power).

Violence

In some respects adjusted democracy may signify the end of external support for tyrannical powers in Africa (and elsewhere), and thus their speedy collapse. But, because the principal consequence of tyranny has been to prevent the organisation of forces of opposition or change, the political transition may be chaotic. The corollory of the decoupling in relation to the conflicts of the North would then be the unleashing of violence (as seen in the civil wars in Somalia, Ethiopia, Sudan and Liberia), the regular demands from the forces of 'order' in Mali, Togo and Zaire, or the macabre trail of refugees and deportees across the continent (Sudan, the Great Lakes region). Even in South Africa, the relaxing of political authoritarianism is marked by the revival of deadly confrontations between African communities.

29. On the notion of 'exit option', see Albert O. Hirschman, *Exit, Voice and Loyalty. Responses to Decline in Firms, Organizations and States*, Cambridge MA., Harvard University Press, 1970. I have analysed the popular styles of international action (then wrongly described as 'diplomatic') in 'Sur les modes populaires d'action diplomatique. Affaires de famille et affaires d'Etat en Afrique orientale', *Revue française de science politique*, 36 (5), 1986, pp. 672–94. See also the series of articles on the general theme of 'Unrecorded Transborder Trade', *Southern African Economist*, 1 (6), December 1988–January 1989.

Such popular violence is not new, as can be confirmed by the peoples of Eritrea, Chad, southern Sudan, the Tuareg, or by Zairean students. It has long been present in the daily life of the shanty towns and the gold fields, and also of the 'smart districts' of Abidjan or Nairobi, where it has gradually increased during the hegemony of powers which before the 'disengagement' were thought to be strong. In simple terms the upheaval in power relations with the North means that the emperors are seen to have no clothes and their victims are supported in the legitimacy of their claims. Furthermore, while political conditionality gave new energy to opposition forces, economic, financial and monetary conditionality linked to structural adjustment helped to reduce the living conditions of vulnerable social groups, notably among the urban populations, the most politically sensitive of these groups. In other words the false loosening of the world order has exacerbated the conditions for a political revolution in Africa. The image of isolation, of exiles cut off from their origins, of Africans cut off from the world, is thus a crude one. Flexible systems of information (pavement radio, the press, travellers) sustain the uninterrupted spread of news on what is happening in the North, and awareness of prevailing thought there. These tenuous networks with their multiple ramifications, corresponding to the manifold forms of sociability at the nerve centre of Africa (networks of kinship, trade and intellect), ensure the dissemination of news of events and opinions in the African peripheries.

Lacking formal channels of expression, the articulation of demands for change tends to be opportunistic (in the street or the bush, by means of clamour, stone-throwing or heavy weapons). Initially dazzled by the complete and peaceful change in the East, the West pretended to take the exception for the rule. It was quick to disregard the very unpeaceful Europe of the last two centuries, the historic authenticity of cultures (Yugoslavia is not Ethiopia even though the Eritrean syndrome is operating there), the diversity of successfully achieved democratic transitions (Portugal, Spain, Namibia, Zimbabwe) and, finally, that change in the East is not exempt from disappointing after-effects (nationalist violence, social crises).

Violence is detestable. But, without it, intolerable political, social and human situations are repeated. Without 'external' violence Idi Amin would still be in power in Kampala; without 'internal' violence Obote would still be in power in Kampala; without the political caution and financial and military aid of the North (and others) in support of these dictatorships, the people of Uganda might perhaps have enjoyed a more peaceful and prosperous fate.[30]

---

30. See D. W. Nabudere, 'External and Internal Factors in Uganda's Continuing Crises', in H. B. Hansen and M. Twaddle (eds), *Uganda Now*, London, J. Currey, 1988, pp. 299–312, or O. Furley, 'Britain and Uganda from Amin to Museveni. Blind Eye Diplomacy' in K. Rupesinghe (ed.), *Conflict Resolution in Uganda*, Oslo, IPRI, 1989, pp. 275–94.

Many of the current episodes of violence are protests against forms of power which lead to oppression and deprivation. The guardians of the new world order, instead of stepping aside, should pay attention. The duty to interfere is imperative not only in support of the Kurds against Saddam Hussein, but also in support of those who resist discredited tyrannies by seeking political change and new methods of government. Should we see here the reason behind American pressure for Ethiopian rebels to enter the capital? In such circumstances we must try hard to overcome our abhorrence of violence and eventually consider a possible 'praise of disorder'.[31]

Connections: Continuities and Innovations

Faced with these situations of serious political and social uncertainty the leaders of the North cannot remain indifferent, if only because, despite everything, they still have some positive interests in Africa. Their new position of hegemony does not mean the end (even within their own ranks) of independent – provided they are not deviant or conflicting – national policies, some hoping to benefit from all the awkwardnesses of the new hegemony (among which would figure the abandonment of Africa), whether they are Japanese or Australian investors or prophets of old or new ideologies.

Disengagement is always relative, and even outside the context of the Cold War a few examples recall that the policy of retreat ultimately turns against its author. At the time of the crisis in Franco-African cooperation, Mauritania turned to Kuwait to support her currency and Niger to Canada for help in building the Unity Road, while in East Africa the Tanzania-Zambia railway gave the People's Republic of China the opportunity for a spectacular achievement in Africa.

Bearing in mind the vitality of the Lomé system and its substantial contribution to international prestige (through the innovative nature of certain arrangements) and to the prosperity of the European Comunity, it is difficult to imagine that the European Community would abandon the region south of the Sahara to face trials of strength with the United States and Japan unsupported and without allies, even purely diplomatic ones. Even if Brussels shares in the new ideology of adjusted democracy, she has no interest whatsoever in bringing despair to Malians who, despite the criticisms of their government, are not wholly losers in the Lomé agreement. One can even suppose that the European Community, by extending the field of its interventions into Eastern Europe, may stimulate a new dynamic of

---

31. See Georges Balandier, *Le désordre. Eloge du mouvement*, Paris, Fayard, 1988. It would appear that the question even has some relevance in fields supposed to require rigorous precision: see 'La science du désordre', special issue of *La Recherche*, 232, May 1991.

European economies and international trade, from which African economies may benefit in the long term, finding in the East more solvent markets and more efficient partners than in the days of the people's democracies. The opening-up of the East is not necessarily bad news for Africa.[32]

It is equally difficult to imagine that, in pushing the mechanics of *laissez-faire* to the limits of despair for the clamouring masses, the westernised North would risk pushing them towards fundamentalisms (such as the Islamism which is the subject of endless fantasies) that predate the fall of the Marxist-Leninist East. The North's future strategy consists not in disengagement, thereby supplying arguments in support of all kinds of protest, but in acting so that an improved standard of living is created as quickly as possible from the adjustments. Such an advance from rigour and privations can in effect, particularly by the new generations which have no credible plans for their future – plans which are more likely be found in some form of 'green revolution' than in the blue-prints of a highly imaginative colonel. The peace of the North still depends on its capacity to (re)create a universally credible purpose.

In fact, the retreat of public or private operators – disappointed, fearful or reluctant North Americans or West Europeans – could be read in several different ways. One reading, prompted by nostalgia for the radicalism of earlier days, consists in emphasising that the Africans will finally be able to organise their decoupling from the international system with full responsibility, and relocate the centre of their development policy.[33] Such nostalgia may prompt another reading: if we recognise that an appreciable proportion of the outflow of capital funds fed the acknowledged technological and financial 'wastage'[34] (quite apart from straightforward corruption), the slowing of the flow of aid may be a good sign, always providing that, as distinct from currency transactions, 'bad' markets are not chasing out 'good' ones. This supposes that the vigilance of opposition parties, stimulated for two years, has not gone to sleep or been bought. It is also (third reading) part of the logic of the structural adjustment to accept a slower flow of aid as long as the reforms demanded by the World Bank and supervised by its brokers (the Paris Club, the London Club) have not been effectively implemented. The 1980s saw the continent-wide expansion of the SAP, under the effective threat of suspension of external capital contributions. Any stepping-up, or even mantaining, of the tempo of these trans-

32. See the World Development Report 1990, *Poverty*, Oxford, Oxford University Press, 1990.

33. Samir Amin, *La déconnexion. Pour sortir du système mondial*, Paris, La Découverte, 1986.

34. See 'Gaspillages technologiques', *Politique africaine*, 18, June 1985.

fers would have indicated lack of cohesive purpose among the guardians of the structural adjustment.

The wait-and-see policy of some of Africa's traditional partners, notably private investors, does not reveal the whole situation. There are still North-South capital flows, particularly from the Far East (maintenance of Japanese public investments throughout the whole of Africa, intervention by Hong Kong in Madagascar) or from 'the Southern North' (Australian involvement in Angola, Ghana, Zimbabwe and Madagascar),[35] to add to the modest but continual operations of the 'new industrial powers' (India, Brazil), more than ever in search of markets and work-sites. The oil-exporting nations themselves, having been concerned with other things between July 1990 and March 1991, have confirmed their selective interest in African affairs which is only partly a function of the oil trade. Finally, it is currently fashionable to enquire as to the repercussions of South Africa's return to the international system in general and the African system in particular. The pessimistic view is that the internal reconstruction of South Africa will absorb national resources and will turn to its own profit what remains of the modest financial resources available on the world market. But it is difficult to see a multiracial government renouncing all African openings. It must accept a considerable symbolic and emotional burden and the relaunching of its sick economic machine (but at what point on the African scale?) requires a rebirth of international trade.[36] Furthermore, in its worldwide strategy, the North needs a prosperous South Africa which, benefiting from the capacity to make a fresh start (which is no longer available to either Nigeria or Zaire), can now accept the call to act as regional leader.

Popular Styles of International Action

Africa's place in the collapsed world order is not determined solely by these lofty strategical considerations. It is too often forgotten that any people in difficulties struggles and builds and that, particularly in the context of a weak state, international status may be as much the result of daily social interaction as of chancellors' gestures.

35. A balance-sheet established for 1990 on the basis of the data in *Africa Research Bulletin* shows that Japan made public payments to most African nations without any clearly visible political or economic logic. Missing from the list of nations were Mozambique, Botswana, Gabon and Liberia; but on the other hand Sudan, Somalia, Tanzania, the Ivory Coast and Nigeria appear on the list. The total is about 350 million dollars.

36. Cf. Peter Vale, *Starting Over. Some Early Questions on a Post-Apartheid Foreign Policy*, Bellville, University of Western Cape, 1990, or Douglas G. Anglin, 'Afrique du Sud. Politique extérieure et rapports avec le continent', *Etudes internationales*, 22 (2), June 1991, pp. 369–91.

Recognition of the importance of local initiatives, whether collective or individual, in international society is still a new concept in the sociology of international relations. To consider only present-day Africa, the failures of public authorities in responding to basic needs have fostered home-grown methods for getting through the crisis and relaunching purchasing power within limits still not properly recognised.

The influence of the new order on African opinion is apparent in the outbreak of claims and disputes which have destabilised all those political systems that, beneath the veneer of different ideologies (which have themselves been borrowed from Northern models), practice the same brand of authoritarianism. It is still apparent in the respectability acquired by a new technocratic élite, trained either in the best schools or in the market-place, and assimilating the managerial culture disseminated by the Northern media and practised by some Africans in their work with the World Bank. Productivity, yield, the conquest of markets, risk-taking – such terms are part of the vocabulary and practices of a new generation of managers who are now attempting to take over the political and economic system.[37]

Here again, it would be wrong to think in terms of a definite break with the past. The entrepreneurial spirit, with its ingredients (profit-seeking, risk-taking, tactical opportunism), is part of popular practice, whether as credit (tontine) systems, clandestine foreign exchange bureaux (now officially recognised in some countries), import-export businesses (unofficial trade with the Gulf), unofficial multinationals (Lebanese, Asian or Mourid), or systems of temporary work (immigrant workers for longer or shorter periods). These local initiatives, which form the basis of micro-processes of accumulation may become development enterprises, an African recreation of the myth of the 'self-made man'. Their diplomatic importance surfaces with the African governments' moderation during the Gulf War, which is to be explained not only by their considerable reservations over Saddam Hussein's methods but also by the conveniently advantageous power relations between the few pro-Iraqi Muslims and discreet business minorities, whose negotiations with the pro-Kuwaiti emirates were the response to genuine local African demands.

These private initiatives share in the construction and operation of transnational networks of alliance and complementarity, with an effectiveness which often operates through the subversion of state networks. Today it is a matter of public notoriety that this economy, awkwardly

37. See the generation of Ouattara (Ivory Coast) or N. Soglo (Benin). Cf. David K. Leonard, 'The Secret of African Managerial Success', *IDS Bulletin*, 19 (4), 1988, pp.35–41. A survey of recent analyses on the emergence of an African form of capitalism has been carried out by Wayne Nafziger, 'African Capitalism, State Power, and Economic Development', *Journal of Modern African Studies*, 28 (1), 1990, pp. 141–50.

described as 'informal', represents a considerable proportion of African economic activity – sometimes the major part – and is the only way in which some basic needs are satisfied against a background of poverty. The networks created are transcontinental; they ensure the circulation of funds, goods, people and ideas throughout the whole of Africa and the Gulf states, the Indian subcontinent, Western Europe and North America: the market economy has an ancient lineage in Africa.[38] Trade which is increasingly less acceptable, but more and more remunerative, completes the network that anchors Africa in the world system: ivory with the Far East and New York, precious stones with Antwerp, Geneva and Israel, arms more or less everywhere, and now drugs.[39] These many popular forms of international activity impose compromises on governments in the South as well as in the North (including the IMF), in addition to negotiations aimed at ensuring at worst some form of regulation and at best control over such trade and occasionally its cessation. These compromises may appear to be the antithesis of the principles of liberalism. The vigour of these principles is sufficient by itself to dismiss any possibility of excluding Africa from the reconstruction of the world order because rulers may know how to combine ancient forms of trade with the new conditions in order to legitimise their domination again, in the name of 'privatisation' and by means of formal electoral suffrage. However, the problem remains that these unofficial initiatives generally occur outside the field of wealth-creating activity; their almost exclusively trading nature sustains a flexibility of movement which fits very well into the new logic of the international system, but their proprietorial attitudes affect the role which they might otherwise play in the fundamental relaunch of African economies. Do-it-yourself methods may well ensure individual survival, but they cannot guarantee collective economic takeoff unless the managerial culture reaches further into these networks – which cannot be taken for granted.

The same comments apply to other forms of private initiative, stemming this time from the North, which appear throughout Africa. Non-governmental organisations (NGOs) are evidence of a considerable will to act.

38. See the study of the spectacular case of Vali Jamal, 'Somalia, Economics for an Unconventional Economy' in Onimode, *The IMF*, vol 1, pp. 99–122, analysing the spontaneous functioning of a free market wholly outside the government, which leads us to question the effects of the '*dirigiste*' measures recommended by the World Bank. Another example is Kate Meagher, 'The Hidden Economy. Informal and Parallel Trade in Northwestern Uganda', *Review of African Political Economy*, 47, 1990, pp. 64–83.

39. Cf. Coussy, 'L'impact des resources extérieures' in *Métamorphoses*. On the new drugs networks, cf. Eric Fottorino, *La piste blanche. L'Afrique sous l'emprise de la drogue*, Paris, Balland, 1991, and 'The Drug Trade', *Southern African Economist*, 5 (5), September 1992, pp. 3–12.

The state of crisis, an altruistic missionary spirit or high self-esteem have resulted in approval (perhaps even over-approval) of their presence in Africa, with some indeed setting themselves up as guardians of universal political virtue.[40] This uneven presence spread across the continent supports networks of privileged relationships whose origins may be very useful (the presence of the Roman Catholic Church in Burkina Faso) but which produce specific actions (education, health, water) which are more important for the peasant than for the analyst of world reconstruction. The question then arises as to which is the most important. Charity is no guarantee of prosperity unless it gets through to investors ready to give a broader perspective to this kind of network.

Africa's place in the world order will also be shaped by the scale and the original axes of these networks. Pilgrims to Mecca or other Islamic or Christian holy places; Mourid brethren in French and North American markets; co-owners of Indian multinationals operating between Nairobi, Bombay and Geneva; clandestine workers or brain-drained intellectuals from Paris or Toronto; Scandinavian expatriates in eastern or southern Africa; seasonal migrations of European or North American tourists (ahead of the Japanese) to Amboseli or the Gambia – all mean enduring shifts of currency and purpose (or the negation of purpose), the long-term effects of which may in future be greater than the lightning missions of financial experts or the chance visits of military advisers who can be easily expelled.

The world order is associated with a frame of reference whose sole true novelty is its universality: market democracy. These words undoubtedly have meaning throughout the whole of Africa and all strata of society, although they have rarely operated together. While the ancient pillars of Afro-Marxism and the planned economy (Angola, Mozambique, Benin, etc.) appear to have rallied to it, it is among the diligent students of the market that the positive adversaries or skilful salvage operators of organised pluralism can be found (Kenya, Malawi). According to all the theories, those who (as in Senegal) were the precursors of the pluralist system can only approve the caution of the World Bank experts in their attempt to establish a correlation between democracy and development,[41] particularly as the great reclassification supervised by the West has added to the troubles of African leaders.

For if, for them, the world time means putting into operation the fairly

---

40. 'Médecins sans frontières' has laid itself open to criticism of this type. See, for example, Desselagn Rahmato, *Famine and Survival Strategies*, Uppsala, Nordiska Afrika Instituet, 1991, pp. 203–7. For a general critique, see Yash Tandon, 'Foreign NGOs, Uses and Abuses. An African Perspective', *Ifda Dossier* 81, April-June 1991, pp. 68–78.

41. World Bank *Report*, 1991, ch. 7.

easily recoverable norms of an adjusted democracy, it may have more destructive effects. The open legitimisation of various secessionist movements in Central Europe and the former Soviet Union means the end of the universal dogma of the inviolability of frontiers. What is acknowledged, or in the process of being acknowledged, for the Baltic, Slav or Caucasian peoples, for whatever reason, cannot easily be forbidden to other groups whose comparable mobilisation has come to fruition through struggles against the exactions of a state power with declining legitimacy. The single purpose now directing the world order holds little promise of harmony or serenity, particularly for this unforgettable continent of Africa.